# Surfiction

# Surfiction

## Fiction Now...
## and Tomorrow

edited by
## Raymond Federman

THE SWALLOW PRESS INC.

CHICAGO

Published by
The Swallow Press Incorporated
1139 South Wabash Avenue
Chicago, Illinois 60605


First Edition
    First Printing


ISBN (CLOTH) 0-8040-0651-2
ISBN (PAPER) 0-8040-0652-0
LIBRARY OF CONGRESS CATALOG CARD NUMBER 73-13215

*In Memory of Jacques Ehrmann*

# Contents

# HOW NOW?

# A Prefatory Note

Samuel Beckett's *The Unnamable* opens with crucial questions not only about the predicament of the narrator-hero whose fiction is about to begin, but more specifically about fiction—about the present-future state of fiction: "Where now? Who now? When now? Unquestioning. I, say I. Unbelieving. Questions, hypotheses, call them that. Keep going, going on, call that going, call that on."

Taking our cue from these typically Beckettian "questions, hypotheses," the essays in this volume are grouped in such a way as to pursue and elaborate the WHERE NOW? WHO NOW? WHEN NOW? of Samuel Beckett, adding to these however, one more question: HOW NOW? These essays have been gathered in an effort to determine, define, analyze what is the present state of fiction—FICTION NOW—and, to some extent, in an effort to suggest, project, propose what will be the future of fiction— ... AND TOMORROW.

The editor does not pretend to have selected or commissioned essays that cover all the possibilities of fiction, nor to have presented a full panorama of fiction writers at work today in various parts of the world. The choice, by necessity, had to be subjective and arbitrary. The authors discussed here have been chosen because their work is recognized as having disrupted the tradition on which fiction has been functioning (for better or for worse) for too many centuries now. It is this dissatisfaction with fiction, this insufficiency, this crisis of fiction which bring many contemporary writers to reexamine, rethink, rewrite fiction in terms and in forms that have not yet been defined. It is hoped that the positions taken by the various authors in this volume will help clarify the present and future state of fiction.

The essays under the heading WHEN NOW? are attempts at pointing out the failings of traditional fiction while proposing new possibilities. Two American novelists, one French novelist, one Italian novelist, and one American critic express their views in this section.

The essays under the category WHERE NOW? present a

*1*

more general view of experimental fiction in America, France, and Germany. Though Italy, Latin America, Japan, and other regions could and might have been covered, the important innovators from these regions receive enough attention in the various essays not to feel that they have been neglected.

WHO NOW? offers a choice of essays dealing specifically with individual authors—authors whose work stands out as the most disruptive of the tradition, and as such the most imaginative and innovative. Many others, of course, could have been discussed in this section. But again, references to the major figures at work today seem sufficient in the other essays to justify this limited choice.

HOW NOW? consists of essays of a more theoretical nature which attempt to formulate, from the reading of certain texts, new avenues for the future of fiction and of literature. Those essays could easily have found a place in one of the other sections. However, the polemical aspect of these essays and their concern for the future, rather than the present, of fiction determined their position as conclusion to this volume.

By a pure coincidence, of the eighteen contributors to this volume, eleven of these are themselves fiction writers—some of national and international reputation. It is, therefore, from the inside, from the very experience of writing fiction (modern fiction) that a number of essays presented here are articulated. The other essays are from literary critics who have proven themselves careful readers and explicators of contemporary fiction. However, it is not a coincidence if some of the fiction writers expressing their views here are also the subject of some of the essays. The editor felt that by having within the pages of this volume a kind of intramural dialogue between those who write fiction and those who read fiction, that is to say by looking at contemporary fiction from the inside and from the outside, one could, perhaps, gain a more valid perception of what is happening to fiction today.

Some of the essays are reprinted from previous publications. Grateful acknowledgments are made to John Barth for permission to reprint "The Literature of Exhaustion," which first appeared in *The Atlantic* (August 1967); to Philippe Sollers and the Editions du Seuil for permission to translate and reprint "The Novel and the Experience of Limits," published in 1968 in a volume of essays entitled *Logiques* (Paris), following its reading as a lecture on December 8, 1965 at a meeting of the Tel Quel Group; to Italo Calvino for permission to translate and reprint "Myth in the Narrative," originally published in French in the review *Esprit* (Paris, April 1971); to Jean Ricardou and the Editions du Seuil for permission to translate and reprint his two essays, "Writing Between the Lines" and "Nouveau Roman, Tel Quel," published in *Pour une théorie du nouveau roman* (Paris, 1971); to Richard Kostelanetz for permission to reprint "Twenty-Five Fictional Hypotheses," first published in the special issue of the review *Panache* ("Future's Fiction," 1971); and finally to Jacques Ehrmann and the editor of *New Literary History* for permission to reprint "The Death of Literature," one version of which appeared in the review *New Literary History* (1972) and another in *"Textes" suivi de la Mort de la littérature* (Paris: Editions de L'Herne, 1971). The other essays were specifically written for this volume, but some of these have been submitted, since they were written, to various journals (with the editor's permission) and may have already appeared at the date of the publication of this volume.

The editor of this volume would like also to express his gratitude to Erica Freiberg and Christine Grahl for the fine work they did in translating some of the essays from the French; to Michael Anania, at Swallow Press, for having supported this project from an idea discussed over a drink in a Chicago bar to its realization and publication; to Durrett Wagner, at Swallow Press; and finally to all the contributors who made this book possible.

RAYMOND FEDERMAN
Buffalo

# raymond federman

# Surfiction—Four Propositions in Form of an Introduction

*Now some people might say that this situation is not very encouraging but one must reply that it is not meant to encourage those who say that!*

RAYMOND FEDERMAN
*DOUBLE OR NOTHING*

*Rather than serving as a mirror or redoubling on itself, fiction adds itself to the world, creating a meaningful "reality" that did not previously exist. Fiction is artifice but not artificial. It seems as pointless to call the creative powers of the mind "fraudulent" as it would to call the procreative powers of the body such. What we bring into the world is per se beyond language, and at that point language is of course left behind—but it is the function of creative language to be left behind, to leave itself behind, in just that way. The word is unnecessary once it is spoken, but it has to be spoken. Meaning does not pre-exist creation, and afterward it may be superfluous.*

RONALD SUKENICK
*a letter (1972)*

Writing about fiction today, one could begin with the usual clichés—that the novel is dead; that fiction is no longer possible because real fiction happens, everyday, in the streets of our cities, in the spectacular hijacking of planes, on the Moon, in Vietnam, in China (when Nixon stands on the Great Wall of China), and of course on television (during the news broadcasts); that fiction has become useless and irrelevant because life has become much more interesting, much more incredible, much more dramatic than what the moribund novel can possibly offer. And one could go on saying that fiction is now impossible (as so many theoreticians and practitioners of fiction have demonstrated) because all the possibilities of fiction have been used up, exhausted, abused, and therefore, all that is left, to the one who still insists on writing fiction, is to repeat (page after page, *ad nauseam*) that there is nothing to write about, nothing with which to write, and thus simply write that there is nothing to write (for instance, the so-called New French Novel of the last 15 years or so).

And indeed, such works as *In Cold Blood*, *The Day Kennedy Was Shot*, *Armies of the Night* and other Mailer books, and all those autobiographies written by people who have supposedly experienced *real* life in the streets of our cities, in the ghettos, in the jails, in the political arena, are possibly better fictions than those foolish stories (love stories, spy stories, businessman stories, cowboy stories, sexual deviate stories, and so on) the novel is still trying to peddle, and make us believe. Indeed, one could start this way, and simply give up on fiction. For, as Samuel Beckett once said: "It's easy to talk about being unable, whereas in reality nothing is more difficult."

Well, I propose that the novel is far from being dead (and I mean now the traditional novel—that moribund novel which became moribund the day it was conceived, some 400 years ago with *Don Quixote*); that, in fact, this type of novel is very *healthy* today (and very *wealthy* too—I know many novelists who can brag that their latest book has brought them 200,000, 300,000, half a million dollars, or more—*Love Story* is but one of those phenomena). But if we are to talk seriously about fiction, this is not the kind of fiction I am interested in. The kind of fiction I am interested in is that fiction which the leaders of the literary establishment (publishers, editors, agents, and

reviewers alike) brush aside because it does not conform to
*their* notions of what fiction should be; that fiction which supposedly has no value (commercial understood) for the common
reader. And the easiest way for these people to brush aside that
kind of fiction is to label it, quickly and bluntly, as *experimental
fiction*. Everything that does not fall into the category of *successful fiction* (commercially that is), or what Jean-Paul Sartre
once called "nutritious literature," everything that is found
"unreadable for our readers" (that's the publishers and editors
speaking—but who the hell gave them the right to decide what
is *readable* or *valuable* for their readers?) is immediately rele-
gated to the domain of experimentation—a safe and useless
place.

Personally, I do not believe that a fiction writer with the
least amount of self-respect, and belief in what he is doing, ever
says to himself: "I am now going to experiment with fiction;
I am now writing an experimental piece of fiction." Others say
that about his fiction. The middle-man of literature is the one
who gives the label EXPERIMENTAL to what is difficult,
strange, provocative, and even original. But in fact, true experiments (as in science) never reach, or at least should never
reach, the printed page. Fiction is called experimental out of
despair. Beckett's novels are not experimental—no! it is the
only way Beckett can write; Borges' stories are not experimental; Joyce's fiction is not experimental (even though it was
called that for some 30 or 40 years). All these are successful
finished works. And so, for me, the only fiction that still means
something today is that kind of fiction that tries to explore the
possibilities of fiction; the kind of fiction that challenges the
tradition that governs it; the kind of fiction that constantly re-
news our faith in man's imagination and not in man's distorted
vision of reality—that reveals man's irrationality rather than
man's rationality. This I call SURFICTION. However, not because it imitates reality, but because it exposes the fictionality
of reality. Just as the Surrealists called that level of man's
experience that functions in the subconscious SURREALITY,
I call that level of man's activity that reveals life as a fiction
SURFICTION. Therefore, there is some truth in that cliché

which says that "life is fiction," but not because it happens in the streets, but because reality as such does not exist, or rather exists only in its fictionalized version. The experience of life gains meaning only in its recounted form, in its verbalized version, or, as Céline said, some years ago, in answer to those who claimed that his novels were merely autobiographical: "Life, also, is fiction . . . and a biography is something one invents afterwards."

But in what sense is life fiction? Fiction is made of understanding, which for most of us means primarily words—and only words (spoken or written). Therefore, if one admits from the start (at least to oneself) that no meaning pre-exists language, but that language creates meaning as it goes along, that is to say as it is used (spoken or written), as it progresses, then writing (fiction especially) will be a mere process of letting language do its tricks. To write, then, is to *produce* meaning, and not *reproduce* a pre-existing meaning. To write is to *progress*, and not *remain* subjected (by habit or reflexes) to the meaning that supposedly precedes the words. As such, fiction can no longer be reality, or a representation of reality, or an imitation, or even a recreation of reality; it can only be A REALITY—an autonomous reality whose only relation with the real world is to improve that world. To create fiction is, in fact, a way to abolish reality, and especially to abolish the notion that reality is truth.

In the fiction of the future, all distinctions between the real and the imaginary, between the conscious and the subconscious, between the past and the present, between truth and untruth will be abolished. All forms of duplicity will disappear. And above all, all forms of duality will be negated—especially duality: that double-headed monster which, for centuries now, has subjected us to a system of values, an ethical and aesthetical system based on the principles of good and bad, true and false, beautiful and ugly. Thus, the primary purpose of fiction will be to unmask its own fictionality, to expose the metaphor of its own fraudulence, and not pretend any longer to pass for reality, for truth, or for beauty. Consequently, fiction will no longer be regarded as a mirror of life, as a pseudorealistic document that informs us about life, nor will it be judged on the basis of its social, moral, psychological, metaphysical, commercial value, or whatever, but on the basis of what it is and what it does as an autonomous art form in its own right.

\* \* \* \*

These preliminary remarks serve as an introduction to four propositions I would like to make now for the future of fiction, but also as an introduction to the essays that follow. My propositions, of course, are but an arbitrary starting point for the possibilities of a new fiction. Each essay, in its own way, represents another position towards fiction. But these positions often overlap, or complement, each other. And that is how it should be.

PROPOSITION ONE — *The Reading of Fiction:*

The very act of reading a book, starting at the top of the first page, and moving from left to right, top to bottom, page after page to the end in a consecutive prearranged manner has become *boring* and *restrictive*. Indeed, any intelligent reader should feel frustrated and restricted within that preordained system of reading. Therefore, the whole traditional, conventional, fixed, and boring method of reading a book must be questioned, challenged, demolished. And it is the writer (and not modern printing technology) who must, through innovations in the writing itself—in the typography and topology of his writing—renew our system of reading.

All the rules and principles of printing and bookmaking must be forced to change as a result of the changes in the writing (or the telling) of a story in order to give the reader a sense of free participation in the writing/reading process, in order to give the reader an element of choice (active choice) in the ordering of the discourse and the discovery of its meaning.

Thus, the very concept of syntax must be transformed—the word, the sentence, the paragraph, the chapter, the punctuation need to be rethought and rewritten so that new ways (multiple and simultaneous ways) of reading a book can be created. And the space itself in which writing takes place must be changed. That space, the page (and the book made of pages), must acquire new dimensions, new shapes, new relations in order to accommodate the new writing. And it is within this transformed topography of writing, from this new paginal (rather than grammatical) syntax that the reader will discover his freedom in relation to the process of reading a book, in relation to language and fiction.

In all other art forms, there are three essential elements at play: the creator, the medium through which the work of art is transmitted from the creator, and the receiver (listener or viewer) to whom the work of art is transmitted. In the writing of fiction, we have only the first and third elements: the writer and the reader. Me and you. And the medium (language), because it is neither auditory nor visual (as in music, painting, and sometimes poetry), merely serves as a means of transportation from me to you, from my meaning to your understanding of that meaning. If we are to make of the novel an art form, we must raise the printed word as the medium, and therefore *where* and *how* it is placed on the printed page makes a difference in what the novel is saying. Thus, not only the writer creates fiction, but all those involved in the ordering of that fiction; the typist, the recorder, the printer, the proofreader, and the reader partake of the fiction, and the real medium becomes the printed word as it is presented on the page, as it is perceived, heard, read, visualized (not only abstractly but concretely) by the receiver.

PROPOSITION TWO — *The Shape of Fiction:*
If life and fiction are no longer distinguishable one from the other, nor complementary to one another, and if we agree that life is never linear, that, in fact, life is chaos because it is never experienced in a straight, chronological line, then, similarly, linear and orderly narration is no longer possible. The pseudo-realistic novel sought to give a semblance of order to the chaos of life, and did so by relying on the well-made-plot (the story line) which, as we now realize, has become quite inessential to fiction. The plot having disappeared, it is no longer necessary to have the events of fiction follow a logical, sequential pattern (in time and in space).

Therefore, the elements of the new fictitious discourse (words, phrases, sequences, scenes, spaces, etc.) must become digressive from one another—digressive from the element that precedes and the element that follows. In fact, these elements will now occur simultaneously and offer multiple possibilities of re-arrangement in the process of reading. The fictitious discourse, no longer progressing from left to right, top to bottom, in a straight line, and along the design of an imposed plot, will follow the contours of the writing itself as it takes shape (unpredictable shape) within the space of the page. It will circle around itself, create new and unexpected movements and figures in the unfolding of the narration, repeating itself, projecting itself backward and forward along the curves of the writing—(much here can be learned from the cinema—that of Jean-Luc Godard in particular). And consequently, the events related in the narration will also move along this distorted curve. The shape and order of fiction will not result from an imitation of the shape and order of life, but rather from the formal circumvolutions of language as it wells up from the unconscious. No longer a mirror being dragged along reality, fiction will not reproduce the effects of the mirror acting upon itself. It will no longer be a representation of something exterior to it, but self-representation. That is to say, rather than being the stable image of daily life, fiction will be in a perpetual state of redoubling upon itself. It is from itself, from its own substance that the fictitious discourse will proliferate—imitating, repeating, parodying, retracing what it says. Thus fiction will become the metaphor of its own narrative progress, and will establish itself as it writes itself. This does not mean, however, that the future novel will be only "a novel of the novel," but rather it will create a kind of writing, a kind of discourse whose shape will be an interrogation, an endless interrogation of what it is doing while doing it, an endless denunciation of its fraudulence, of what *it* really is: an illusion (a fiction), just as life is an illusion (a fiction).

PROPOSITION THREE — *The Material of Fiction:*
If the experiences of any man (in this case the writer) exist only as fiction, as they are recalled or recounted, afterwards,

and always in a distorted, glorified, sublimated manner, then these experiences are inventions. And if most fiction is (more or less) based on the experiences of the one who writes (experiences which are not anterior to, but simultaneous with, the writing process), there cannot be any truth nor any reality exterior to fiction. In other words, if the material of fiction is invention (lies, simulation, distortions, or illusions), then writing fiction will be a process of inventing, on the spot, the material of fiction.

The writer simply materializes (renders concrete) fiction into words. And as such, there are no limits to the material of fiction —no limits beyond the writer's power of imagination, and beyond the possibilities of language. Everything can be said, and must be said, in any possible way. While pretending to be telling the story of his life, or the story of any life, the fiction writer can at the same time tell the story of the story he is telling, the story of the language he is manipulating, the story of the methods he is using, the story of the pencil or the typewriter he is using to write his story, the story of the fiction he is inventing, and even the story of the anguish (or joy, or disgust, or exhilaration) he is feeling while telling his story. And since writing means now filling a space (the pages), in those spaces where there is nothing to write, the fiction writer can, at any time, introduce material (quotations, pictures, diagrams, charts, designs, pieces of other discourses, doodles, etc.) totally unrelated to the story he is in the process of telling; or else, he can simply leave those spaces blank, because fiction is as much what is said as what is not said, since what is said is not necessarily true, and since what is said can always be said another way.

As a result, the people of fiction, the fictitious beings, will also no longer be well-made-characters who carry with them a fixed identity, a stable set of social and psychological attributes —a name, a situation, a profession, a condition, etc. The creatures of the new fiction will be as changeable, as unstable, as illusory, as nameless, as unnamable, as fraudulent, as unpredictable as the discourse that makes them. This does not mean, however, that they will be mere puppets. On the contrary, their being will be more genuine, more complex, more true-to-life in fact, because they will not appear to be simply what they are; they will be what they are: word-beings.

What will replace the well-made-personage who carried with him the burden of a name, a social role, a nationality, parental ties, and sometimes an age and a physical appearance, will be a fictitious creature who will function outside any predetermined condition. That creature will be, in a sense, present to his own making, present to his own absence. Totally free, totally uncommitted to the affairs of the outside world, to the same extent as the fiction in which he will exist (perform that is), he will participate in the fiction only as a grammatical being (sometimes not even as a pronominal being). Made of fragments, disassociated fragments of himself, this new fictitious creature will be irrational, irresponsible, irrepressive, amoral, and unconcerned with the real world, but entirely committed to the fiction in which he finds himself, aware, in fact, only of his role as fictitious being. Moreover, not only the creator but the characters (and the narrator, if any) as well will participate (in the same degree as the reader) in the creation of the fiction. All of them will be part of the fiction, all of them will be responsible for it—the creator (as fictitious as his creation) being only the point of junction (the source and the recipient) of all the elements of the fiction.

PROPOSITION FOUR — *The Meaning of Fiction:*

It is obvious from the preceding propositions that the most striking aspects of the new fiction will be its semblance of disorder and its deliberate incoherency. Since, as stated earlier, no meaning pre-exists language, but meaning is produced in the process of writing (and reading), the new fiction will not attempt to be meaningful, truthful, or realistic; nor will it attempt to serve as the vehicle of a ready-made meaning. On the contrary, it will be seemingly devoid of any meaning, it will be deliberately illogical, irrational, unrealistic, non sequitur, and incoherent. And only through the joint efforts of the reader and creator (as well as that of the characters and narrators) will a meaning possibly be extracted from the fictitious discourse.

The new fiction will not create a semblance of order, it will offer itself for order and ordering. Thus the reader of this fiction will not be able to identify with its people and its material, nor will he be able to purify or purge himself in relation to the actions of the people in the story. In other words, no longer being manipulated by an authorial point of view, the reader will be the one who extracts, invents, creates a meaning and an order for the people in the fiction. And it is this total participation in the creation which will give the reader a sense of having created a meaning and not having simply received, passively, a neatly prearranged meaning.

The writer will no longer be considered a prophet, a philosopher, or even a sociologist who predicts, teaches, or reveals absolute truths, nor will he be looked upon (admiringly and romantically) as the omnipresent, omniscient, and omnipotent creator, but he will stand on equal footing with the reader in their efforts *to make sense* out of the language common to both of them, *to give sense* to the fiction of life. In other words, as it has been said of poetry, fiction, also, will not only mean, but it will be!

*    *    *    *

One should, I suppose, in conclusion to such a presentation, attempt to justify, or at least illustrate with examples, the propositions I just made for the future of fiction. But justifications and illustrations are readily available, and to a great extent most of the writers discussed in the following essays have already forged the way into this new type of fiction. For, I must confess, I am not alone in these wild imaginings. Many contemporary writers, each in his own personal "mad" way, have already successfully created the kind of fiction I tried to define in the preceding pages: Samuel Beckett, of course, in French and in English, Jorge Luis Borges and Julio Cortazar in Spanish, Italo Calvino in Italian, Robert Pinget, Claude Simon, Philippe Sollers, Jean Ricardou, J.M.G. Le Clézio, and many others, in France, and in their own individual manner, a number of American writers such as John Barth, John Hawkes, Ronald Sukenick, William Burroughs, Donald Barthelme, Richard Kostelanetz, Jerzy Kosinsik, to mention only those who receive particular attention in this volume, but many others too who should deserve mention here, and who are discussed in the following pages. But perhaps it is preferable to let the reader (wherever he might be) reflect on these propositions, and discover for himself the fiction of which he has now become an integral part.

The essays that follow deal with some of the problems I have exposed here. These essays are about some of the writers just mentioned, but also written by some of these writers. None of them, however, would pretend to have solved, singlehandedly, the problems of fiction, nor to have presented the only possible way for future fiction. I, like them, only know that this is the path I, as a fiction writer, want to explore in order, perhaps, not to succeed (commercially, socially, or otherwise), but in order to give fiction another chance, or, as one of the greatest fiction writers alive, Samuel Beckett, once said, in order "to make of failure a howling success."

# When now?

# john barth

# The Literature of Exhaustion

*The fact is that every writer* creates *his own precursors. His work modifies our conception of the past, as it will modify the future.*

JORGE LUIS BORGES
*LABYRINTHS*

*You who       listen       give me life in a manner       of speaking. I won't hold you responsible.       My first words weren't my first words. I wish I'd begun differently.*

JOHN BARTH
*LOST IN THE FUN HOUSE*

I want to discuss three things more or less together: first, some old questions raised by the new intermedia arts; second, some aspects of the Argentine writer Jorge Luis Borges, whom I greatly admire; third, some professional concerns of my own, related to these other matters and having to do with what I'm calling "the literature of exhausted possibility"—or, more chicly, "the literature of exhaustion."

By "exhaustion" I don't mean anything so tired as the subject of physical, moral, or intellectual decadence, only the used-upness of certain forms or exhaustion of certain possibilities—by no means necessarily a cause for despair. That a great many Western artists for a great many years have quarreled with received definitions of artistic media, genres, and forms goes without saying: pop art, dramatic and musical "happenings," the whole range of "intermedia" or "mixed-means" art, bear recentest witness to the tradition of rebelling against Tradition. A catalogue I received some time ago in the mail, for example, advertises such items as Robert Filliou's *Ample Food for Stupid Thought*, a box full of postcards on which are inscribed "apparently meaningless questions," to be mailed to whomever the purchaser judges them suited for; Ray Johnson's *Paper Snake*, a collection of whimsical writings, "often pointed," once mailed to various friends (what the catalogue describes as The New York Correspondence School of Literature); and Daniel Spoerri's *Anecdoted Typography of Chance*, "on the surface" a description of all the objects that happen to be on the author's parlor table—"in fact, however . . . a cosmology of Spoerri's existence."

"On the surface," at least, the document listing these items is a catalogue of The Something Else Press, a swinging outfit. "In fact, however," it may be one of their offerings, for all I know: The New York Direct-Mail Advertising School of Literature. In any case, their wares are lively to read about, and make for interesting conversation in fiction-writing classes, for example, where we discuss Somebody-or-other's unbound, unpaginated, randomly assembled novel-in-a-box and the desirability of printing *Finnegans Wake* on a very long roller-towel. It's easier and sociabler to talk technique than it is to make art, and the area of "happenings" and their kin is mainly a way of discussing aesthetics, really; illustrating "dramatically" more or less valid and interesting points about the nature of art and the definition of its terms and genres.

One conspicuous thing, for example, about the "intermedia" arts is their tendency (noted even by *Life* magazine) to eliminate not only the traditional audience—"those who apprehend the artist's art" (in "happenings" the audience is often the "cast," as in "environments," and some of the new music isn't intended to be performed at all)—but also the most traditional notion of the artist: the Aristotelian conscious agent who achieves with technique and cunning the artistic effect; in other words, one endowed with uncommon talent, who has moreover developed and disciplined that endowment into virtuosity. It's an aristocratic notion on the face of it, which the democratic West seems eager to have done with; not only the "omniscient" author of older fiction, but the very idea of the controlling artist, has been condemned as politically reactionary, even fascist.

Now, personally, being of the temper that chooses to "rebel along traditional lines," I'm inclined to prefer the kind of art that not many people can *do*: the kind that requires expertise and artistry as well as bright aesthetic ideas and/or inspiration. I enjoy the pop art in the famous Albright-Knox collection, a few blocks from my house in Buffalo, like a lively conversation for the most part, but was on the whole more impressed by the jugglers and acrobats at Baltimore's old Hippodrome, where I used to go every time they changed shows: genuine *virtuosi* doing things that anyone can dream up and discuss but almost no one can do.

I suppose the distinction is between things worth remarking —preferably over beer, if one's of my generation—and things worth doing. "Somebody ought to make a novel with scenes that pop up, like the old children's books," one says, with the implication that one isn't going to bother doing it oneself.

However, art and its forms and techniques live in history and certainly do change. I sympathize with a remark attributed to Saul Bellow, that to be technically up to date is the least important attribute of a writer, though I would have to add that this least important attribute may be nevertheless essential. In any case, to be technically *out* of date is likely to be a genuine defect: Beethoven's Sixth Symphony or the Chartres Cathedral if executed today would be merely embarrassing. A good many current novelists write turn-of-the-century-type novels, only in more or less mid-twentieth-century language and about contemporary people and topics; this makes them considerably less interesting (to me) than excellent writers who are also technically contemporary: Joyce and Kafka, for instance, in their time, and in ours, Samuel Beckett and Jorge Luis Borges. The intermedia arts, I'd say, tend to be intermediary too, between the traditional realms of aesthetics on the one hand and artistic creation on the other; I think the wise artist and civilian will regard them with quite the kind and degree of seriousness with which he regards good shoptalk: he'll listen carefully, if noncommittally, and keep an eye on his intermedia colleagues, if only the corner of his eye. They may very possibly suggest something usable in the making or understanding of genuine works of contemporary art.

The man I want to discuss a little here, Jorge Luis Borges, illustrates well the difference between a technically old-fashioned artist, a technically up-to-date civilian, and a technically up-to-date artist. In the first category I'd locate all those novelists who for better or worse write not as if the twentieth century didn't exist, but as if the great writers of the last sixty years or so hadn't existed (*nota bene* that our century's more than two-thirds done; it's dismaying to see so many of our writers following Dostoevsky or Tolstoy or Flaubert or Balzac, when the real technical question seems to me to be how to succeed not even Joyce and Kafka, but those who've *succeeded* Joyce and Kafka and are now in the evenings of their own careers). In the second category are such folk as an artist-neighbor of mine in Buffalo who fashions dead Winnies-the-Pooh in sometimes monumental scale out of oilcloth stuffed with sand and impaled on stakes or hung by the neck. In the third belong the few people whose artistic thinking is as hip as any French new-novelist's, but who manage nonetheless to speak eloquently and memorably to our still-human hearts and conditions, as the great artists have always done. Of these, two of the finest living specimens that I know of are Beckett and Borges, just about the only contemporaries of my reading acquaintance mentionable with the "old masters" of twentieth-century fiction. In the unexciting history of literary awards, the 1961 International Publishers' Prize, shared by Beckett and Borges, is a happy exception indeed.

One of the modern things about these two is that in an age of ultimacies and "final solutions"—at least *felt* ultimacies, in everything from weaponry to theology, the celebrated dehumanization of society, and the history of the novel—their wc
in separate ways reflects and deals with ultimacy, both tech-

nically and thematically, as, for example, *Finnegans Wake* does in its different manner. One notices, by the way, for whatever its symptomatic worth, that Joyce was virtually blind at the end, Borges is literally so, and Beckett has become virtually mute, musewise, having progressed from marvelously constructed English sentences through terser and terser French ones to the unsyntactical, unpunctuated prose of *Comment C'est* and "ultimately" to wordless mimes. One might extrapolate a theoretical course for Beckett: language, after all, consists of silence as well as sound, and the mime is still communication—"that nineteenth-century idea," a Yale student once snarled at me—but by the language of action. But the language of action consists of rest as well as movement, and so in the context of Beckett's progress immobile, silent figures still aren't altogether ultimate. How about an empty, silent stage, then, or blank pages[1]—a "happening" where nothing happens, like Cage's *4' 33"* performed in an empty hall? But dramatic communication consists of the absence as well as the presence of the actors; "we have our exits and our entrances"; and so even that would be imperfectly ultimate in Beckett's case. Nothing at all, then, I suppose: but Nothingness is necessarily and inextricably the background against which Being et cetera; for Beckett, at this point in his career, to cease to create altogether would be fairly meaningful: his crowning work, his "last word." What a convenient corner to paint yourself into! "And now I shall finish," the valet Arsene says in *Watt*, "and you will hear my voice no more." Only the silence *Molloy* speaks of, "of which the universe is made."

After which, I add on behalf of the rest of us, it might be conceivable to rediscover validly the artifices of language and literature—such far-out notions as grammar, punctuation . . . even characterization! Even *plot!*—if one goes about it the right way, aware of what one's predecessors have been up to.

Now J. L. Borges is perfectly aware of all these things. Back in the great decades of literary experimentalism he was asso-

---

[1] An ultimacy already attained in the nineteenth century by that *avant-gardiste* of East Aurora, New York, Elbert Hubbard, in his *Essay on Silence*.

ciated with *Prisma*, a "muralist" magazine that published its pages on walls and billboards; his later *Labyrinths* and *Ficciones* not only anticipate the farthest-out ideas of The Something Else Press crowd—not a difficult thing to do—but being marvelous works of art as well, illustrate in a simple way the difference between the *fact* of aesthetic ultimacies and their artistic *use*. What it comes to is that an artist doesn't merely exemplify an ultimacy; he employs it.

Consider Borges' story "Pierre Menard, Author of the Quixote": the hero, an utterly sophisticated turn-of-the-century French Symbolist, by an astounding effort of imagination, produces—not *copies* or *imitates*, mind, but *composes*—several chapters of Cervantes' novel.

> It is a revelation [Borges' narrator tells us] to compare Menard's *Don Quixote* with Cervantes'. The latter, for example, wrote (part one, chapter nine):
>
> ... truth, whose mother is history, rival of time, depository of deeds, witness of the past, exemplar and adviser to the present, the future's counselor.
>
> Written in the seventeenth century, written by the "lay genius" Cervantes, this enumeration is a mere rhetorical praise of history. Menard, on the other hand, writes:
>
> ... truth, whose mother is history, rival of time, depository of deeds, witness of the past, exemplar and adviser to the present, the future's counselor.
>
> History, the *mother* of truth: the idea is astounding. Menard, a contemporary of William James, does not define history as an inquiry into reality but as its origin. ...

Et cetera. Now, this is an interesting idea, of considerable intellectual validity. I mentioned earlier that if Beethoven's Sixth were composed today, it would be an embarrassment; but clearly it wouldn't be, necessarily, if done with ironic intent by a composer quite aware of where we've been and where we are. It would have then potentially, for better or worse, the kind of significance of Warhol's Campbell's Soup ads, the difference being that in the former case a work of art is being reproduced instead of a work of non-art, and the ironic comment would therefore be more directly on the genre and history of the art than on the state of the culture. In fact, of course, to make the valid intellectual point one needn't even re-compose the Sixth Symphony any more than Menard really needed to re-create the *Quixote*. It would've been sufficient for Menard to have *attributed* the novel to himself in order to have a new work of art, from the intellectual point of view. Indeed, in several stories Borges plays with this very idea, and I can readily imagine Beckett's next novel, for example, as *Tom Jones*, just as Nabokov's last was that multivolume annotated translation of Pushkin. I myself have always aspired to write Burton's version of *The 1001 Nights*, complete with appendices and the like, in twelve volumes, and for intellectual purposes I needn't even write it. What evenings we might spend (over beer) discussing Saarinen's Parthenon, D. H. Lawrence's *Wuthering Heights*, or the Johnson Administration by Robert Rauschenberg!

The idea, I say, is intellectually serious, as are Borges' other characteristic ideas, most of a metaphysical rather than an aesthetic nature. But the important thing to observe is that Borges *doesn't* attribute the *Quixote* to himself, much less re-compose it like Pierre Menard; instead, he writes a remarkable and original work of literature, the implicit theme of which is the difficulty, perhaps the unnecessity, of writing original works of literature. His artistic victory, if you like, is that he confronts an intellectual dead end and employs it against itself to accomplish new human work. If this corresponds to what mystics do—"every moment leaping into the infinite," Kierkegaard says, "and every moment falling surely back into the finite"—it's only one more aspect of that old analogy. In homelier terms, it's a matter of every moment throwing out the bath water without for a moment losing the baby.

Another way of describing Borges' accomplishment is in a pair of his own favorite terms, *algebra* and *fire*. In his most often

anthologized story. "Tlon, Uqbar, Orbis Tertius," he imagines
an entirely hypothetical world, the invention of a secret society
of scholars who elaborate its every aspect in a surreptitious encyclopedia. This *First Encyclopaedia of Tlon* (what fictionist
would not wish to have dreamed up the *Britannica*?) describes
a coherent alternative to this world complete in every aspect
from its algebra to its fire, Borges tells us, and of such imaginative power that, once conceived, it begins to obtrude itself into
and eventually to supplant our prior reality. My point is that
neither the algebra nor the fire, metaphorically speaking, could
achieve this result without the other. Borges' algebra is what
I'm considering here—algebra is easier to talk about than fire—
but any intellectual giant could equal it. The imaginary authors
of the *First Encyclopaedia of Tlon* itself are not artists, though
their work is in a manner of speaking fictional and would find
a ready publisher in New York nowadays. The author of the
story "Tlon, Uqbar, Orbis Tertius," who merely *alludes* to the
fascinating *Encyclopaedia*, is an artist; what makes him one
of the first rank, like Kafka, is the combination of that intellectually profound vision with great human insight, poetic
power, and consummate mastery of his means, a definition
which would have gone without saying, I suppose, in any century
but ours.

Not long ago, incidentally, in a footnote to a scholarly edition
of Sir Thomas Browne (*The Urn Burial*, I believe it was), I
came upon a perfect Borges datum, reminiscent of Tlon's self-
realization: the actual case of a book called *The Three Impostors*, alluded to in Browne's *Religio Medici* among other
places. *The Three Impostors* is a non-existent blasphemous
treatise against Moses, Christ, and Mohammed, which in the
seventeenth century was widely held to exist, or to have once
existed. Commentators attributed it variously to Boccaccio,
Pietro Aretino, Giordano Bruno, and Tommaso Campanella, and
though no one, Browne included, had ever seen a copy of it, it
was frequently cited, refuted, railed against, and generally discussed as if everyone had read it—until, sure enough, in the
*eighteenth* century a spurious work appeared with a forged date
of 1598 and the title *De Tribus Impostoribus*. It's a wonder

that Borges doesn't mention this work, as he seems to have read absolutely everything, including all the books that don't exist, and Browne is a particular favorite of his. In fact, the narrator of "Tlon, Uqbar, Orbis Tertius" declares at the end:

> ... English and French and mere Spanish will disappear from the globe. The world will be Tlon. I pay no attention to all this and go on revising, in the still days at the Adrogué hotel, an uncertain Quevedian translation (which I do not intend to publish) of Browne's *Urn Burial.*[2]

This "contamination of reality by dream," as Borges calls it, is one of his pet themes, and commenting upon such contaminations is one of his favorite fictional devices. Like many of the best such devices, it turns the artist's mode or form into a metaphor for his concerns, as does the diary-ending of *Portrait of the Artist As a Young Man* or the cyclical construction of *Finnegans Wake*. In Borges' case, the story "Tlön," etc., for example, is a real piece of imagined reality in our world, analogous to those Tlönian artifacts called *hronir*, which imagine themselves into existence. In short, it's a paradigm of or metaphor for itself; not just the *form* of the story but the *fact* of the story is symbolic; "the medium is the message."

Moreover, like all of Borges' work, it illustrates in other of its aspects my subject: how an artist may paradoxically turn the felt ultimacies of our time into material and means for his work—*paradoxically* because by doing so he transcends what had appeared to be his refutation, in the same way that the mystic who transcends finitude is said to be enabled to live, spiritually and physically, in the finite world. Suppose you're a writer by vocation—a "print-oriented bastard," as the McLuhanites call us—and you feel, for example, that the novel, if not narrative literature generally, if not the printed word altogether, has by this hour of the world just about shot its bolt,

[2] Moreover, on rereading "Tlön," etc., I find now a remark I'd swear wasn't in it last year: that the eccentric American millionaire who endows the *Encyclopaedia* does so on condition that "the work will make no pact with the impostor Jesus Christ."

as Leslie Fiedler and others maintain. (I'm inclined to agree, with reservations and hedges. Literary forms certainly have histories and historical contingencies, and it may well be that the novel's time as a major art form is up, as the "times" of classical tragedy, grand opera, or the sonnet sequence came to be. No necessary cause for alarm in this at all, except perhaps to certain novelists, and one way to handle such a feeling might be to write a novel about it. Whether historically the novel expires or persists seems immaterial to me; if enough writers and critics *feel* apocalyptical about it, their feeling becomes a considerable cultural fact, like the feeling that Western civilization, or the world, is going to end rather soon. If you took a bunch of people out into the desert and the world didn't end, you'd come home shamefaced, I imagine; but the persistence of an art form doesn't invalidate work created in the comparable apocalyptic ambience. That's one of the fringe benefits of being an artist instead of a prophet. There are others.) If you happened to be Vladimir Nabokov you might address that felt ultimacy by writing *Pale Fire*: a fine novel by a learned pedant, in the form of a pedantic commentary on a poem invented for the purpose. If you were Borges you might write *Labyrinths*: fictions by a learned librarian in the form of footnotes, as he describes them, to imaginary or hypothetical books.[3] And I'll add, since I believe Borges' idea is rather more interesting, that if you were the author of this paper, you'd have written something like *The Sot-Weed Factor* or *Giles Goat-Boy*: novels which imitate the form of the Novel, by an author who imitates the role of Author.

If this sort of thing sounds unpleasantly decadent, nevertheless it's about where the genre began, with *Quixote* imitating *Amadis of Gaul*, Cervantes pretending to be the Cid Hamete Benengeli (and Alonso Quijano pretending to be Don Quixote), or Fielding parodying Richardson. "History repeats itself as farce"—meaning, of course, in the form or mode of farce, not

---

[3] Borges was born in Argentina in 1899, educated in Europe, and for some years worked as director of the National Library in Buenos Aires, except for a period when Juan Peron demoted him to the rank of provincial chicken inspector as a political humiliation. Currently he's the *Beowulf*-man at the University of Buenos Aires.

that history is farcical. The imitation (like the Dadaist echoes in the work of the "intermedia" types) is something new and *may be* quite serious and passionate despite its farcical aspect. This is the important difference between a proper novel and a deliberate imitation of a novel, or a novel imitative of other sorts of documents. The first attempts (has been historically inclined to attempt) to imitate actions more or less directly, and its conventional devices—cause and effect, linear anecdote, characterization, authorial selection, arrangement, and interpretation—can be and have long since been objected to as obsolete notions, or metaphors for obsolete notions: Robbe-Grillet's essays *For a New Novel* come to mind. There are replies to these objections, not to the point here, but one can see that in any case they're obviated by imitations-of-novels, which attempt to represent not life directly but a representation of life. In fact such works are no more removed from "life" than Richardson's or Goethe's epistolary novels are: both imitate "real" documents, and the subject of both, ultimately, is life, not the documents. A novel is as much a piece of the real world as a letter, and the letters in *The Sorrows of Young Werther* are, after all, fictitious.

One might imaginably compound this imitation, and though Borges doesn't he's fascinated with the idea: one of his frequenter literary allusions is to the 602nd night of *The 1001 Nights*, when, owing to a copyist's error, Scheherezade begins to tell the King the story of the 1001 nights, from the beginning. Happily, the King interrupts; if he didn't there'd be no 603rd night ever, and while this would solve Scheherezade's problem —which is every storyteller's problem: to publish or perish—it would put the "outside" author in a bind. (I suspect that Borges dreamed this whole thing up: the business he mentions isn't in any edition of *The 1001 Nights* I've been able to consult. Not *yet*, anyhow: after reading "Tlön, Uqbar," etc., one is inclined to recheck every semester or so.)

Now Borges (whom someone once vexedly accused *me* of inventing) is interested in the 602nd Night because it's an instance of the story-within-the-story turned back upon itself, and his interest in such instances is threefold: first, as he himself declares, they disturb us metaphysically: when the characters in a work of fiction become readers or authors of the fiction they're in, we're reminded of the fictitious aspect of our own existence, one of Borges' cardinal themes, as it was of Shakespeare, Calderón, Unamuno, and other folk. Second, the 602nd Night is a literary illustration of the *regressus in infinitum,* as are almost all of Borges' principal images and motifs. Third, Scheherezade's accidental gambit, like Borges' other versions of the *regressus in infinitum,* is an image of the exhaustion, or attempted exhaustion, of possibilities—in this case literary possibilities—and so we return to our main subject.

What makes Borges' stance, if you like, more interesting to me than, say, Nabokov's or Beckett's is the premise with which he approaches literature; in the words of one of his editors: "For [Borges] no one has claim to originality in literature; all writers are more or less faithful amanuenses of the spirit, translators and annotators of pre-existing archetypes." Thus his inclination to write brief comments on imaginary books: for one to attempt to add overtly to the sum of "original" literature by even so much as a conventional short story, not to mention a novel, would be too presumptuous, too naive; literature has been done long since. A librarian's point of view! And it would itself be too presumptuous, if it weren't part of a lively, passionately relevant metaphysical vision and slyly employed against itself precisely, to make new and original literature. Borges defines the Baroque as "that style which deliberately exhausts (or tries to exhaust) its possibilities and borders upon its own caricature." While his own work is *not* Baroque, except intellectually (the Baroque was never so terse, laconic, economical), it suggests the view that intellectual and literary history has been Baroque, and has pretty well exhausted the possibilities of novelty. His *ficciones* are not only footnotes to imaginary texts, but postscripts to the real corpus of literature.

This premise gives resonance and relation to all his principal images. The facing mirrors that recur in his stories are a dual *regressus.* The doubles that his characters, like Nabokov's, run afoul of suggest dizzying multiples and remind one of Browne's remark that "every man is not only himself . . . men are lived over again." (It would please Borges, and illustrate Browne's point, to call Browne a precursor of Borges. "Every writer," Borges says in his essay on Kafka, "creates his own precursors.") Borges' favorite third-century heretical sect is the Histriones —I think and hope he invented them—who believe that repetition is impossible in history and therefore live viciously in order to purge the future of the vices they commit: in other words, to exhaust the possibilities of the world in order to bring its end nearer.

The writer he most often mentions, after Cervantes, is Shakespeare; in one piece he imagines the playwright on his deathbed asking God to permit him to be one and himself, having been everyone and no one; God replies from the whirlwind that He is no one either; He has dreamed the world like Shakespeare, and including Shakespeare. Homer's story in Book IV of the *Odyssey*, of Menelaus on the beach at Pharos, tackling Proteus, appeals profoundly to Borges: Proteus is he who "exhausts the guises of reality" while Menelaus—who, one recalls, disguised his own identity in order to ambush him—holds fast. Zeno's paradox of Achilles and the Tortoise embodies a *regressus in infinitum* which Borges carries through philosophical history, pointing out that Aristotle uses it to refute Plato's theory of forms, Hume to refute the possibility of cause and effect, Lewis Carroll to refute syllogistic deduction, William James to refute the notion of temporal passage, and Bradley to refute the general possibility of logical relations; Borges himself uses it, citing Schopenhauer, as evidence that the world is our dream, our idea, in which "tenuous and eternal crevices of unreason" can be found to remind us that our creation is false, or at least fictive.

The infinite library of one of his most popular stories is an image particularly pertinent to the literature of exhaustion; the "Library of Babel" houses every possible combination of alphabetical characters and spaces, and thus every possible book and statement, including your and my refutations and vindications, the history of the actual future, the history of every possible future, and, though he doesn't mention it, the encyclopedias not only of Tlön but of every imaginable other world—since, as in

Lucretius' universe, the number of elements, and so of combinations, is finite (though very large), and the number of instances of each element and combination of elements is infinite, like the library itself.

That brings us to his favorite image of all, the labyrinth, and to my point. *Labyrinths* is the name of his most substantial translated volume, and the only full-length study of Borges in English, by Ana Maria Barrenechea, is called *Borges the Labyrinth-Maker*. A labyrinth, after all, is a place in which, ideally, all the possibilities of choice (of direction, in this case) are embodied, and—barring special dispensation like Theseus'— must be exhausted before one reaches the heart. Where, mind, the Minotaur waits with two final possibilities: defeat and death, or victory and freedom. Now, in fact, the legendary Theseus is non-Baroque; thanks to Ariadne's thread he can take a shortcut through the labyrinth at Knossos. But Menelaus on the beach at Pharos, for example, is genuinely Baroque in the Borgesian spirit, and illustrates a positive artistic morality in the literature of exhaustion. He is not there, after all, for kicks (any more than Borges and Beckett are in the fiction racket for their health): Menelaus is *lost*, in the larger labyrinth of the world, and has got to hold fast while the Old Man of the Sea exhausts reality's frightening guises so that he may extort direction from him when Proteus returns to his "true" self. It's a heroic enterprise, with salvation as its object—one recalls that the aim of the Histriones is to get history done with so that Jesus may come again the sooner, and that Shakespeare's heroic metamorphoses culminate not merely in a theophany but in an apotheosis.

Now, not just any old body is equipped for this labor, and Theseus in the Cretan labyrinth becomes in the end the aptest image of Borges after all. Distressing as the fact is to us liberal Democrats, the commonality, alas, will *always* lose their way and their souls: it's the chosen remnant, the virtuoso, the Thesean *hero*, who, confronted with Baroque reality, Baroque history, the Baroque state of his art, need *not* rehearse its possibilities to exhaustion, any more than Borges needs actually to *write* the *Encyclopaedia of Tlön* or the books in the Library of Babel. He need only be aware of their existence or possibility, acknowledge them, and with the aid of *very special* gifts—as extraordinary as saint- or hero-hood and not likely to be found in The New York Correspondence School of Literature—go straight through the maze to the accomplishment of his work.

**ronald sukenick**

# The New Tradition
# in Fiction

*Fiction constitutes a way of looking at
the world. Therefore I will begin by considering how the world looks in what I
think we may now begin to call the contemporary post-realistic novel. Realistic
fiction presupposed chronological time as
the medium of a plotted narrative, an
irreducible individual psyche as the subject of its characterization, and, above
all, the ultimate, concrete reality of things
as the object and rationale of its description. In the world of post-realism, however, all of these absolutes have become
absolutely problematic.*

*The contemporary writer—the writer
who is acutely in touch with the life of
which he is part—is forced to start from
scratch: Reality doesn't exist, time doesn't
exist, personality doesn't exist.*

RONALD SUKENICK
*THE DEATH OF THE NOVEL
AND OTHER STORIES*

Obviously there's no progress in art.
Progress toward what? The avant-garde is a convenient propa-
ganda device, but when it wins the war everything is avant-
garde, which leaves us just about where we were before. The only
thing that's sure is that we move, and as we move we leave
things behind—the way we felt yesterday, the way we talked
about it. Form is your footprints in the sand when you look
back. Art consists of the forms we leave behind in our effort to
keep up with ourselves, define ourselves, create ourselves as we

move along, like Malone dying or Genet in prison. Traditions, also, are after the fact. Traditions are inventions—a decision accumulates about which part of the museum is most useful to us in the ongoing present. Now and then a reorganization seems in order. We suddenly discover a kinship with Donne or Greek Antiquity. Pieces are moved up from the basement and dusted off, there's a major turnover in the catalogue, we "discover" Japanese art. It's hard to believe the novel has a future because, like certain women, it has the wrong kind of past. What we think of as the novel has lost its credibility—it no longer tells what we feel to be the truth as we try to keep track of ourselves. There's no point pushing ahead with fiction; we might as well write autobiography and documentary, or social criticism and other how-to books. But suppose fiction is something other than what we tend to think it is? I would like to propose the invention of a new tradition for fiction.

You can't manufacture a tradition with a whole body of work, its examples, its interconnections, its ways of thinking and proceeding. By definition it must already be there awaiting only one final element—that we say it exists. We have already had some work that talks about a new line of fiction as if it exists. Such people as Robert Scholes, Ihab Hassan, Hugh Kenner, Alain Robbe-Grillet have already digested some of this material for us, and an important new book by Sharon Spencer talks about a very large group of modern novelists, many of them unfamiliar in this country, as if they had the coherence of a school. *Space, Time and Structure in the Modern Novel*[1] begins with a quote from Anaïs Nin's *The Novel of the Future*: "It is a curious anomaly that we listen to jazz, we look at modern paintings, we live in modern houses of modern design, we travel in jet planes, yet we continue to read novels written in a tempo and style which is not of our time and not related to any of these influences." There is no shortage of a renewed fiction, as Spencer's book amply demonstrates, and many of its examples have already gained a wide audience. The phenomenon of which Nin speaks is no longer a "curious anomaly"—it is simply a function

---

[1] New York University Press, 1971; Swallow Press, 1974.

of the economics of the publishing industry and a lagging criticism. Given the situation, the initial virtue of the Spencer book is its choice of subject. It responds to necessity. Fiction is one of the ways we have of creating ourselves and the lives we lead. We speak of a new fictive tradition as if it exists because we need to.

The first thing that must be said about the new tradition of the novel is that it's not modern. The modern is now a period— both an era and an end of something. It implies 1939, the New York World's Fair, the Trylon and Perisphere. The modern behaved as if a new age were due tomorrow, and as if it were it, the final goal of progress. Here in tomorrowland we have a more tragic sense of things. We know there's no such thing as progress, that a new age may be a worse one, and that since the future brings no redemption, we better look to the present. In consequence the new tradition makes itself felt as a presence rather than a development. Instead of a linear sequence of historical influences it seems a network of interconnections revealed to our particular point of view. Like Eliot's view of tradition, it would resemble a reservoir rather than a highway project, a reservoir that is ahistorical, international, and multilingual. Our curriculum would probably start with *Don Quixote* in which we would note the split between the pragmatic and the fantastic, the empirical and the imaginative, the objective and the subjective, between meaning and feeling, finally, represented by Sancho and the Don. We would then use this split to illustrate the old novel's inception in a schizophrenia of the word and we would show how the realism descending from Sancho required an initial depoeticization. From here we would move to Rabelais as an example of how such dissociations in fiction can be avoided through the unity of a style that treats creation in both its senses as "all the same river." From Rabelais we might go almost anywhere—to encyclopedic multiplicity unified by wordplay in *Finnegans Wake*, or to Sterne via a joke borrowed from Rabelais in *Tristram Shandy*. In the case of *Tristram Shandy* we would point out how the new tradition coexisted with the old tradition from the beginning, not as the exception that proves the rule but as an alternative rule. We would then proceed to articulate the new tradition through groups of similar novels without regard to period or nationality. We would talk about the qualities common to each of these types of fiction, qualities that in many cases they would share with other types within the tradition as a whole.

The Spencer book deals with one such type, in fact it creates the type—that is, the books were there (Butor, Cortazar, Nabokov, Nin, Musil, Robbe-Grillet, Gertrude Stein, Gide, many others) but the type wasn't before Spencer got hold of them. The "archetectonic novel," as she calls it, is characterized by the spatialization of its form. The spatialization of form serves as an alternative to the old novel's sequential organization in plot and narrative. Through such techniques as juxtaposition and manipulation of the print on the space of the page, the novelist can create a structure that communicates by means of pattern rather than sequence in a manner approaching that of the plastic arts. This kind of writing—one immediately thinks of the prose of John Cage and Raymond Federman's *Double or Nothing*—can be taken in with something like the simultaneous apprehension of someone looking at a box in a comic strip. One model for a work of fiction is the jigsaw puzzle. The picture is filled out but there is no sense of development involved. When you feel that things are happening to you without logic or sequence, this is a good model to use—situations come about through a cloudburst of fragmented events that fall as they fall and finally can be seen to have assumed some kind of pattern. The sequential organizations of the old novel are coming to seem like an extravagant, if comforting, artifice—things don't appear to happen according to Aristotle any more.

A novel is both a concrete structure and an imaginative structure—pages, print, binding containing a record of the movements of a mind. The form is technological, the content is imaginative. The old novel tends to deny its technological reality, but, as Spencer points out with reference to Hugh Kenner, the book is "a spatial phenomenon by its very essence." A canvas is flat: a painter may wish to affirm its flatness or deny it through perspective. A writer may wish to convey an illusion, an imitation of reality, or he may wish to create a concrete structure among the other concrete structures of the world, although one which, like a piece of music, may alter our perceptions of the rest. The novel as illusion is no longer credible, so why bother (Spencer might disagree). But if we treat the novel as a concrete technological structure there is no reason why we can't go ahead in that direction and try to improve the technological structure to suit the purposes of our imaginations. There is the example of the Frenchman, Marc Saporta, who has published a novel in a box so that its pages may be shuffled to read in various orders determined by chance. One can envision novels printed on scrolls, on globes, on moebius strips (see John Barth's *Lost in the Funhouse*), on billboards—or not printed at all but produced on electronic or video tape, or acted out on a stage. Beyond the frame is certainly one possible direction to go, though, as in the history of painting from cubism's "painting out" to the total displacement of the work of art into reality in the "happening," there is some indefinable line beyond which the art you are working in becomes some other art, or no art at all. Fine. Who's to say that painters can't put on plays, and if novelists want to try a little skywriting, that could be fun too. The other direction lies in acknowledgment of the nature of the medium, as in the history of American painting from Gorky to Pop Art in painting "flat," which may permit as much exploitation of the genre without the danger of departure from it. A. R. Ammons wrote his poem *Tape for the Turn of the Year* on a roll of adding machine tape but, while retaining the resultant verse form, cut up the tape and published it in the pages of a book. The consequence is an interesting tension between the vertical thrust of the tape and the consecutive pull of the pages. The book contains the tape form and accommodates it to its own. To complain that the novel can't escape from its binding, as one critic does, is like complaining that the mind can't escape from its skull.

We badly need a new way of thinking about novels that acknowledges their technological reality. We have to learn how to look at fiction as lines of print on a page and we have to ask whether it is always the best arrangement to have a solid block of print from one margin to the other running down the page from top to bottom, except for an occasional paragraph indentation. We have to learn to think about a novel as a concrete structure rather than an allegory, existing in the realm of experience rather than of discursive meaning and available to multiple interpretation or none, depending on how you feel about it—like the way that girl pressed against you in the subway. Novels are experiences to respond to, not problems to figure out, and it would be interesting if criticism could begin to expand its stock of responses to the experience of fiction.

I presume that the movement of fiction should always be in the direction of what we sense as real. Its forms are expendable. The novelist accommodates to the ongoing flow of experience, smashing anything that impedes his sense of it, even if it happens to be the novel. Especially if it happens to be the novel. But it takes form to destroy form and a new form is highly noticeable. It's almost inevitable that a writer who is merely trying to get close to his experience will at first be called self-conscious, formalistic, or literary. The kind of form employed by Laurence Sterne is, in this sense, still new to us. "Writing about writing" the critics like to sneer about this type of novel—too self-conscious. Nevertheless I'll bet that the multifaceted, anti-sequential, surrational *Tristram Shandy* is closer to the truth of your experience these days than *Robinson Crusoe*. Sterne's calculated demolition of the conventions of "the" novel is a thrust into reality rather than a retreat into literature. Let's do away with make-believe, we aren't children. Why suspend disbelief—is Disneyland really necessary? It's as if we have to make believe before we can work up the confidence to believe, as if belief in good conscience were the privilege of primitives or maybe Europeans. Disney, like Coleridge, found an excuse to escape statistics, but Sterne knew we never needed an excuse.

One slogan that might be drawn from Sterne's anti-art technique is that, instead of reproducing the form of previous fiction, the form of the novel should seek to approximate the shape of our experience. In this respect and in many others, Diderot's ignored masterpiece, *Jacques the Fatalist*, which literally begins and ends with *Tristram Shandy*, is the direct descendant of Sterne. In its emphasis on the act of composition, among other things, Gide's *The Counterfeiters* has much in common with

Sterne and Diderot on the one hand, and Genet and Beckett on the other. And of course there is Viktor Shklovsky's great novel of the Russian Revolution, *A Sentimental Journey*, translated only in 1970, which is as deeply indebted to Sterne as is Diderot's *Jacques*. The Russian Formalist's book, in turn, has many similarities with *The Counterfeiters*, especially in its technique of "retardation," which comes to much the same thing as Gide's intentional destruction of continuity. Perhaps the fundamental assumption behind this line of fiction is that the act of composing a novel is basically not different from that of composing one's reality, which brings me back to a slogan I draw from Robbe-Grillet's criticism that the main didactic job of the contemporary novelist is to teach the reader how to invent his world. Writers like Genet, Beckett, and Nabokov, especially in *Pale Fire*, move away from the pretense of imitation and representation to pure and undisguised invention.

There have to be many ways for fiction to deal with the multiplicity of experience, and still another live alternative to "the" novel might be grouped around the axis of Kleist, Kafka, and Borges. If Borges is like a Kafka without anguish, then another important but little known novelist who can be associated with this line, Raymond Roussel, is like Kafka without anything, a castle without a moat, without walls, without buildings—an absence. *The Castle* can be read as an allegory of everything, Roussel's *Impression of Africa* reads like an allegory of nothing, gratuitous inventions, puzzles solved by further puzzles, insignificance explained by what turns out to be even less significant until, as with Kafka, one is driven out of the depths back to the cryptic surface of experience that exists despite interpretation and beyond interpretation. The connection with the French "new novel" is clear, especially with Sarraute and Robbe-Grillet —Butor having moved off into the archetectonic mode. With a twist of the surreal in the direction of the fantastic you arrive at Donald Barthelme, and with another twist in the direction of the psychological you come to John Hawkes. Somewhere in this area you also find: Leonard Michaels, Ishmael Reed, and, lately, Jonathan Baumbach, as well as Kenneth Patchen, whose *The Journal of Albion Moonlight* is another excellent book elbowed out of the way by "the" novel. Here also, and especially in connection with this line's recoil from the idea of profundity, you might run across Witold Gombrovicz, whose *Pornografia* reads like an eroticized Henry James, with all the latter's suppressed devils unchained and raging.

There are two important types of modern fiction that disappeared almost completely during the literary depression of the forties and fifties, although in this case we tend to bury them with critical lip service. "The revolution of the word," as they used to call the Paris experiments of Joyce, Stein, and the Surrealists, is probably still the crucial element in a renewed fiction, and the one least reckoned with by contemporary novelists. The reason it is crucial is that it deals with the nature of language itself, and any art, after all the other things it may be about, is fundamentally about its medium. Both the impossibly overloaded punning in *Finnegans Wake*, and the impossibly opaque wordplay in Stein's *Tender Buttons*, raise the question of whether it is really the pragmatic, discursive, rationally intelligible side of language that best puts us in touch with our experience of the world and of ourselves. All writers are in love with nonsense as the water in which everyone swims, and Rimbaud's desperate assertions as well as Mallarmé's desperate negations are the extreme strategies of lovers attempting union with our native element. John Ashbery wrote recently that there are two ways of going about things: one is to put everything in and the other is to leave everything out. Joyce tends to put everything in and Gertrude Stein tends to leave everything out, and they both arrive at enigma. The only way to confront an enigma is to leave behind what you know in the hope of discovering something that you don't—understanding requires a release from understanding.

The other important line that was almost completely submerged during the counterrevolution of the oldfangled is that descending from D. H. Lawrence through Henry Miller and Anaïs Nin. After Lawrence's first impact as a sexual iconoclast it came to be recognized that his real subject was the crisis of the modern psyche, and I believe the same shift is due to come about with respect to Miller's reputation. These writers are primarily psychological novelists. I think of their books as wisdom books, more analagous to *Job* or *Ecclesiastes* than to what we ordinarily think of as fiction, and of course Lawrence consciously made use of the gospel form. People read such books to find out how they should live their lives, and they are often very popular with the young, who presumably need most to find out. Hesse and Brautigan, for example, are also more or less in this line. The books of Carlos Casteneda, which though not novels have the texture and style of fiction, quite specifically transmit the widsom of Casteneda's teacher, the medicine man Don Juan. They remind me of Hassidic and Sufic teaching stories, but unfold with the advantages of the novel's sophisticated techniques for rendering experience. The recent popularity of the autobiographical form may be attributed partly to the need for such books—as well as to the general voracious and often misguided appetite for facts—though the quality of recent autobiography (as well as of the "documentary novel") seems to depend on what kind of novel it happens to be imitating. Nin's *Diaries*, on the other hand, seem to be a counterpart to and a completion of her novels, and may in fact be her best novel.

One could go on to speak of other alternatives—the revitalization of narrative in the exuberant inventions of writers like John Barth and Gabriel Garcia Marquez, or the work of the mythmakers and fairytalers like William Gass and Robert Coover. Such types are approximate and arbitrary anyway, though one's need to define them from a particular point of view is not. I prefer instead to cut the pie another way, and make note of a new thing that has recently been spotted from my observation post in California, where I and my students in the M.F.A. program in writing at the Irvine Branch of the University were suddenly struck by many similarities in the fiction we were writing, in the fiction that was being submitted in applications from all over the country, and in certain writers of growing reputation. This new thing is a style that we have come to call the Bossa Nova, an elaboration of the new tradition. Needless to say the Bossa Nova has no plot, no story, no character, no chronological sequence, no verisimilitude, no imitation, no allegory, no symbolism, no subject matter, no "meaning." It resists interpretation: as with Kafka's fiction, you can explain it and explain it, but it won't go away. The Bossa Nova is non-representational—it represents itself. Its main qualities are abstraction, improvisation, and opacity. The degree of abstraction may be great, as in Donald Barthelme, a writer who is very bossanova, or it may be slight as in Douglas Woolf, whose fiction seems to hover a fraction of an inch above the level of common experience, just enough to show that no experience is ever common. Woolf, who is in other respects not very bossanova, is nevertheless different enough to have been shouldered aside by "the" novel—or is it just that we can't tolerate anything serious in fiction unless it's dull or comes from Europe? His *Wall to Wall* and especially *Fade Out*, which is a kind of geriatric *Huckleberry Finn*, should be enough to get him generally recognized as one of the best writers going.

The best contemporary example of improvisational style that I know is the fiction of Steve Katz, a leading bossanovan, who writes like a seal with the ball continually about to fall off its nose. He is a surfer on the wave of chaos and the closest thing to Rabelais since Rabelais, but try to find a man of the street who has read *The Exaggerations of Peter Prince* or *Creamy and Delicious* and you will probably be taking a long walk. As abstraction frees fiction from the representational and the need to imitate some version of reality other than its own, so improvisation liberates it from any *a priori* order and allows it to discover new sequences and interconnections in the flow of experience. In a situation where traditional patterns of order seem false or superfluous it may be better to open oneself as completely as possible to the immediacy of experience and allow, in William Carlos Williams' phrase, "nothing that is not green." One way of doing this is through collage, which in fact Williams uses extensively in *Paterson*, and which Paul Metcalf, a descendant of Melville, puts to similar use in a fascinating and forgotten novel published in 1965 called *Genoa*.

Rudolph Wurlitzer is a writer whose work gets very close to the quality that I have in mind when I speak of opacity. His novels have the interesting effect of passing through your mind the way ice cream passes over your tongue—you get the taste and that's it. The experience exists in and for itself. It is opaque the way that abstract painting is opaque in that it cannot be explained as representing some other kind of experience. You cannot look through it to reality—it is the reality in question and if you don't see it you don't see anything at all. This quality, which is perhaps most brilliantly managed in Eugene Wildman's work and some of Barthelme's stories, is a good antidote for that way we have of fending off experience by explaining it. Opacity implies that we should direct our attention to the surface of a work, and such techniques as graphics and typographical variations, in calling the reader's attention to the technological reality of the book, are useful in keeping his mind on that surface instead of undermining it with profundities. The truth of the page is on top of it, not underneath or over at the library.

Admittedly the Bossa Nova is nothing but a hopeful fabrication. In fact, the whole paradoxical idea of a "new tradition" for fiction is a mere product of the imagination. Still, who knows but that one day you may look up to find that a writer as peculiar as Jerzy Kosinski has won the National Book Award, or that Richard Brautigan's far-out fables have become best sellers, or even that such esoteric artists as Beckett and Agnon have been awarded the Nobel Prize, and you may begin to wonder if something is happening Mr. Jones.

**richard pearce**

# Enter the Frame

*The Cartesian focus is something more
than a pedantic coincidence. The philosophy which has stood behind all subsequent philosophies, and which makes the
whole of intelligible reality depend on
the mental processes of a solitary man,
came into being at about the same time
as the curious literary form called the
novel, which has since infected all other
literary genres. The novel, for all its look
of objectivity, is the product of an ar-
duous solitary ordeal: you can sing your
poems, and arrange to have your plays
acted, but all you can do with your novels
is write them, alone in a room, assembling
what memories you can of experiences
you had before your siege in the room
commenced, all the time secretly perhaps
a little ashamed of the genre you are
practicing.*

HUGH KENNER
*SAMUEL BECKETT*

The narrative is distinguished from all
other forms of art by the voice of the solitary narrator that
intercedes between the subject and the listener or reader.

The "curious literary form called the novel" is distinguished
by the narrator's view—a self-contained visual entity that stands
between the subject and the reader. The narrator's view follows
from his choosing a detached and fixed vantage, even when he
narrows his focus to the mind of a central intelligence, and from
his enclosing the subject within the frame of his visual imagination. It is in this sense that the whole of reality depends on the
mental processes of a solitary man. And the narrator's view

gains in objectivity and clarity through a suppression of the frame which he imposes upon his subject, and a suppression of the medium through which he fashions his narrative picture.

A new fiction, aptly termed "surfiction," derives from a radical change in narrative dynamics. The narrator is no longer situated between the subject and the reader, he no longer stands on a fixed vantage, and he no longer encloses the subject within the frame of his visual imagination. Indeed, as he enters the frame, the medium asserts itself as an independent source of interest and control. The narrative voice loses its independent and dominant status. And what the reader sees is no longer a clear picture contained within the narrator's purview, but an erratic image where the narrator, the subject, and the medium are brought into the same imaginative field of interaction, an image that is shattered, confused, self-contradictory but with an independent and individual life of its own.

Samuel Becket may be considered the progenitor of surfiction, and each in his own way—Robbe-Grillet, Pinget, Calvino, Cortazar, and Barth—has followed his lead. In what follows I shall expand on the dynamics of traditional fiction in order to focus on the transition to surfiction.

Let us return to Descartes through a series of innovations by solitary men who made the whole of intelligible reality depend on their mental processes and established a new intellectual and imaginative approach to reality. In his *Dialogue of the New Sciences*, Galileo shows how he arrived at the principle of inertia: "I conceive as the work of my own mind a moving object launched above a horizontal plane and freed of all impediment." In a solitary ordeal and a break not only from tradition but from reality, Galileo imagined an ideal picture of an object freed from the impediments which it naturally encounters. And, as Ortega y Gasset remarks, it was by just this imaginative act that Galileo founded the new science. But Ortega, in seizing on the relationship between science and art, only begins to realize the potential of his subject. For it was a particular pattern of imaginative activity that distinguished Galileo's achievement—a pattern like that which established the new philosophy, the new art, and the new literature. Galileo's pattern can be divided into three stages, although Galileo himself might not have conceived them this way. First, he created an ideal picture; that is, from the detached perspective of a solitary but ideal viewer, he framed his subject or isolated it from the clutter and continuity of its context. Second, he reintroduced the impediments to reconstitute the "full" or "real" picture, implying a relationship between the impediments or a quantity of visible elements and a sense of reality. Third, he transformed his three-dimensional mental picture of a moving object into a two-dimensional and static model—a series of dots framed by the coordinates of time and space.

Now Galileo did not invent the system of coordinates, nor did he realize their geometrical potential, and the history of this mathematical construct has two interesting parallels in the history of Western arts and letters. Shortly after the coordinates were invented, Alberti invented a system of perspective. By looking through a tiny opening in a small box, he found that he could translate the exact proportions of a three-dimensional object onto a two-dimensional plane. Alberti established a new art, like Galileo, by imposing a frame upon a cluttered and continuous field from the detached perspective of an ideal viewer, by filling his frame with a quantity of "realistic" detail, and by reducing a three-dimensional and dynamic perception to a static, two-dimensional form.

The second interesting point in the development of coordinate geometry came shortly after Galileo used the system to discover the principle of inertia, when Descartes helped develop it into a major scientific tool. For Descartes applied the same imaginative pattern in his *Discourse on Method* to establish the new philosophy. As Descartes doubted the lessons of custom, habit, authority, and the senses, he imposed a frame upon the clutter and continuity of history from the perspective of an ideal, solitary, and detached viewer; his ideal picture, freed from all but the necessary elements, consisted of the fact of his doubting and, hence, of his existence. From this certain fact he reconstituted the "full" or "real" world: the First Cause, the heavens, the stars, the earth, water, air, fire, minerals, etc. And he arrived at his picture of the world through deductive logic. That is, he reduced and translated a dynamic field into that static language of geometry—a system of points whose relationship, he tells us, could be best understood if viewed as "subsisting between straight lines."

Alberti imposed his frame upon the whole field of visual experience, Galileo upon a universe filled with moving objects and impediments, Descartes upon a history of assertions about the real and the true. And a similar step was taken soon afterwards by Defoe, Fielding, and, in a less obvious way, Richardson in the art of narrative fiction. Of course the frame was not invented in the Renaissance, but it did serve a new purpose and carry a new message. In the Middle Ages the frame was an outer edge —a limit to the imaginative construction which called attention to the act of imagination and to the fact of its being shaped in a particular medium. In the Renaissance the frame began to be a limit imposed upon the real world. As the novel developed, the narrator gradually shifted his role from that of professional storyteller toward that of witness. He found ways to disguise or suppress the fact that he was conveying a fiction through artificial conventions, and he imposed the frame upon reality itself. Boccaccio, following in the specific tradition of the fourteenth century *favellatore* and in the general tradition of storytellers from the epic to the *fabliaux*, was retelling stories with eloquence and evocative power. His "Preface to the Ladies" called attention to itself as a frame that enclosed his stories. Chaucer created a narrator who claims to have witnessed the events of his narrative; but his pretense is an obvious convention, and his frame is seen only as a more skillfully created device than Boccaccio's. What distinguishes the novel from the epic, the early short narrative, and the stories told within the walled garden of a plagued city or the time encompassed by a journey to Canterbury is our sense of the narrator not as a storyteller but as a witness who has imposed his frame upon reality. Whether his story is told in the first or third person, the narrator is present as a witness who holds a world of time and space within his solitary purview. And the epistolary novel conveys the presence of an arranger with the same function.

Indeed, the narrator of the novel, with his detached and fixed viewpoint and his enclosing frame, is very much like the ideal intellect postulated by Laplace at the end of the eighteenth century and which would serve as a scientific model for the next hundred years. This "intellect which at a given instant knew all the forces acting in nature, and the position of all things of which the world consists . . . would embrace in the same formula the motions of the greatest bodies in the universe and those of the slightest atoms; nothing would be uncertain for it, and the future, like the past, would be present to its eyes."

In the Renaissance a stance was developed to view objects defined not by their inherent qualities or limits but by their relation to a fixed observer governing a closed system.[1] And the term "realistic"—deriving from the Latin *"res,"* or thing— aptly applies to this kind of objectification. It applies, that is, to Galileo's ideal picture, which he transformed to a coordinate graph; to the view through Alberti's little box, which he transformed onto a two-dimensional canvas; to the world picture generated by the solitary mind of Descartes, which he structured on the principles of geometry. And to the purview of the narrative persona who imposes his frame on a continuous stream of events, holds the past, present, and future before him, and fits the complicated details of character, setting, commentary, motivation, and action into the grid of his plot.

It is the frame that gives the narrator's picture its peculiar clarity—a clarity, for all the novel's illusion of movement through time, that is essentially geometrical. And yet, in order to evoke an illusion of objective reality, the frame, as an idealized or esthetic limit, was suppressed. The frame would seem to say, "The world of space and time outside of me is qualitatively the same but is unnecessary and would blur my focus. Moreover, you should forget that only *some* of the visual details (not every blade of grass) and only some moments in the sequence of time (not every word or action) are actually included within me." As realism in the arts and sciences developed, more and more details were included within the frame and more skill was manifested in their representation, and the message was always that

---

[1] For a fuller discussion of the closed system see my "Limits of Realism," *College English* (January 1970), 31: 335-343.

the creation was real and full.

And the picture's clarity was achieved through a suppression of the medium, for not only was the frame suppressed, the canvas as a two-dimensional object, the stage as a framework for carefully plotted and skillfully executed action, and the novel as an artfully contrived sequence of words virtually disappeared. The two-dimensional canvas would seem to say, "I am three-dimensional reality." The proscenium stage would seem to say, "I am a real room with the fourth wall removed." The novel would seem to say, "I am really happening."

Let me try to demonstrate my point and develop a transition to the dynamics of surfiction by focusing on four works where the story-frame plays an important role: Henry James' *Turn of the Screw*, an apparently simple illustration of fiction reaching for a sophisticated extreme of objectivity; Joseph Conrad's *Heart of Darkness*, where the story as story asserts itself as the true subject; William Faulkner's *Absalom, Absalom!*, where the story as main subject is beyond the grasp of the storytellers and the reader; and Samuel Beckett's trilogy (*Molloy, Malone Dies,* and *The Unnamable*), where the central conflict becomes that between the storytellers and the story, indeed, between the storyteller and the storytelling voice—or between various formal elements of the fiction itself.

Henry James' novella, *The Turn of the Screw,* is a useful illustration of traditional fiction reaching a limit, not only because it is short but because one of its chief aims is to bring an ostensibly fantastic story within the grasp of realistic objectivity. The narrative structure begins with the frame of a detached and fixed narrator, who underscores his detachment by remaining nameless. Within his frame is the frame of Douglas, who is telling a story to the guests of the manor. Douglas is not so detached from the story, for he had been involved for twenty years with the protagonist in a way that he can only intimate, and he has preserved this relationship in his memory for the twenty years since she died. Within Douglas' frame is the frame of the governess, this time not the voice of a living character telling a story from memory, but the manuscript of a woman long since dead, who, as the style suggests, composed a traumatic experience into an extremely controlled story. Hence the real subject, contained within her frame, is absolutely beyond our grasp. This does not mean that the ultimate picture is unclear. Quite the contrary. We see the frame imposed by each narrator and the story contained within these frames with absolute clarity. It is only our interpretation of the story that remains beyond our final grasp. The story is not unclear but ambiguous. And our perception is like that of the viewer who tries to fix on the ambiguous picture of the duck-rabbit, which E. H. Gombrich describes in *Art and Illusion*. This is a picture that can be seen as either a duck or a rabbit. But, as Gombrich points out, it can never be seen as both at once. The images may be contradictory, but no single perception contains a self-contradiction. This distinction should become more meaningful when we later examine an illustration where the subject image is self-contradictory.

Joseph Conrad's *Heart of Darkness* is also structured on the principle of a frame within a frame, but the dynamics are entirely different. Again the largest frame is provided by an unnamed narrator. He is not so detached as the first narrator in James' novella; as a comparison of his opening and closing descriptions show, the story has a profound effect on his consciousness. Nonetheless, he imposes his frame from a detached and fixed vantage. Within his frame sits Marlow, in the lotus-flower position, who tells the main story. But Marlow's stories are not like those of the typical seaman—or those of the traditional narrator, including the narrators of *Turn of the Screw*—"the whole meaning of which lies within the shell of a cracked nut." For Marlow, "the meaning of an episode was not inside like a kernel but outside, enveloping the tale which brought it out." The subject of the *Heart of Darkness* is not a series of events contained within a frame but Marlow's story as story, a dynamic process where style, description, characters, symbols, actions are constantly evolving—and where all these elements are brought into the same field of imaginative perception and meaning. The resulting picture is not clear, partly because Marlow tends to generalize and to keep his focus from the "heart of darkness," but more because his focus is not on the kernel, a static entity within the shell or frame, but on the "enveloping" and developing "tale." The reader is offered a stable vantage, even though the first narrator's perspective changes as a result of his vicarious experience, for the first narrator encloses his subject within a traditional frame. And hence we can designate *Heart of Darkness* as an ideal transitional work between fiction and surfiction.

Faulkner's *Absalom, Absalom!* aims directly at the kernel, or at the character of Sutpen, whose story would seem to provide the meaning of Western history—from its sources in classical and biblical times to those of frontier America and the ante-bellum South—and to provide the link between the past and the present. But the kernel is approached from the vantage of four characters with different preconceptions, needs, obsessions, and degrees of relationship to Sutpen: Rosa, the one character who ever saw Sutpen, who was the object of a traumatic insult, and who was obsessed by puritanic repressions and a gothic imagination; Mr. Compson, who heard a great deal of the story from his grandfather, an apparently reliable witness, and who has come to terms with the outrages of history; Quentin, who is obsessed by chivalric values and the love for his sister, who is ambivalent about a history where the sources of affirmation and negation are one; and Shreve, historically, emotionally, and psychologically detached from the central situation but genu-inely curious and possessing a sympathetic imagination.

What we see in our experience of *Absalom, Absalom!* is not a clear or even an ambiguous picture of Sutpen or the events of his legend, and while the novel leads us to reconstruct the events and fit the pieces of the picture puzzle together, to end at this point is to lose sight of the experience as a whole. For the legend of Sutpen is beyond our perception, due to the psychological and historical limitations of each narrator. Indeed the gaps between each narrator and the central story assert themselves as a dramatic part of the novel's fabric. Nor, as in *The Turn of the Screw*, do we see a series of frames, one within the other. What we see are four partially overlapping and con-stantly shifting frames attempting to enclose a subject that is not there. The subject of the novel is not an enveloping or developing story but a montage of storytellers as they try to impose a frame and reconstitute the "full" or "real" picture.

To illustrate the dynamics of montage, let me refer to Sergei Eisenstein's first film, a short comedy designed to fit into his production of Ostrovsky's play *Enough Simplicity in Every Sage*. The play, as Eisenstein describes it in *Film Form*, is an elaborate intrigue in which Glumov deceives his uncle by courting his aunt, while at the same time deceiving the aunt by courting their niece. For the film insert, Eisenstein made use of the play's stage set, which was shaped like a circus arena with a small raised platform at one end. The scene with the uncle took place downstage in the arena; the fragments with the aunt took place on the platform. "Instead of changing scenes, Glumov ... ran from one scene to the other and back—taking a fragment of dialogue from one scene, interrupting it with a fragment from the other scene—the dialogue thus colliding, creating new meanings and sometimes wordplays. Glumov's leaps acted as *caesurae* between the dialogue fragments."

Eisenstein's montage is more immediately applicable to Joyce's *Ulysses*, which was contemporaneous with the production of Ostrovsky's play; but the key elements and the dynamics of montage are also applicable to Faulkner's novel, which, of course, was influenced by Joyce. The key elements are fragmentation, collision, leaping, and *caesurae*. The picture which we hold of *Absalom, Absalom!* in our imaginations is of the dynamic pattern of the storytellers, of their fragments and their collisions—and of the *caesurae* over which we leap as we turn from one page to the next. As in *Heart of Darkness*, the various elements of the subject and the medium are all brought into the same field of imaginative perception; but they are not enclosed within the frame or purview of a solitary, fixed, and detached narrator. Indeed, the shifting frames that attempt to enclose the subject are themselves dramatic elements that collide and leap. And the *caesurae*, or the main story's gaps, assert themselves as equally dynamic and important.

What we have seen so far in this development from fiction to surfiction (a development that is not historical but paradigmatic) is that as the narrator relinquishes his detached stance and reduces his distance from the subject, he can no longer enclose the subject within his frame. The medium, instead of being suppressed, asserts itself as an independent and vital part of the subject. And the resulting picture or view loses its traditional clarity. In the trilogy of Samuel Beckett, not only the view but the very voice of the narrator is called into question. And the medium itself—indifferent, threatening, capricious—comes to dominate the narrator, the characters, and the story.

In *Molloy* the question of the narrator's voice can have two answers: either Molloy is telling his own story, in part one, and then telling the story of Moran; or Moran is telling of his conversion to Molloy, and the chronological beginning is in part two. But this dual interpretation is not like that of James' *Turn of the Screw* or Gombrich's duck-rabbit, where only one picture presents itself to the imagination at a time. Given the symmetrical structure of the novel and the *caesura* or gap between its two parts, and given the contradictory nature of Molloy's voice or the voice which Moran finally achieves, the culminating picture is self-contradictory. The images leap the *caesura* and collide, and they are kept in continual and erratic motion. When we are introduced to Malone in the next novel, who seems very much like the first two narrators but whose identification is precluded by the *caesura* between the novels, we cannot be sure whether he is the first narrator, who has told the stories of Molloy and Moran while waiting to die, or whether he is one of the characters in a story being told by Molloy or Moran. Another shifting frame is added to our montage. And when we are introduced to the Unnamable, a stump of head and torso living in a jar beneath a restaurant sign, and who tells us that he sees Malone passing before him, "unless it is I who pass before him," the shifting frames are multiplied to a point suggesting infinity. But the Unnamable brings the trilogy to a further extreme when he claims that the voice with which he is compelled to speak is not his own. He tries to tell the story of Mahood but finds it was Mahood who "told me stories about me . . . his voice continued to testify for me, as though woven into mine, preventing me from saying who I was."

A key word in the vocabulary of the trilogy is *aporia*, the rhetorical device of doubting. But unlike Descartes', the Unnamable's doubting cannot end with the affirmation of a doubter, and hence of his existence. For the Unnamable goes so far as to doubt the very voice with which he speaks and thinks. The narrative voice, at once liberated from its traditional position between the subject and the reader and gratuitiously imposing itself upon the narrator, usurps the main character and his narrative view. In breaking from traditional fiction, Beckett creates a new subject: the conflict between his narrator and the narrative voice, or between his main character and the limits of his medium.

Hugh Kenner has shown how Beckett extends and parodies the line of Descartes, who, like those followers who gave birth to the novel, "made the whole of reality depend on the mental processes of a solitary man." But we might go further and see how Beckett stretches this line to its breaking point—and destroys not only the Cartesian enterprise and the strategy that gave rise to classical physics, perspective painting, and the novel, but the very essence of the narrative.

The achievement of Beckett's trilogy is in its ability to evoke a positive, indeed vital and creative, sense of personality, even though all the sources of personality—the narrator's view and the narrator's voice—are denied. This potential is achieved from a medium which has a life of its own, and from *caesurae*, narrative gaps, and silences that can assert themselves as positive elements and collide in our imaginative picture. With his trilogy Beckett completes the transition from fiction to surfiction and opens a pandora's box for practitioners who succeed him.

## philippe sollers

# The Novel and the Experience of Limits

*You must pierce the wall. Piercing it is
not difficult; it is made of thin paper.
What is difficult is not to be deceived by
the fact that there is already a painting
on paper representing the way you pierce
the wall, so exceedingly deceptive that
you are tempted to say, "Don't I pierce
it continually?"*

FRANZ KAFKA
*THE CASTLE*

MYTHOLOGY — Admittedly, the novel
has become a harmless topic. Humanists play the role of humanists in this ritualistic discussion, and the modern are modern
with conviction: each speaks according to defined rules of opposition and no one expects the least surprise. Although it protests
as part of the game, the old school willingly yields to the new
one. Today, things happen fast; and once inaugurated the new
school hastens to point out the great historical movement whose
clear, definite incarnation it is. Before this new school illuminates
it, history took a number of detours; but from now on the novel
repudiates its false gods (Balzac and Tolstoy): supposedly, it
has found its trinitary gospel—Proust, Joyce, and Kafka. Dialectical necessity requires that the new novelists *accomplish* what
was embryonic in these three authors, in whom revolutionary
genius is universally recognized. Other names can be cited as
reinforcement; nevertheless it is essential to know how to extract from the pioneering work of these three novelists a linear
evolution which ensures the Assumption of the contemporary
novelist. Despite temporary setbacks, this Assumption promptly

appears in the now infallible museum of cultural values. Thereafter, everything continues as before: increasing numbers of Balzacian novels are printed; humanists are no less humanistic and young humanists soon take their places; and the moderns, the exception which proved the rule, show that their hidden desire was ultimately to gain the modest distinction of having been modern at the correct moment. No one could reproach them. Such, it seems, is today's fashionable mythology.

Thus, everything runs smoothly and a certain determined literary genre (but why precisely this one?) becomes capable of assuming its own good and bad consciousness at the same time. There seems to be a definite division between dogma and heresy, but above all there is an ecumenicism which permits their peaceful coexistence. The law tolerates those transgressions which recognize it and need it in order to manifest themselves. This critic defends eternal classical values; that writer negates them with great sincerity. On this basis they take their places around a circular table. The satiated listener will think that this gathering poses the problem in its true scope, that this confrontation is a good example of democracy, and that literature has finally become the synthesis and consciousness of itself. Enemies use exactly the same language if they can oppose each other with mutual comprehension by doing so. Besides, *"avant-garde"* includes the word *garde*. Strange combat and strange complicity.

Our society needs the myth of the "novel." It is not merely an economic matter, a ceremonial by which society can acknowledge literature cheaply by controlling it very closely, by carefully filtering out deviations (think of the sordid taint of the notion of *"prix littéraire"*). Also, more subtly, it is a way to ensure the influence of a permanent conditioning effect far beyound the mere sale of the book. THE NOVEL IS THE WAY THIS SOCIETY SPEAKS TO ITSELF; to be accepted in it, the individual MUST LIVE this way. Thus, it is essential that the "novelesque" viewpoint be clear, omnipresent, and untouchable and that its masterpieces as well as its difficult trials, half-successes, and failures be casually cited, commented on, and recalled. It is essential that it encompass all the modes: naturalistic, realistic, fantastic, imaginary, moral, psychological and infra-psychological, poetic, pornographic, political, and experimental. Moreover, everything happens as though these books were henceforth written in advance: as if they were part of this all-powerful, anonymous language and thought which reign inside and outside, from public information to the mutest intimacy, with an exaggerated visibility which renders them invisible. Our *identity* depends on it: what is thought of us, what we think of ourselves, and the way our life is insensibly arranged. In oneself one recognizes only a character from a novel. (In me, speaking to you, you recognize only a character from a novel.) What language would escape this insidious, incessant language which always seems to be there before we think of it? It is possible to be recognized, preferably posthumously, as a great thinker or great poet; but the "great thinker" and "great poet" are *primarily* characters from a novel. The "great writer" is *primarily* a character from a novel. The novel, as mute as science, is the *value* of our age: it is the law we instinctively refer to, the manifestation of power in our time and the key to its mechanical, closed everyday unconsciousness.

A book which seems to recognize none of the genre's rules yet dares to call itself a *novel* provokes the anger and irritation of the guardians of this law, the literary traffic cops. It is an intimate journal, they say, or an essay, or a poem; but it is not a *novel.* Nevertheless, such books are usually neither intimate journals, essays, nor poems. If it calls itself "novel" it may be precisely to stimulate a controversy which should be taking place. If we were attentive we would first note that what is in question is a book. But after all, what is a novel? It is a book. And what is a book today? That is the question.

In our civilization the book was originally written language. Then it became printed writing. Perhaps it is in the process, and has been for a long time, of assuming a totally different significance which would pose the real, misunderstood question of *writing,* of which the written volume would be only a limited particular case. There have never been so many books, yet there have never been so few. If the book pretends to challenge the present means of communicating information, it reveals its poverty, inertia, and ponderousness. Evidently it can no longer depend on its author's "style": from now on there is a complete, definitive repertoire of beautiful language (which does not, however, prevent incessant plagiarism). If on the contrary the book wants to constitute itself as *object*, it doubles its fatality and becomes a drifting project destined to be realized (better) by another technique. Perhaps one no longer reads except by allusion to the finished Library or to the mass audiovisual media: almost all books now published are replacement products as soon as they appear.

But by the same token, another dimension, which the book had always preserved for itself, appears in the margin. At first sight it is a negative dimension opposed to the idea of power, to aesthetic values, and to narrative or spectacular objectification. The book which would be a real book, that is, a text, no longer informs, convinces, demonstrates, tells, or represents. If it does, it must only be in relation to its own outdated history or in reference to means other than its own. Of course the genre can prosper for a long time (verse tragedy was very successful in the eighteenth century). But the mainsprings of the classical theater are increasingly well understood despite efforts to prevent their coming to consciousness. And some day a machine will invent supremely engrossing, human, profound novels in which imagination will be at maximum efficiency. After all, the imagination is poor and will be more and more easily *encoded*. Increasingly, men will ask machines to make them forget machines; perhaps the apotheosis of the civilized individual will be to live in an entirely novelized way. In any case this fiction allows us to envisage maximum alienation, lived as liberty and physical gratification. We should not be surprised if the accent is henceforth placed increasingly with perfunctory, confused haste on Epinal's surrealism, the fantastic, the neo-baroque, cheap sexuality, more or less contrived fabulation, the cinema-novel, and the novel-cinema. A previously intransigent writer recently decided the time had come to reassure the convention, which was worried for a moment about irresponsible *forms*: "My novels," wrote this less and less new novelist, "are not of thought, they are of life." This declaration of humility should disarm censure. Let us rest assured that the novel's readers are not to be pitied: it is *la belle époque*, and we are not bored.

"Not thought but life." Or: "not question but spectacle." These are the mottoes of all the reactions, mystifications, and regressions. It is no longer "when I hear talk of culture, I take my revolver out of my pocket"; but rather we are entitled to hear: "culture is so well established in my pocket that talk of thought makes me smile." Obscurantism has never been so aggressive; the strangest part of it is that now it takes the form of an apology of *literature as literature*, as though literature had not been an irrepressible movement of progress and negation for over a hundred years and as though the birth of literature in the middle of the last century had not been violent: *"Literature is not literature, literature is everything."* But pseudocultural inconsequence has become the rule. Increasingly sure of themselves, bourgeois journalists judge from above and decide with enviable impunity. The orientation toward publicity and the biographical exploitation of writers have never been so energetic: as though it were important above all to discover the man behind the author, a man whose photograph should be large enough to hide the text. Soured by the obscurity in which their conformist education rightly maintains them, certain professors suddenly assume the posture of ardent pamphleteers against what is rigorous in contemporary criticism. They are immediately applauded with relief. In psychoanalysis itself, which by definition should be the area of redoubled attention, the sense of intellectual comfort has become such that an increasingly dubious dogmatism resists all research aimed at elucidating the field. Writers suspected of wanting to strike a blow at the health of the novel, and thus of life itself, are treated, in the words of Sainte-Beuve, the still living god of Frenchmen, like eunuchs, impotents, and fetuses. Their writings are sterile, disembodied, and unreadable; the authors are decadent mandarins, pregnant women who cannot deliver, or larvae. To sum it up, they are the opposite of what the novelist's function demands: a capable virility creating stories and carelessly violating nature, a creator, a *procreator*. "We need beings of flesh and blood, we need sperms!" says one. "Exoticism, eroticism!" the other replies. "The imaginary!" they chorus. And we must remember the essential element, "humor," if we ask them to be accountable. But it is fairly obvious that humor which declares its humorousness is not quite humor. Instead, it resembles fear.

Thus, a strange logic desires that any true revolution be followed by a pseudorevolution, not to say a counterrevolution, which is recognized at this moment as "revolutionary." This is the situation, and one could demonstrate the simplistic, repetitive mechanism of its appearance since it began. Proust, Joyce, Kafka, and the rest may after all have accomplished something very different from laying the groundwork for what is presented with tiring and academic obstinacy as the modern novel. They might be very surprised to be taken for novelists in the sense which the word has assumed today. Perhaps, far from founding the renewal of a literary genre or its pseudorenovated exploitation, the limits these authors reach in their writing signal, in disappearing, a rupture which we pretend (or our money pretends) to recognize by the name *avant-garde*, in order to avoid seeing it (along with other simultaneous mutations, notably in "poetry"). But what are these limits? And how is the term *novel* appropriate to designate them?

## WRITING, READING

The incessant, unconscious, mythical discourse of individuals is what we call *novel*. This discourse relates to an interpretation which tends to underline its *determinations*, whereas it is officially declared spontaneous and natural. Whether we like it or not, the unconscious is henceforth at the heart of our existence; thus, optimistic declarations about "creation" find only skeptical listeners among us. We are undoubtedly beginning a period of general interpretation which will leave no domain untouched; and language less than any other will remain as it is, since it is precisely language whose insistent appearance in the primary plane of our attention should elicit a global revision of our knowledge. It seems increasingly necessary, for example, no longer to consider literature only in time but equally, so to speak, *in space*, in its *meaning* and *function*: i.e., in its different levels of enunciation, which are more or less constant. This assumes our *right* to demand of writers a critical and practically scientific attitude toward themselves which represents a definitive rupture with the individualism of the pretended creator of forms. There are no innocent forms: brutal, original, pure, immediate, popular, first, or last; there is no degree zero of meaning. Thus, there is no "true" or "realistic" novel *a priori*, no matter what degree one considers it in, whether the most evident or the most profound. This distinction between superficial and hidden has become incomprehensible, like all arbitrary dualistic classifications (interior-exterior, thought-life, imaginary-real, good-evil, God-Devil, etc.). In our transitional age, the difficulty is evidently to be able to situate ourselves outside these distinctions and the limitations they impose permanently on us without our knowing it. The novel, or the literary genre called novel, has survived for a long time as inoffensive fiction on the condition that we hypocritically ignore the most significant event in its history as well as the novelist who destroyed in advance the laborious production of characters, intrigues, and social and psychological nonsense. The one novelist who gave this event its name was the author of *Idée sur les romans*, in which one can read this question: "When the very deviations of man no longer seem to be anything but *errors* legitimated by his studies, shouldn't one then not speak to him with the same energy he uses in his conduct?" This event and this novelist were excluded with the same force with which they showed the novelesque hypocrisy of an entire culture in the brightest light of day, in the clearest and firmest language. We mean, of course, Sade. Even today, Sade is the fire in which to throw most novels. But despite the clarifications brought to this subject by recent thinkers, Sade's language may long remain illegible in its true perspective, which is not that of pathological sexuality but of the will to *say all*. Maurice Blanchot recently recalled this admirable phrase of Sade's: "Whenever men tremble before it, philosophy should say all." This might also be the definition of literature. Today, to *say all* would mean something very different from a kind of indefinite and manifestly scandalous verbalization. To say all (and the phrase contains no paradox) would be instead to energetically refuse to say anything *except by saying it*, or to denounce a verbalization to the extent that it conceals and justifies with ceasing to practice novelesque mystification. This position immediately entails a concrete choice: as social individuals (and beyond simple material necessity), we may accept the guarantee of reality this society gives us in exchange for an implicit abandonment of all fundamental claims and all attacks on the society's principles. In this case language becomes a secondary phenomenon: it is "art." Otherwise, we decide to live, no matter what the price, as *fiction*: here, a decisive reversal occurs which is undoubtedly scandalous but whose uniqueness constitutes the literary experience. Literature is nothing if it does not touch this reversal.

This experience is the basis for calling into question the novel as *expression*, and consequently the basis for the life given to us. To formulate an idea of it, we must leave the closed space of culture, our habits, and our sleep. The easy, frivolous opinion that such an experience would interest only him (the author) who lives it reveals the misconception on which it rests. The new dimension of the book of which we have spoken, a dimension which is new and yet has always been in it, which it seems to have given itself as an explicit goal as though arising from itself or doubling back on itself, is on the contrary its *reader*— its present reader—and with him the drama of fixed, admitted, described communication. Significantly, it is precisely on this communication that the strongest taboos are placed. Sometimes the accent is on the author as character, an author whose works basically confirm his mythological existence; sometimes—but it is often the same movement—a sort of fetishism of the work, as dogma and as absolute, is constituted. On the one hand, we have the author without the work; on the other, the work without the reader. But it is elementary to remark that an author is not really the cause of what he writes but its product; thus, he is incessantly potential and plural in relation to his writing. A work exists for itself only potentially, and its actualization or production depends on its readings and the moments when these readings are actively accomplished.

The attempt is made to hide this evidence by antinomical

sacralizations. On the one hand, we are told "not forms but sense"; thus the old humanism indefatigably continues its sermon on the SOUL and the salvation of the author by his SOUL. On the other hand, we are told "not sense, forms" and are thrown into the middle of aestheticizing gratuitousness, a barely disguised reincarnation of "art for art's sake" in the appearance of an OBJECT and the more or less fruitful commerce of this OBJECT. One wants to exclaim, as Michelet did about indulgences sold in Rome; "Magical virtue of the equivocal! Thanks to the phrase *work of art,* money and philosophy speak the same language!" Everything happens as though surrealism, for example, had not occurred; but it is nevertheless impossible not to *take it into account,* even though the formula "automatic writing" introduces an ambiguity from which many have tried to profit automatically, with only superficial results. This formula, as we all know, had to refer, in fact, to other sorts of *simulations,* and, finally, to the control and the almost mundane fabrication of the "surrealistic" genre. Nonetheless, one must give André Breton credit, despite some of his unjustified condemnations (Poe and Joyce), for having unmasked in advance all that would return to an attitude of regression or historical omission. Now, more than ever, this attitude seems to be the order of the day. In 1953, Breton wrote: "We have not insisted enough on the meaning and extent of the operation which tends to return language to its true life: rather than trace the signified thing to the sign which survives it—which would prove impossible at any rate—much better to proceed in a single leap to the birth of the signifier." He underlines an event whose undue neglect up until then permitted Blancot, for example, to write "the quest of literature is the quest for the moment which precedes it." But this event carries with it the disclaimer of so-called *realism* (no matter by what name it is disguised, be it naturalistic or mental). This prejudice consists in the belief that writing should *express* something not given in it, something on which unanimity could be immediately reached. But this agreement can relate only to pre-existing conventions, since the notion of *reality* is itself a convention and a conformity, a sort of tacit contract between the individual and his social group. What is

declared real in given historical conditions is what the greatest
number (expressed through those in power, for precise economic
reasons) is obliged to hold as real. This reality, on the other
hand, is not manifested anywhere except in language; and the
language of a society, its myths, is what it decides its reality
to be. Thus, discussions on realism are often interminable, each
participant believing more or less honestly that he is more realistic than the others. Basically, the social censure to which we
are subjected could be defined as what our society prevents by
its network of codes, its monetary obsession, its legislation, and
its *literature*: the coming to consciousness that we are signs
among others—sign-producing signs. In Marxian terms, as long
as *social classes* exist there will also be *reality classes*, the ones
opposing the others indefinitely by contradictions which only a
radical de-psychologization could abolish. But what kind of
liberation would that be? Is it possible? It may seem strange
to ask Nietzsche for a glimpse of this possibility, but according
to Nietzsche we can never think freely if we have not "unlearned
our antinomies." "The contradiction is not between the 'false'
and the 'true' but between the 'abbreviations of signs' and the
signs themselves. The essential is the construction of forms
which represent many movements, the invention of signs which
sum up entire varieties of signs." Thus, we must pose the problem from within language, recognized somewhat mathematically
as our *transformational milieu*. That is to say, it must be posed
outside the notion of *character*: to the extent that we—actors,
authors, and readers of this life—see ourselves as characters,
we submit to our society's mythology and identify with a ridicu-
lously limited identity which is not ours. It must be posed
outside the notion of *product*: to the extent that we value the
product, we suppose the existence of the museum and, sooner
or later, the academy; we favor the collection of fixed, rigidified
things in the pseudo-eternity of value, whereas what we seek
should carry us beyond all value.

The essential question today is no longer the *writer* and the
*work* (still less the "work of art") but instead *writing* and *reading*. Consequently, we must define a new space including these

two phenomena as reciprocal and simultaneous: a curved space, a *milieu* of exchanges and reversibility in which we would finally be on the same side as our language. This difficulty lies in our mistake about the specific nature of writing. We habitually consider it a simple ficticious image of the spoken word or of its imitative transcription (by which we show mainly our obsession with *time*, our perception giving us predominance to the sonorous element and becoming more and more blind to the spatiality of signs). But the experience of writing cannot be assimilated to that of speaking: increasingly, one writes to keep quiet and to attain the written silence of memory, which paradoxically returns the world to us in its ciphered movements, this world whose hidden, irreducible cipher each of us is. Writing would be linked to a space in which time had somehow *turned*, being only the circular operative movement. If writing is genetic, it is at once the most peripheral and most central phenomenon; and thus it contains language and uses it as second-degree material. To clarify *what the literary experience* is, and to show that in no way is it "literature" but, on the contrary, that it touches each of us *in its life*, we must insist on the point which makes it unique and hides it from gossip. It would be easy to show that research on this *real* point was the only preoccupation of writers, as different as writers can be. Our society has unceasingly attempted to brake this research by denigrating or celebrating those writers' lives or works to avoid drawing the consequences from them, to avoid reading them. Let us consider Proust, Joyce, and Kafka. Near death, Proust alerts us to the meaning of his research and of all research: "I fixed on . . . a cloud, a triangle, a steeple, a flower, a pebble, feeling that perhaps underneath these signs there was something else entirely, which I should try to discover, a thought which they translate like these hieroglyphics, which one would think represented only material objects. No doubt this deciphering was difficult, but it alone gave some truth to reading. . . . No one could help me with any rules for reading the interior book of these unknown signs (of signs in relief, it seemed, which my attention exploring my subconscious went to find, bumped against, and circled around like a probing diver). This reading consisted in an act of creation in which no one can supplant us or even collaborate with us. Also, how many turn away from writing, how many tasks would one not assume to avoid that one. . . . The book with figured characters, not written by us, is our only book. . . . When he reads, each reader is the reader of himself. The writer's work is only a kind of optical instrument which he offers the reader to permit him to discern what he might not have seen in himself without the book. The reader's recognition in himself of what the book says is the proof of the book's truth and vice-versa, at least to some extent, the difference between the two texts often being imputed not to the author but to the reader. . . ."

The movement of *Le Temps Perdu*, that of found time, is fully expressed in these obvious, understood sentences; and it is this movement which is important and which must be understood and translated into writing other than Proust's (since it is obviously not a question of writing like him). For Joyce, the question is even clearer, and without the "aesthetic" ambiguity of discourse which in a certain way delays the Proustian experience. In Joyce, legibility is created in the very heart of illegibility; at the border between the world and dream, the sedimentation of languages becomes the world and the dream of one person and of all humanity. The limit reached by *Finnegans Wake* is paramount: the reader is put in the position of becoming the deciphering act which can never be definitive and global but which manifests itself as circular metamorphosis and sliding: "While writing on night, I really couldn't, I felt that I could not use words in their ordinary relationships. Used in that way they do not express the way things are during the night, in their various stages: consciousnes, semiconsciousness, unconsciousness. I discovered that it was not possible when using words in their original relations and connections. But when the day dawns, all becomes clear again." Into the night which Joyce entered through his writing, languages untangle themselves and become alive: they reveal their ambiguity and multiplicity, of which we are the reflections in broad daylight: reflections, images which believed themselves protected and clear. We live in the false daylight of a dead language with limited meanings: we miss the day to the extent that we miss the night which we are. But we are only this nocturnal and diurnal move-ment of the legible and the illegible, in us and out of us, and we do not want to know that. We prefer to think that Joyce made a baroque mistake. We speak calmly of the "failure" of Mallarmé; we imply that Lautréamont was insane; that Ray-mond Roussel pushed the joke a little too far; that in the final analysis Kafka did not detest his sickness; that Artaud should have been locked up; that Nerval or Nietzsche did not fail anywhere else but in the interval which anyone can avoid: it is a matter of good sense. Or else we romanticize the existence of those writers who absolutely did not want to be "writers" in the common sense of the word, whereas they themselves declared and repeated their impersonality. In summary, we make the *reason* these names designate, a textual reason, into the object of sentimental luxury. And that is always done for the same reason: a certain mentality finds it impossible to read what is written; impossible to think in terms other than "products" or "persons"; impossible to notice that it is itself radically com-promised in its language and in the night where it would not want to let us open our eyes. Wishing to reduce this *vigil* of writing, one can say that a writer like Kafka has *become* it entirely. He defined himself thus: "I am a memory become living, therefore the insomnia." This writing without sleep, which is as external to the world as to the dream, but which is nonetheless established in their center and carries them along in its interrogative succession, is what Kafka wanted to live. Until death, he lucidly denounced in terms of death the invisible situation whose objects we are: "He who looks does not find, but he who does not look is found. . . . In literature, I have ex-perienced some states (very few) which, according to me, are very close to visionary—and during which I was entirely and absolutely in everything that came to my mind, without that preventing my accomplishing every idea while feeling myself having reached not only my own limits but the limits of the human in general." And here is another passage where every-thing we are trying to say is assembled in the simplest and most enigmatic manner, primarily the relationship between writing and reading, pushed to a limit where it seems to double back and reverse upon itself: "Three houses touched each other and formed a small courtyard. However, this courtyard contained two workshops in sheds and a large pile of small boxes in a corner. One extremely stormy night—the wind brutally chased the floods of water in the courtyard over the lowest of the houses —a student still awake in a mansard bent over his book distinctly heard a plaintive noise coming from the courtyard. He trembled and listened, but everything remained silent, indefinitely silent. 'No doubt it is a mistake,' the student said to himself; and he began reading again. 'No mistake,' said the letters after a short instant, composing the phrase in the book. 'Mistake,' he repeated, and guiding them with his index finger, he came to the assistance of the lines which were becoming agitated."

Thus, for these people, writing was not an activity undertaken in order to tell this or that better or worse, to express, imagine ("fantasize"), or produce this or that. On the contrary, it was an abrupt, and by definition unachievable, experience which could only engage their lives in fundamental risk, an act which consisted not only in tracing words but in reversing the perspective of the world in which they were found, touching its limits concretely and by themselves. This action can be enunciated triply: "*He who writes is concerned with the whole.*" "*He who does not write is written.*" "*He who writes encounters death.*"

Mallarmé says: "To think is to write without accessories." Thus, we can affirm that "life" and writing mingle, and "writers" (these bizarre individuals usually so incomprehensibly proud of their privileges) merely accentuate the reality which is everyone's. In the last analysis, we are only our system of reading/ writing, in a concrete and practical way. This proposition permits us, without reducing them, to understand Lautréamont's enigmatic declarations, which one must not tire of reiterating. "Poetry should have practical truth as its goal"; "poetry must be made by all, not by one." To write, to make writing appear, is not to dispose of privileged knowledge: it is to discover what everyone knows but no one can say. It is to try, *just once*, to raise the veil which maintains us in an obscurity we have not chosen.

On this level the distinctions between "literary genres" destroy themselves. They are generally maintained only by a convention which ignores the economy and the field of writing, a repressive convention which permits falsified limits (those of an evident pseudo-communality) to be assigned to the novel and to confine "poetry," for example, to an inexpressible obscurity. But we should not let our society dictate the definition of literary activity any more than our artificial roles as producers and consumers. We must think otherwise, according to the following circular, periodical schema: the novel would say what poetry is made not to say; criticism would be the foundation of the great *translation* which goes on in these operations, linked by the same experience, engaging the subject's entire life up to its ultimate consequences. Therefore it is no longer a question of the usual appropriative relationship writer-work-critic, but instead a moving constellation: writing-reading-fiction-thought. This is an impersonal, necessary movement, since one will notice more and more that writing must be thought, that our reality must become thought of writing and reading. If we want to act, we can do so at the level which seems to be that of non-power and retreat but which in fact commands all possible action and at the same time restores chance and ungraspable necessity, whose key in us is *desire*. We do not speak here for an ideology, of a certain conception of the world, of a pathological mania, or even from the viewpoint of a fabricator of illusions. We want to point out a concrete, living experience, the most concrete and living one possible, something each of us can claim, something each of us *is* anyway. What good is there today in talking about literature, about writing, if the most psychic effects are not produced behind these words? We do not childishly desire to be told stories; at the risk of being blinded, we want to open our eyes on the point from which all stories begin, knowing that this activity is and should be *guilty* in relation to the reigning myths and stories. A novelist, poet, critic, and philosopher of our age has lived this silent adventure, tensely proposing these two apparently contradictory affirmations: "To write is to impose one's will." "To write is to pursue chance." To passivity and resignation we must always oppose will and chance, will as chance; and that is effectively what Georges Bataille marked by his writing. These words are dedicated to him.

*Translated from the French*
*by Christine Grahl*

# italo calvino
# Myth in the Narrative

> *Making signs that weren't that sign no*
> *longer held any interest for me; and I*
> *had forgotten that sign now, billions of*
> *years before. So, unable to make true*
> *signs, but wanting somehow to annoy*
> *Kgwgk, I started making false signs,*
> *nitches in space, holes, stains, little tricks*
> *that only an incompetent creature like*
> *Kgwgk could mistake for signs.*
>
> ITALO CALVINO
> *COSMICOMICS*

The primitive tribe's first storyteller
began the word of his first story not in order to elicit other,
predictable words from his listeners, but rather as an experiment, to find out how far his words could be combined, to
what extent they would engender each other reciprocally. And
to deduce an explanation of his universe from the thread of all
narrative discourse, from the arabesque formed by nouns and
verbs, subjects and predicates, in their ceaseless ramifications.
The narrator's repertory of figures was a meager one: jaguar,
coyote, toucan, man-eating piranha, or else father, son, brother-
in-law, uncle, wife, mother, sister, daughter-in-law. The actions
these characters could perform were no less limited: be born,
die, copulate, sleep, fish, hunt, climb trees, dig holes, eat, defe-
cate, smoke vegetable fibers, make taboos, violate them, offer or
steal objects and fruits—which objects and fruits were in turn
classifiable in a limited catalogue of their own. The narrator
explored the possibilities implicit in his own language by combinations and permutations of the characters and actions and
the objects on which the characters could accomplish the actions. This was the basis on which his stories were built, as

linear constructions that inevitably presented symmetries and oppositions: earth and heaven, fire and water, each term with its own set of attributes, its own repertory of acts. The development of the stories allowed certain relations between the various elements and no others, certain sequences and no others: prohibition had to precede violation, and punishment to follow it; the magical gift had to come before performance of the task. Tribal man was confronted with a fixed world of signs and symbols, and with ephemeral, shifting relations between words and things, that came alive in the narrator's flow where each word acquired new values and transmitted them back to the ideas and images to which it referred. Each animal, object, and relationship acquired beneficient or maleficient powers, which were to be called magical powers and should instead have been called narrative powers, potentials inherent in words, the faculty of combining with other words at the level of discourse.

The primitive oral narrative, like the folktale which has been handed down from generation to generation almost to the present day, is modelled on fixed structures—practically on prefabricated components—which, however, allow for an enormous number of combinations. Popular imagination is not endless like an ocean, but that is no reason to think of it as a reservoir of limited capacity. In civilizations having attained similar levels of development, narrative operations, like arithmetical operations, will not differ very much from one to the other. Yet that which is constructed on the basis of these elementary procedures may produce unlimited combinations, permutations, and transformations.

Let me now try to combine two opposite points of view, for that is the best way to avoid remaining prisoner of my own ideas. On the one hand, I believe that all of literature is implicit in language and that literature itself is merely the permutation of a finite set of elements and functions. But surely literature is constantly straining to escape from the bonds of this finite quantity, surely literature is constantly struggling to say something it does not know how to say, something that cannot be said, something it does not know, something that cannot be known? One can say of something that it cannot be known as long as the words and the concepts for saying and thinking it have not yet been used in that particular juxtaposition, as long as they have not yet been arranged in that particular order, in that particular sense. The whole struggle of literature is in fact an effort to escape from the confines of language. Literature reaches forth from the extreme edge of the effable. It is the demand made by that which no dictionary contains which stimulates literature.

The tribal storyteller combines sentences and images: the youngest son gets lost in the woods, spots a light in the distance, walks, walks, walks. The tale unfolds sentence by sentence, but where is it heading? Toward the point where something still unspoken, something still only dimly anticipated is revealed, takes hold of us, and tears at us like some man-eating witch. That is when the vibrations of myth pass like a rustling wind through the forest of fairy tales.

Myth is the hidden part of every story, the underground part, the zone still unexplored because there are still no words to take us there. The telling of a myth required more than the storyteller's voice at daily tribal gatherings. It required special locations and times, special assemblies. The spoken words were not enough either: there had to be a combination of many-valued signs, i.e. a rite. Myth feeds on silence as much as on the spoken word; a myth makes its presence felt in an ordinary story, in commonplace words; it is like a linguistic void which sucks words into its whirlpool and gives shape to the fable. Yet what else is a linguistic void but the sign of a taboo forbidding talk of certain subjects, pronunciation of certain words—the sign of an old or recent prohibition? Literature follows courses that skirt the barriers of interdictions or cross them, that lead you to say what you could not say before; invention, in literature, is the rediscovery of words and stories that had been lost from individual and collective memory. Hence myth acts on the fable like a repetitive force: it compels the fable to re-trace its own steps even when it had started off on paths that seemed to be leading in a completely different direction.

The unconscious is an ocean of the ineffable, of that which has been evicted from language, abandoned because of primitive taboos. The unconscious speaks out—in the dream, the lapsus, in spontaneous association—through borrowed words, stolen symbols, smuggled linguistic effects, until literature finally salvages this domain and annexes it to the language of the conscious self.

The strength of modern literature lies in the fact that it is conscious of giving voice to all that which has remained unspoken in the individual or collective unconscious. That is the challenge with which it continues to confront us. The more our homes are well-lit and prosperous, the more their walls stream with ghosts; the dreams of progress and rationality are haunted with nightmares. Is this the triumph of the irrational? Or is it rather the refusal to believe that the irrational exists, that something in the world may be considered foreign to the rationale of existing things, even though it cannot be accounted for by the rationale dictated from our historical condition, by a so-called rationalism which is in fact limited in scope and defensive in action?

The relationship between combinatorial analysis and the unconscious in artistic activity is the central theme of one of the most persuasive aesthetic theories in circulation today. It is that of E. H. Gombrich as developed in his essay on *Freud and the Psychology of Art,* where he analyzes an idea from Freud's famous study on *Wit and the Unconscious.* Gombrich, following in the steps of Freud, points out that the pleasure derived from plays on words, puns and riddles is obtained by means of the possibility of permutation and transformation proper to language itself. It starts with the specific pleasure imparted by all combinatorial play. At a certain stage, one among the many possible combinations of words having similar sounds takes on a special value that provokes laughter. What has happened is that the juxtaposition of concepts arrived at by sheer chance releases a preconscious idea, i.e., one that was partly buried and erased from the conscious mind, or else only cast aside and kept at a certain distance, but in such a way that it could again become conscious if prompted not by deliberate intention but by some objective process.

Gombrich argues that poetry and art follow the same procedure as wit. It is the childish delight at combinatorial play that induces the painter to try out patterns of lines and colors and the poet to attempt combination of words. At a certain stage something clicks, and one of the combinations obtained by its own mechanisms, independently of any search for meaning or effect on some other level, takes on an unexpected sense or produces an unforeseen effect that consciousness could not have achieved intentionally. It is an unconscious meaning or at least the premonition of one.

Now my two lines of argument may be seen to merge. Literature is a combinatorial game which plays on the possibilities intrinsic to its own material, independently of the personality of the author. But it is also a game which at a certain stage is invested with an unexpected meaning, a meaning having no reference at the linguistic level on which the activity takes place, but which springs from another level and brings into play something on that other level that means a great deal to the author or to the society of which he is a member. Now, a writing machine could perform all the possible permutations on any given material, but the poetic result would be the specific effect of one of these permutations on a single individual endowed with consciousness and an unconscious. On society, on historical man, the effect would be that of the shock which is produced only when the writing machine is placed in a human environment, i.e., surrounded by a society with its own hidden ghosts.

To return to our tribal storyteller, quite unperturbed he goes on permuting jaguars and toucans until there comes a moment when one of his innocent little stories explodes into a terrible revelation: a myth, which demands to be recited in secret and in a sacred place.

Here I realize that my conclusion contradicts the most authoritative theories about the relationship between myth and fable. Up to now, it was generally thought that the folktale— the non-sacred story—came after the myth, that it was either a corruption or a vulgarization or a lay version of the myth. Or else it has been argued that folktale and myth co-exist and counterbalance each other, as different functions within the same culture. The logic of my argument, on the other hand, entails the precedence of fable-making over myth-creation. The myth-value would thus be something you finally encountered if you kept on obstinately playing with the various narrative functions.

The myth which has sprung from the storyteller's combinatorial game then tends to crystallize, to become a series of set formulas. It passes from the myth-creation stage to a ritualistic phase, from the hands of the storyteller to those of the tribal organizations in charge of the preservation and celebration of myths. The tribe's sign-system is established in relation to the myth; some signs become taboo and the lay storyteller is no longer allowed to use them directly. He continues to circle around them, inventing new arrangements, until this methodic and objective labor touches off a new illumination of the unconscious and the interdiction, obliging the tribe to find a different system of signs.

In this perspective, literature's role changes according to the situation. Long periods go by when literature appears to work toward the consecration of values, toward the confirmation of established authority. At a certain stage something in the mechanism clicks and literature becomes the promoter of a process of refusal to see and say things the way they had been seen and said up to that very moment.

So now the various strands of my argument converge with the central thesis of Vittorini in his notes for an essay against "authoritarian" literature: when books and writing come into being, humanity is already divided into a civilized world—that part of humanity which was the first to reach the neolithic age —and a so-called savage world, which has not progressed beyond the paleolithic age and in which the neolithic group is no longer able to recognize its ancestors. In the civilized world, people think that things have always been what they now are, that for instance there have always been masters and slaves. When written literature comes into being, it already bears the burden of the duty to confirm and consecrate the established order of things, a burden from which it slowly frees itself in the course of a process that takes thousands of years, by becoming a private event where poets and prose writers are able to express the very oppressions they labor beneath, to bring them into full consciousness and to transmit this consciousness to the culture and thought of a whole society.

I would add that literature achieves this when it can at last afford to indulge in a playful attitude, a combinatorial game that may at a certain stage take on preconscious content and finally give it voice. It is this path blazed toward freedom by literature that enables man to develop a critical attitude which he is attempting to turn into the society's common inheritance (although the development of this process is still quite precarious).

*Translated from the French*
*by Erica Freiberg*

# Where now?

# richard kostelanetz

# New Fiction in America

> *Every fresh idea, every original theory,*
> *every new machine cancels or replaces*
> *something which had previously held*
> *sway—and simultaneously annoys, dis-*
> *concerts, and frightens those people who*
> *were very tied to the old.*
>
> THEODORE L. SHAW
> *CRITICAL QUACKERY*

A myth dominant in the fifties and taught as well to all its "creative" children held that everything imaginative had already been done—a predicament that, we were told, brought Art to an end through the exhaustion of intrinsic possibilities; but the great truth of artistic modernism, especially reaffirmed in the late sixties, is that there need be no end to experiment and innovation in any of the arts. There continue to be genuine stylistic leaps in literature, signifying the invention of imaginative possibilities not seen before, since creative motives as old as man will always generate radically unprecedented forms. Just as, say, James Joyce's elaborately detailed portrait of one man in a big city—a subject matter typical of naturalism—eventually took a counter-naturalistic style, so the innovative fictions discussed ahead echo traditional fictional concerns and yet, in crucial respects, scarcely resemble ninety-nine per cent of the fiction we have known.

Not all that is new is automatically good, of course; and just as some alternative developments will prove more fertile than others, now as well as in retrospect, so certain examples of any new artistic direction are better than most. (And weak innovations may have the subsidiary virtue of suggesting, if not directly stimulating, stronger possibilities.) Indeed, some new styles are destined to have a more commanding influence upon artists and/or the discriminating audiences than others. Nonetheless, the crucial rule to remember, in a serious appraisal or analysis of any new art, is that *only the good ones count,* for anything less than first-rate will be as surely forgotten as the bulk of Elizabethan theater. Indeed, one measure of excellence is the capacity to inspire in the reader, especially an experienced one, that rare and humbling awe that here, before one's eyes, is something that is quite marvelously different from what has gone before, and yet intrinsically successful and fine. Since the aim of creation in our time is to make a crucial contribution that extends an established artistic concern or tradition, nearly all attempts to create a "masterpiece for all time" succumb to academic rules, which are honored only between snickers of embarrassment. In truth, the dynamics of artistic change invariably sabotage the masterpiece-mentality.

Literary innovations not only expand the vocabulary of human communication but they also resuscitate modern arts that are incipiently senile, in part by inspiring the controversy that revives what might otherwise be moribund, but also by making artists aware of neglected by-ways in their respective traditions. In practice, new fiction usually rejects or ignores the recently dominant preoccupations of literature to draw selectively upon unmined or unfashionable strains of earlier work, recording an esthetic indebtedness that may not be immediately apparent. Therefore, thanks to innovative work, certain otherwise forgotten precedents are revived in literature's collective memory. Furthermore, new work tends to draw upon materials and structures previously considered beneath or beyond fiction, as well as upon new developments in the other arts; and much of it articulates levels of consciousness that reflect both fresh historical understandings and the influence, say, of mind-expanding drugs.

Some of this new fiction seems at first so different from established styles that conservative mentalities are apt to question whether these works are "fiction" at all, even though the modern history of subsequently canonized innovative literature endlessly illustrates that the new work is, upon its first appearance, customarily dismissed as "not poetry" or "not art." This charge is usually as ignorant as the similarly conservative contention of "formlessness," even though any sort of definable coherence (as in the following examples) establishes not only the existence of both a particular form and esthetic selection but, in turn, the presence of the poet's shaping hand. In my judgment, then, fiction is anything that descends from accepted fiction, or more closely resembles traditional fiction than anything else, such as poetry or painting; and it would be stupid to forget Marianne Moore's classic aphorism, radical in its time, that she calls her own pieces "poetry" because no other classification is more appropriate. Another factor worth mentioning is that stylistically new literature suffers at its beginnings a miniscule audience and critical neglect, for it is unlikely that even ten per cent of the works discussed ahead are familiar to readers (and perhaps the editors) of the esthetically conservative reviewing media—*The New York Times Book Review, Saturday Review/World*, or *The New York Review of Books.*

The milestones are those stylistic positions that, though puzzling at first, are now increasingly easy to understand and even imitate. One is the creation of an unusual narrative voice, or voices, a technique spectacularly realized in the classic fictions of William Faulkner and Ford Madox Ford, but also informing the more recent novelistic monologues of, say, Saul Bellow, John Hawkes, and Philip Roth, as well as most of Donald Barthelme's shorter stories; nearly all of these works take as their subject the madness and/or "vision" of their protagonists. (Indeed, creating a fictitious voice is nowadays the favorite exercise in sophisticated fiction workshops, which typically teach not how to write but how literature was recently written.) A second contemporary milestone appropriates the poetic-painterly technique of collage-composition and applies it to fiction, either as shrewdly placed juxtapositions, as in Michel Butor's magnificent *Mobile* (1963), or through the more random "cut-up" technique of William Burroughs; and the successful examples of either method display a narrative line more various and jagged than before and, at times, a realized multiple perspective, in addition to a continuity of style and/or vision over a sharply discontinuous narrative.

The stories of Jorge Luis Borges and Vladimir Nabokov's *Pale Fire* epitomize a third position, defined by turning the forms and trappings of literary scholarship into ironic fiction; and this has influenced John Barth and Ronald Sukenick, among others. Physically separate words and images constitute a fourth fictional tradition dating back at least as far as Kenneth Patchen's *The Journal of Albion Moonlight* (1944); and both Donald Barthelme's captioned prints and R. Crumb's beloved anti-comix are still, in form as well as contents, essentially funny books, differences in motives and imagery notwithstanding. The principal new structure of short fiction in the early sixties, as I suggested in a 1965 essay on the short story (subsequently reprinted in my 1967 anthology, *Twelve from the Sixties*), was the scrupulously flat work, in which the standard inflections of narrative are eschewed as the story simply goes on and on, all of its parts, whether paragraphs or just sentences, contributing equally to the whole. Generally dealing with social absurdity, these works typically come to conclusions that seem intrinsically arbitrary. A major influence here was Samuel Beckett's novels, though an earlier precursor, actually concerned with something else (ostinato repetition), was Gertrude Stein's *The Making of Americans* (originally written in 1906-12). A more recent gem in this mode, Kenneth Gangemi's *OIT* (1969), portrays a certain psychopathology; yet by the seventies, this scrupulously flat narrative form seems more past than present, as, incidentally, are the French "new novel" explorations in phenomenal perception.

Another early classic, Joyce's *Finnegans Wake*, holds a singular position because its multilingual techniques continue to be widely misunderstood, rarely imitated, and never exceeded—the closest approximation being *Fa!m' Ahniesgwow* (1959), a predictably neglected and unexported book-plus-record by the German polymathic critic Hans G. Helms; and for these reasons, among others, does the *Wake* still seem the great unsurpassable achievement of literary modernism. (Indicatively, were the *Wake* itself to arrive unsolicited in a publisher's office tomorrow, it would surely be rejected as "unpublishable in its present form.") In short then, the greatest fictions of recent decades established several definite, post-realist positions that, in turn, can be successfully used to classify most other prominent works of lesser rank. When Philip Roth charged, in the early sixties, that fiction could scarcely compete, as imaginative experience, with the far-fetched "realities" found in American newspapers, he was really judging, it is now clear, the prosaic quality of fictional ideas, and fiction-reading, at that time.

The past decade also witnessed numerous experiments with alternative forms of literary coherence, such as ellipses analogous to the associational form of post-Poundian poetry, as in the following passage from "Idaho" (1962), a short fiction by the poet John Ashbery:

> Carol laughed. Among other things,
>     till I've finished it. It's the reason of
> dropped into Brentano's.
>     get some of the
> a pile of these. I just grabbed one...
>     —Oh, by the way, there's a tele-
> "See?" She pointed to the table.

so that between the clear fragments remains much of the fiction's unclear action. This elliptical technique is extended to novelistic length in Willard Bain's *Informed Sources* (1969) and G. S. Gravenson's far superior *The Sweetmeat Saga* (1971), in which the fragments are splayed rectilinearly across the manuscript page. (Both books draw heavily upon the elliptical lingos of wire services, and both depend so much upon the typography of typewriters that their manuscripts were photographed, rather than typeset, for final publication—typing incidentally revealing far more of the authorial hand than typography.) Other examples of recent prose that seem acoherent sometimes represent attempts to use words to transcend language, largely for unusual perceptual effects; but the master of this fictional motive, as well as much other formal invention besides, remains Gertrude Stein—not only in the unabridged *The Making of Americans*, which is considerably different from the shorter paperback edition, but also in *Geography and Plays* (1922) and *Mrs. Reynolds* (1952), all of which serve contemporary fiction as Pound's *Cantos* inadvertently stands to poetry today—as a compendium of pioneering techniques that need no longer be done. In practice, the acknowledgment of definite milestones implicitly makes the forging of new art not only more necessary but also more possible, for only by knowing exactly what has already been imagined can the fictionalizing artist create, or the critical reader discern, something radically new.

Whereas poetry usually strives for concentration and stasis, fiction, by contrast, creates a universe of circumscribed activity, which may be human or naturalistic, imagistic or merely linguistic; for within fictional art there is generally some kind of movement from one place to another. Precisely by containing diversity and change within an encompassing frame does fiction differ from poetry; for, as Marvin Mudrick noted, "In the beginning of poetry is the word; in the beginning of fiction is the event." For this reason, even experimental fiction favors sequential forms, as the difference between the material on one page and its successors (and predecessors) generates the work's internal life. For instance, a single page of visual poetry might stand as a picture or a "word-image," but such frames in sequence begin to evoke a fictional world not evident in one alone. Nonetheless, a linear reading experience is not a necessary characteristic of fiction, since many innovative books, like the *Wake*, are best dipped into, rather than read from beginning to end. Also, certain examples of new fiction are very short, some just a single page in length, and others just a single line, such as this by Toby MacLennan:

On the table sat a grapefruit made out of a hole.

For even within an isolated space can sometimes be compressed a comprehensive world of artistic activity that is, like several one-page pieces collected in my anthologies of *Future's Fictions* (1971) and *Breakthrough Fictioneers* (1973), ultimately more fictional than poetic. By and large, these rough distinctions separate nearly all literary creations, although I can think of a few, such as Armand Schwerner's ongoing *The Tablets* (1969, 1971), that straddle them, largely by mixing poetic forms with aspirations more typical of fiction.

## II

New fiction, like new art in other genres, can be divided into those that deal only with the traditional materials of the medium, and those that miscegenate with other arts; and the roots of fiction have been prose and ways of structuring it in narrative forms. Serious writers have always tried, in the first respect, to transcend prosaic language for extraordinary styles; so that one measure of novelty in fiction is magical language that is genuinely unlike anything read before, such as the elliptical prose of Stanley Berne and Arlene Zekowski, or the following from bpNichol's *Two Novels* (1969):

> lay on his bed and gazed at the desk
> ties below the levels he'd
> existed on body becoming his falling into her river joining
> every motion she made merely his own body entering
> himself loving noone but himself hating himself because
> his body wasn't his tho she had made her body his alive
> inside himself blobby mass of her breasts swaying against
> his chest choking mamma mamma steam rising

or this inventive pornography from Ed Sander's *Shards of God* (1970):

> He prayed over the sexual lubricant in the alabaster jar
> and swirled his cock directly into it, signaling to one
> of the air corps volunteers to grab her ankles as he oiled
> himself up like a hustler chalking a pool cue. He fucked
> this way, in the anklegrab position, until he heard the
> starter's gun, at which point he whirled about, faced the
> bed, and leaped up into the air toward it, executing a
> forward one-and-a-half somersault with a full twist and
> landed on all fours on the mattress, ready to grope.

Whereas Berne and Zekowski, as well as Nichol and Sanders,

generally favor familiar vocabularies, a more obvious stylistic originality comes from the simulated Africanisms of William Melvin Kelley's *Dunford Travels Everywhere* (1970):

> They ramparded, that reimberserking evolutionary band, toring tend, detiring waygone, until that foolephant (every litre having a flow) humpened to pass Misory Shutchill's open wide oh to be, and glanzing in, unpocked his truck, GONG to D-chel (musically),....

Or by the Joycean overlappings of Kenneth King's "Print-Out" (1967). Critical praise of inventive language needs no more support than an extended citation; but discussions of structural innovation in fiction are more problematic in an essay this short.

Innovative art nowadays tends to be either much more or much less, in terms of quantity of information (words and/or events in space), than art has previously been; and if *Finnegans Wake* represents an epitome of linguistic abundance, creating so many original words out of a rather hackneyed subject (familial conflict), the contrary motive, analogous to minimalism in art, endeavors to tell a story with much fewer words than before, as well as avoiding the familiar perils of normal paragraphs. Sections of Kenneth Gangemi's two-page "Change" (1969), originally published in his collection of "poetry," make huge leaps with every new line (if not, at times, with every new word), typically compressing great hunks of experience into succinct notations:

> White face and red whiskers
> Red face and white whiskers

or:

> Prophase
> Metaphase
> Anaphase
> Telophase

all of his short lists vividly illustrating the fiction's announced subject. Bill Knott's "No-Act Play" (1971) tells a less definable story in a few physically separate lines, while my own "Milestones in a life" (1971) uses one word (or occasionally two) to define the important events in the life of a fictitious successful American:

0 birth
1 teeth

it begins, on the left side of the page, concluding with columns that creep to the right:

76 measles
77 death

and in another of my one-pagers, "On Fortune and Fate" (1969), the skeletal form of a family tree is filled with nothing more than names and professions—fictitious data—that weave their own story about the irregular pattern of fortune in an elaborate family. The pages of Emmett Williams' pioneering *Sweethearts* (1967) consist only of that title word, subject to sequential typographic variations that evoke a heterosexual relationship. Reduced fictions are not synonymous with very short stories, such as Russell Edson's very fine collections or those cute anecdotes comprising John Cage's "Indeterminacy" (1958), both of which contain, to cite two current criteria of archaism, sentences and paragraphs.

Some new fictional forms depend upon either material or structures taken from outside literature. In a witty pastiche that successfully masks its collage-composition, Frederic Tuten's *The Adventures of Mao on the Long March* (1971) mixes paragraphs of conventional historical narrative with fictitious incidents, such as Greta Garbo propositioning Mao, and such extrinsic material as verbatim (but unidentified) quotations from a variety of literary sources (Hawthorne, Melville, Wilde, Jack London, Marx-Engels, et al.). Exploiting not only nonfictional materials but a non-literary structure, Jan Herman's brilliant *General Municipal Election* (1969) takes the format of an elaborate election ballot, and fills the 12″ by 24″ space with fictional (and sometimes satirical) choices, while John Barth's "Frame-Tale" (1968) must be cut from the book, and then folded and pasted into a Moebius strip (an endless geometrical surface) that reads, "Once upon a time there was a story that began" in an interminable circle. Perhaps the extended masterwork in this mode of extrinsically imposed form is Richard Horn's novel *Encyclopedia* (1969), in which alphabetized notations (filled with cross-references worth following) weave an ambiguous fiction about human interrelationship, paradoxically disordering by reordering; and this novel, like many other examples of new fiction, deliberately frustrates the bourgeois habit of continuous reading. One might say that both the rectangular page and the process of turning pages are as essential to fiction as prose and narrative form; but if the reader must skip around so much, how can he tell whether or not he has "finished the book"?

Another of the supremely inventive recent novels, Madeline Gins' *Word Rain* (1969), also ranks among the most difficult, dealing with the epistemological opacity of language itself. The first sign of the book's unusual concerns and its equally special humor is its extended subtitle: "(or A Discursive Introduction to the Philosophical Investigations to G,R,E,T,A,G,A,R,B,O, It Says)"; a second is the incorporation of several concerns of new fiction—special languages, expressive design, extrinsically imposed form. Perhaps the surest index of this novel's originality was either the neglect of reviewers or Hayden Carruth's sneer, in *New American Review*, at novelists' "fooling away at their talents in endless novelistic puzzles, a pastime which seems to have reached an ultimate reduction—I hope it's ultimate—in *Word Rain* by Madeline Gins."

"The saddest thing is that I have to use words," announces the narrator, not only echoing the opening sentence of Ford Madox Ford's fictional study of human opacity, *The Good Soldier* (1927), but also exemplifying that Gertrude Steinian paradox of using language to reveal the limitations of both language and the reading process. That theme is reiterated in every chapter, rather than developed in a cumulative way, suggesting that the indicatively unpaginated book is best read in snatches, rather than straight through. That method which is the book's theme is revealed through a variety of opaque styles; but some of the passages remain more illuminating, if not more definite, than others:

> Each word on the page seemed ossified. The word face was a stone. The word guess was a flint. The words a, the, in, by, up, it, were pebbles. The word laughter was marble. Run was cartilage. Shelf was bone. Talk was an oak board. See was made of quartz. The word refrigerator was enameled. The word afternoon was concrete. The word iron was iron. The word help was wrought-iron. The word old was crag. The word touch was brick. The word read was mica and I was granite.

The book's pages are also distinguished by numerous inventive displays of printed material—lists of unrelated words with dots between them, whole sides filled mostly with dashes where words might otherwise be, pseudo-logical proofs, passages in which the more mundane expressions are crossed out, an appendix of "some of the words (temporary definitions) not included," even a photographed hand holding both sides of a printed page, and a concluding page of print-over-print which reads at its bottom: "This page contains every word in the book." *Word Rain* suffers from the perils of its theme—a linguistic opacity that prevents most readers from discovering its purpose and entering its imaginative world—a fault of Frederick Barthelme's comparable, though lesser effort, *War and War* (1971); but precisely by allowing its philosophical obsession to remain uncompromised, *Word Rain* becomes, inevitably for the few, a touchstone of innovative prose.

## III

The other strain of new fiction resembles certain parts of *Word Rain* in mixing fictional concerns with materials and techniques from the other arts, as *Word Rain* does in certain parts. Visualization is probably a more feasible kind of miscegenation than sound-fiction, which N. H. Pritchard and W. Bliem Kern, for two, have begun to broach. In this new fiction, visual dimensions are not auxiliaries to language, as in certain Wright Morris photographic works, but entwined within the verbal material, as in word-image poetry. In Nancy Weber's "Dear Mother and Dad" (1970), a rather prosaic tale of the narrator's breakdown is brilliantly enhanced by photographically reproduced handwriting that expressively changes (and, thus, interprets the language) in the course of the four-page story; so that without the visual dimension, the fiction would be uninteresting. In Pritchard's "Hoom" (1970), two-page spreads filled entirely with "sh" are punctuated by a progressively increasing number of spreads with other kinds of wordless typographical arrangements; "Oab" by Robert Zend, a Canadian born in Hungary, brilliantly mixes poetry and prose in various typographies with even more various designs.

In Raymond Federman's masterpiece, *Double or Nothing* (1971), a form is established for each page—usually a visual shape, but sometimes a grammatical device such as omitting all the verbs—and the words of his fiction fill the allotted structure. Over these individually defined pages which reveal an unfaltering capacity for formal invention, he weaves several sustained preoccupations, including the narrator's immigration to America, his obsessive memories, his poverty, his parsimonious passion for noodles, etc. In *Double or Nothing,* as in much other visual fiction, the page itself becomes the basic narrative unit, superceding the paragraph or the sentence, the work becoming a succession of extremely distinctive, interrelated pages. No other "novel" looks like it; none of the other visual fictions is so rich in traditional "content." Reflecting this new sense of fictional unit, several otherwise less substantial recent novels include reproduction of the typewritten manuscript (e.g., Earl Conrad's *Typoo* [1969]) and full-page graphics (e.g., Steve Katz's *The Exagggerations of Peter Prince* [1967]): and also blank pages and totally black ones, the latter two usually signifying the absence of action or an extended, otherwise undefinable pause.

Predominantly visual fictions emulate the structure of film

in the sequential development of related images, with or without words; but even in totally visual stories, the narrative exposition is far more selective and concentrated than in film—as is the audience's perceptual experience and subsequent memory of the work. Many stories that are primarily, or exclusively, pictorial strive to implant an "after-image"—a sense of the whole visually embedded in the viewer's mind long after he has experienced the work; for in this process too can the medium of printed pages be more selective and concentrated than film. However, since visual fictions, unlike film, cannot simulate the experience of time, much of the "story," and nearly all of its elapsed duration, occurs *between* the fiction's frames.

The best of Duane Michals' wordless photographic *Sequences* (1970) is a set of six pictures collectively entitled "The Lost Shoe," the first showing a deserted urban street, with the fuzzy backside of a man walking away from the camera and up the street. In the second frame he drops on the pavement a blurred object which in the third frame is seen to be a lady's shoe; and this frame, as well as the next two, suggest that he departs up the street in a great hurry. In the sixth frame the man is nowhere to be seen, while the shoe is mysteriously inflamed. The realism of all the photographs starkly contrasts with the mysteriousness of the plot, while the movements portrayed accent the absolute stationariness of the camera. For this reason, the authorial perspective is as Chekhovian as both the work's title and its acceptance of something very inexplicable and perhaps forbidding; and although "The Lost Shoe" would conventionally be classified as a photographic sequence, its ultimate impact is decidedly fictional and, as fiction, very fine and clearly new. M. Vaughn-James, Edward Ruscha, and Eleanor Antin are among those working successfully in this way.

Some visual fictions contain words, which create patterns that change, as can the words, over the sequence's duration. One of my own opens with that multiply defined word "GOODS" repeated into the shape of an open rectangular frame, which, as the pages turn, becomes progressively more filled with "GOODS" until all that remains open is the shape of a cross and then just an open rectangle perhaps reminiscent of a coffin; for in the next frame the rectangle falls away for the first time and the repeated word "GOODS" forms a cross. The final frame duplicates the first except that in the open middle is a rectangular shape formed by repeating the words "PEACE/CEASE!" The fiction depends upon the repeated word for its subject, the accumulation of goods (which could be taken as either objects or virtues); but the story's narrative development comes from visual, rather than linguistic manipulations. One of my novellas, *In the Beginning* (1971), contains just letters; another, *Accounting* (1972), only numbers.

Other visual fiction differs from both "The Lost Shoe" and my novellas by compressing all of its material into a single page, like those of Lee DeJasu and Norman Ogue Mustill, or by its total abstraction, presenting just a sequence of related shapes. In Marian Zazeela's "Lines" (1969) are five pages of related meditative shapes that become more complex for four pages prior to a delicate resolution on the fifth; and Jess Reichek's *etcetera* (1965) is an unpaginated succession of abstract, black and white shapes superficially resembling Rorschach blobs that echo and complement each other for sixty frames, all presented without any preface or explanation. The progression seems at times symbolic, perhaps of a descent; but the frames remain largely loyal to their own narrative terms. In this and similar pieces, "Form *is* content, content *is* form," to quote Samuel Beckett's classic remark about *Finnegans Wake;* so that both of these dimensions are by necessity experienced simultaneously. And visual fiction can articulate kinds of stories and perceptions— and offers kinds of "reading" experience—simply unavailable to prose.

It should be clear by now that the writings described here represent something radically new and undefined, and as yet probably undefinable, in literary history—a "post-Modernism," if you will; and these examples repudiate conclusively any intimations of either literature's evolutionary death or the creative mind's reported inability to compete imaginatively with the exaggerations of contemporary life. They also suggest not just a new development in American literature but further radical possibilities for change in imaginative forms, thereby testifying to the continuing inventive capacities of literary men. This new writing surpasses as well most earlier forms of avant-garde literature, constituting an advance perhaps best defined by the critic-poet Hugh Fox in the course of distinguishing "beat" from "hip": "The Beats were still 'linear,' the Hippies are 'curvilinear,' the Beats were 'sequential,' the Hippies are 'instantaneous,' the Beats were 'natural,' the Hippies are 'electronic.' " More crucially, the expressionistic Beats emphasized authorial voice, which goes masked in nearly all strains of new literature.

Most of the writers discussed here are still underground— disaffiliated and disorganized, rarely surfacing into public print, inhabiting a culture of little magazines and small press (or self-published) books, somewhat known to each other, but unrecognized by more orthodox poets and novelists, all but totally invisible to the larger reading public and then totally excluded from all anthologies except their own; so that their creative adventure is, for the while at least, doomed to be isolated and frustrated. Since established critics ignore this literature, reputations are primarily made among fellow avant-garde artists who, in spite of inevitable jealousies, generally acknowledge genuine achievements and advances; and as in other contemporary arts, stylistic imitation implicitly becomes not only the sincerest form of flattery but also the most honest way of bestowing honor. Despite all the pressures toward cultural alienation and literary hermeticism, most of this new literature is remarkably accessible, once the open-minded reader overcomes the superficial difficulties posed by anything original.

It is my considered estimate, as both an avant-garde critic and experimental literary practitioner, that three-quarters of the potentially innovative works done today do not get into print, and more than half of those that do probably never broach even my attentive interest; for two decades from now, it will probably seem that as much ignorance as knowledge marked even this pioneering essay. Indeed, the current editorial situation is so comprehensively discouraging that the mere existence of something innovative is itself a tribute to human imagination and perseverance. That there exists an intelligent audience for this work there is no doubt, as the success of earlier kinds of avant-garde literature (or, say, almost everything that I champianed in *The New American Arts* [1965]) demonstrates that a large literary public does undoubtedly appreciate genuinely step-ahead writing; and that fact alone provides reason for hope. In the end, the fate of literature and imaginative reading depends, to a degree, upon the public fortunes of this new work. If writers coming of age in the twenties thought poetry was king, and those in the thirties and forties were most awed by fiction (and those in the sixties by personal journalism, perhaps), it is my hunch that the seventies will become an era marked by innovative literature—by writing in any form that successfully surpasses what has been written before.

**jean ricardou**

# Nouveau Roman, Tel Quel

*The most imaginative people have the sense of theory because they are not afraid that it will curb their imagination, on the contrary. But the weak fear theory, and any kind of risk—they fear it the same way they fear draughts.*

PIERRE BOULEZ

*What would that event be? It would have the external form of a rupture and a reduplication.*

JACQUES DERRIDA

Those who confine themselves endlessly to mere labels thereby grant themselves the precarious privilege of manipulating peculiar syncretisms—such, as Paul Valéry often observed, is the very common way of eluding singular texts. Conversely, those who let themselves be captivated by the individuality of literary work thereby expose themselves to the mirage of originality—at the risk of omitting the very precise relations that prevail between the texts. Avoiding both those temptations, and citing the texts to document our case, we shall examine the complementary play of their divergencies and similarities. A small number of specific problems shall constitute the basis for a classification of several recent works of fiction. Con-

---

"Nouveau Roman": the French "new novel"; "Tel Quel": a French formula which means "as is", "as it stands", but also the name of a contemporary French literary review and group of writers whom Jean Ricardou compares to the so-called "new novelists".

sidered in themselves, the eventual superpositions will enable us to transcend the singular toward an outline of typical procedures; their probable respective oppositions, on the other hand, will suggest some of the differences which distinguish two kinds of fiction. *La Maison de rendez-vous*, by Alain Robbe-Grillet (1965), *Le Libera*, by Robert Pinget (1968), on the one hand and, on the other, *Personnes*, by Jean-Louis Baudry (1967), and *Nombres*, by Philippe Sollers (1968) shall constitute the field of inquiry. The problems of *character*, *formalization*, and *representation* shall be the topics of investigation. Thus, starting from an essential aspect of fiction, the technical and the ideological will ultimately be brought into relation.

### I. DEATH OF THE FICTIONAL CHARACTER

It is common knowledge that the traditional notion of character has been attacked from every conceivable angle by the movement of modern literature. It was certainly not by accident that Claude Ollier chose "The Death of a Character" as the title for one of his radio plays: today it is in fact possible to construct an entire fiction as the ironic allegory of that irremissible degradation. Yet what is that metaphor, if not the contemporary echo of a prophetic announcement which attracted little attention, in another age, at the dawn of the modern era? In his famous letter to Sainte-Beuve about his novel *Salammbô*, Flaubert made the confession that in his book the pedestal was incommensurate—too big for the statue. Yet Flaubert's meticulous accuracy is a little too well known for us not to suspect him of having exercised, there too, his usual extreme caution. What! The author of *Salammbô* who wouldn't hazard a description of some Carthaginian door without first having checked its every detail in Ammien Marcelin; who relentlessly pursued in all points of his text the most microscopic involuntary alliteration; this same Flaubert would yet have tolerated, in his book, after years of labor, such a monumental disproportion? No, let us rather read that, addressing himself in an unfavorable time to a powerful and retrograde critic, he had hardly any other means of suggesting that the novel, in the future, would no longer be comparable to a statue on a pedestal; that, ever more severely subjected to novel literary procedures, the character had started along the path of his downfall. Before long, Bouvard and Pécuchet would be no more than the pure and simple convenience of an encyclopedic inventory.

A. "Now, that was a real character!"
*La Maison de rendez-vous* not only pursues that course, but even tends to accentuate it. If, for instance, the title of a play is mentioned, it is "The Death of Edouard Manneret." This title is an obvious counterpart to that of Ollier's play: isn't Edouard Manneret in fact the only one about whom Robbe-Grillet's novel asserts, somewhat comically: "now, that was a real character"? It is this same Edouard Manneret who, eternally resuscitated in the plot, is the victim, innumerably, of the widest assortment of murders. No doubt this is a case of one of those internal fables whereby the novel, in some point or another, signals the techniques of its own production. The moral: on the continually reborn character, the novel shall inflict the violence of ceaselessly recurring massacres.

This attack on the character, i.e. on the singleness of an identity, is one means of producing problems of classification. The operation consists of two phases: the dissociation of an individual into incompatible fragments; the distribution of the pieces according to completely new units. As is the case in the phenomenon of animal mimicry, where disruptive spots disperse the specimen into new figures by analogy with the variety of the environment, so here the problem is to dissolve a unity, then to amalgamate the various parts. Needless to say, these perturbations take as their object the traditional attributes of the solid Balzacian character: surname, social role, nationality, parentage, and sometimes even age and physical appearance.

In *La Maison de rendez-vous*, this disjunctive activity seems at first to obey two inverse tendencies: the one connecting the permanence of the name to a diversity of roles; the other linking a plurality of names to the continuity of role. Manneret is a perfect example of the first case. Although his surname appears to remain stable, his occupation undergoes some strange metamorphoses which, in their successive stages, while these are not

all incompatible, cumulatively result in the excesses of a disquieting miscegenation. On page 70 [of the French edition, of
course] he is a writer: "He is at his desk. He is writing." On
page 84, he is the character of a play: "The Assassination of
Edouard Manneret." On page 85, he turns out to be a painter:
"The Maïa, a famous painting by Edouard Manneret." On page
117, he is characterized as a usurer, notorious for his meanness.
Page 167 reveals that he is a "doctor, chemist, vaguely fetishist
at the same time", while on page 208 he is denounced as a
curious kind of secret agent:

> Edouard Manneret was just murdered by the Communists,
> on the pretext—obviously false—that he was a double
> agent for Formosa. Actually it was a much more compli-
> cated and disturbing act of retaliation.

Finally, a major discrepancy, his death hardly seems to inter-
rupt his life ... Conversely, cast in the role of Lauren's fiancé
is a certain Dutch merchant whose name undergoes a series of
phonetic transformations. A first alternative is proposed on
page 13: "This Marchat or Marchand was not a habitué"; a
second is offered on page 210: "It was Georges Marchat or
Marchant" [Trans. note: *marchand* = merchant; *marchant* =
walking (marching)].

However, a closer reading reveals that the stable element is
actually challenged in both cases. The solidity of the surname
Manneret is compromised by transparent allusions to the names
of two painters, Manet and Man Ray, which tend respectively
to shorten and to split it. And as for Lauren's fiancé, the merchant Marchat, are we so sure of his trade after all? Page
185 seems rather to suggest that he, no less than Manneret,
is a well-known painter:

> I had had hundreds of opportunities to contemplate at
> leisure these sculptures, paintings and pastels. I even know
> their signatures, practically all famous. Edouard Manneret,
> R. Jonestone, G. Marchand, etc.

And that is not the only hint of conflict: in a book where theater plays as insistent a role as in this one, the obvious phonetic references to such well-known French performers as Jean Marchat or Georges Marchal continue, somewhat insidiously, to lend our character the traits of an actor. And even his nationality is none too certain: a question which presumes him French is answered, page 97, with a dubious: "No, Dutch I think". And, finally, perhaps this suitor is merely, page 56, "that insignificant young man to whom Lauren is generally supposed to be engaged."

Thus, ultimately, nothing really solid subsists of either names or roles. The most surprising example is no doubt provided by the reversible transformations of Lady Ava, the beautiful proprietress of the Maison Bleue, into the German Eva Bergmann, then into Jacqueline, the old actress born in the low-class Parisian neighborhood of Belleville, who babbles old tales she once heard about the place. . . . But the most complex disjunction is the one that produces the impossible R. Jonestone, Jonstone, "the one they call Johnson or often even 'the American' although he's British and a baron" (page 46), Sir Ralph, "that freshly debarked American" whose indifferent manner "probably earned him his British title" (page 53) and who, a Portuguese from Macao on page 95, is alternately painter, planter, white slaver, pusher, political undercover agent, and even, on occasion, doctor.

As we have observed, the disparate elements which dislocate each identity concomitantly provide resources whereby the effects of similarity may produce some disquieting amalgams. Writer, actor, usurer, doctor, vaguely fetishistic chemist, undercover agent: such an excessive accumulation thoroughly splits the identity of Manneret the painter. And, from then on, the latter has an even greater tendency to be confused, if not fused, with any other character who, no less deteriorated, happens to be a painter, too. Thus a series of curious hybrids, transient combinations born of strange encounters, appear throughout the book. And in fact, systematically, the common roles are multiplied. Manneret, Johnson, Marchand are all painters. Johnson and Manneret are doctors of a sort. Manneret, Johnson, and

Lady Ava are pushers who double as spies. From Manneret, Johnson, and Marchand to Lady Ava and Lauren, there is no one who is not involved in some kind of commercial activity. And, finally, practically all have names reminiscent of well-known actors and actresses: Marchand (Georges Marchal), Johnson (Van Johnson), Bergmann (Ingrid Bergman), Kim (Kim Novak), Ralph (George Raft), Lauren (Sophia Loren)— which, in addition, suggests the possibility that the fragmentation of their beings may be attributed to their actually being mere appearances.

Hardly less than their roles, their names, too, display factors in common. They also function as insidious sieves: the reader is tempted to use names to shift from one character to another. Ki is common to Kim and Kito, To to Kito and Jonestone, Man to Manneret and Bergmann, Chan to Marchand and Tchang. In this cosmopolitan world, the connection between rocks (stone) and mountains (berg) provides a link betwen Bergmann and Jonestone. Thus the reader's thirst for identification is constantly frustrated by a perfect system of quid pro quo, the upshot of which is that, as no one is ever exactly himself, everyone is always more or less everybody else. This comes to a comical climax on the final pages, where Johnson, i.e. Sir Ralph, ends up being taken for Sir Ralph, i.e. Johnson:

> First Manneret takes Johnson for his son; he takes him for Georges Marchat or Marchant, he takes him for Mr. Tchang, he takes him for Sir Ralph, he takes him for King Boris.

Nor do things stop there: since the monopolization of a proper name contributes to the unity of identity, a new type of decadence may be surmised. If various collusions associate the weaving of the plot with the interwoven names, the latter will somehow tend to become synonyms of mere common nouns. Jonestone, precisely, the name of a sculptor, contains the common name Jones as well as the common noun stone; Edouard Manneret and Marchand, names of artists, include the French pronunciation of *art* ("ar"); Marchand (merchant) negotiates,

which is doubtless why his phonetic relative Tchang is a middle-
man. Manneret, naturally enough, takes Johnson for his *son;*
better still, the name Jonestone is restored by the word *fiston*
(youngster, son); Sir Ralph is involved in a *rafle* (raid). As for
the merchant Marchat, who marches so obediently to Lauren's
tune, he is the object of the patent phonetic plot woven by
the paragraph:

> It was Georges *Marchat*, Lauren's ex, who wandered around
> so long endlessly ruminating (*remâchant*) on the elements
> of his lost happiness and his despair. Having left the party
> very early, as his presence was hardly justified any longer,
> he, too, first walked (*marché*) . . . (page 120).

Manneret is *Manne* (manna) and *rets* (net): the person from
whom Johnson expects to receive miraculous assistance but who
turns out instead to be a dangerous trap. Lauren is *l'or* (gold)
and *reine* (queen): if Johnson, who has just left her to get the
*money* he needs to purchase her, follows a specified itinerary,
it is down *Queens* Road, then *Queen* Street, etc.

But there is another type of aggression. Once we remark the
episodic presence of King Boris, who is reminiscent of two characters from Robbe-Grillet's early, unpublished novel, *Un
Régicide*, an excerpt of which appeared in a literary review
(*Médiations* n° 5), we are led to relate Georges Marchat to the
merchant Adolph Marchat of *The Erasers*; Jacqueline to Jacqueline Leduc from *The Voyeur*; Lady Ava to A., the heroine of
*Jealousy*. As for Manneret, he belongs to one of *In the Labyrinth*'s groping series: Matadier, Montoret, Montaret, Montalet.
No doubt these similarities lend additional aptitudes to the
groups of possibilities that by now we can hardly persist in
calling characters. And these pinpoint references to other works
are further reinforced by innumerable allusions, such as:

> There's no point insisting further on that scene everyone
> is familiar with. It's very late at night again, already. I
> hear the crazy old king (*Un Régicide*) walking up and down
> the hallway, on the floor above. He's looking for something,

in his memories, something solid, and he doesn't know what (*The Voyeur*). The bicycle (*The Voyeur*) has disappeared. There's no more wood tiger, no dog either, no dark glasses (*The Immortal*), no heavy drapes (*In the Labyrinth*). And there's no more garden (*Marienbad*), nor shutter (*Jealousy*).

The point here being to interline the current fiction with the previous ones, so as to enable past characters, with precisely the effects we would expect, to come and haunt the present narrative.

Last but not least, the very notions of character, hero, and heroine are detached from their meanings by three puns. Character (*personnage*): Lady Ava, that aged Jacqueline, is the lady who has lost her age (*perd-son-âge*). Heroine: heroin, obviously, with which so many pages deal. Hero (*héros*): stripped of its *h* [silent in French anyway—Trans. note], it is revealed as Eros, implicated in the novel's incessant litany of stripteases. Character, hero, and heroine are only allowed to figure in the narrative, or, if you prefer, to serve to construct it, on one condition: that of their literal defacement.

B. "Frankly, names, you know . . ."

In *Le Libera*, the notion of character is challenged in a similar manner by two complementary techniques: the fission of unities and the fusion of diversities. No doubt there are some differences in procedure. Thus for instance the character breakdown does not occur on the level of their occupations, which remain stable from one end of the book to the other. Rather, that which most strikes the reader is the stupefying profusion of protagonists that Pinget brings into play. An approximate count places their number at some one hundred and fifty. Not surprisingly, under the circumstances, most of them hardly manage to reach any degree of consistency: materially, they lack sufficient continuity.

Their ages, too, are manipulated relentlessly. Far from serving as points of reference, the dates that are slipped into the text serve instead to promote confusion. If La Lorpailleur was twenty when she told the story of Serinet's murder, and forty at the time of her bicycle accident, the dates mentioned in connection with these events would make her no less than one hundred and nine when, after school, at forty, she starts off on her bike. Yet any attempt to rearrange the adventures in order to give her a less incongruous longevity displaces in time all the other characters involved, piling incongruity on top of incongruity until any hint of a reasonable chronology is thoroughly swamped. There is no one, in this novel, whose age is not suspect.

The character is further discomposed by the interaction of incompatible events. Pinget resorts to the tried and true procedure: provide a set of variants, establish their equal claim to "reality", and string them out in narrative succession. With the order of a truthful scene surrounded by a collection of lies thus excluded, their collusion determines a perfect dissecting machine that operates on whatever character gets involved with it. Judge by the following:

> Coming out of school La Lorpailleur mounted her bicycle, sat down and right then let go of the handlebars, she falls, thrashing about and screaming . . . foaming at the mouth. She was lying in the road, the kids in a circle at a distance, poor teacher how'd she do that, the truckdriver kept saying she ran right into me . . . the doctor who lives at the corner leaning over the dead woman feeling for her pulse listening for her heartbeat declaring she was dead (p. 11). Or else she wasn't killed instantly. Or else the truck just passed her (p. 12). The truck ran over her, no trace of epilepsy (p. 13). I bet she just let herself slide from her bike when she saw the truck either out of fear or on purpose, she's so mean, make it look like the truck ran her down (p. 15). . .

If, in addition, as is obviously the case here, the variants are recounted by different narrators, all of the accounts, enmeshed in the ensuing play of contradictions, lose their power of persuasion: each version becomes phantasmic, each actor, ectoplasmic.

Once this dismemberment is achieved, the way is clear for various combinatorial formulas to exploit the precious assistance provided by the lavish supply of protagonists. Innumerable in their succession, minor or secondary most of the time, at the slightest resemblance these become the object of irreparable mistakes. Thus Pinget grants an astonishing extension to family ties: sisters, mothers, brothers, fathers, cousins, uncles, and aunts proliferate all over the place, and of course those natural promoters of confusion: twins.

Among the similarities, we should include the suggestions of related professions: Ronzière the postmistress and Lorpailleur the schoolmistress, for instance, are both involved with local papers. But, more insistently, all sorts of anecdotes are common to the most varied characters. Sometimes it is a simple house-keeping activity, as in the case of the no-less-than five different women, in the space of 53 pages (pp. 9 to 62), who are depicted washing their windows or else having visited Argentina. This country in fact receives, more or less, the visit of La Lorpailleur's sister (p. 8), Mrs. Ducreux's sister (p. 19), Etiennette Piede-vant's sister (p. 62), Pinson's son (p. 66), the youngest of the Moignon children (p. 68), an unspecified woman (p. 141), and Odette Magnin (p. 186).

The profusion of characters has a third function: it allows Pinget to exaggerate, paroxysmally at times, the similarity of names that *La Maison de rendez-vous* utilized quite modestly in comparison. The teachers are called Lorpailleur, Lattirail, Loiseleur. A simple contraction separates Verveine the phar-macist from a man called Vernes. Ducreux, Cruze, Crottard, Crottet, Descreux have *cr* in common. *Ar* links Ariane, Aristide, Topard, Monnard, Charpy, Maillard, Marie, Chottard, Edouard, Mottard, Dondard, Crottard, Ménard, Poussardin, Cossard, Paillard, Marin, Marchin. Like the names that begin with *S* in Proust's *Jean Santeuil*, in *Le Libera* the names that start with *M* are legion: Monneau, Monnard, Mortin, Moine, Mail-lard, Marie, Magnin, Mottard, Moineau, Moignon, Ménard, Monette, Morier, Miquette, Mireille, Machette, Marin, Marchin. Better still, constellations are sometimes established by analogy, first terminal then initial, until the end of the last name in the series rejoins the beginning of the first one. Piedevant, Passavant, Passetant, Passavoine, Passepied. Whereupon cer-

tain remarks in the narrative read like comments on these procedures: "Frankly, names, you know..." (p. 134), or "a trick
facilitated by a rhyme" (p. 172). Added to these effects of
consonance is what we might call a patronymic theme: a curious
collection of proper names that refer to a common idea. Serinet,
Moine, Monneau, Pinson, Moinneau, Paquerot, Poussardin,
Poussinet are all names of birds in French, while Loiseleur is
the bird-catcher.

And, not surprisingly, we soon find this kind of deliberate
coaxing of similarities resulting, here, too, in a permanent possibility of confusion:

> What he had to say concerned Monnard or Dondard (p.
> 148). But his mother Mrs. Ducreux no that is Mrs. Moineau
> (p. 173). I can still see Monnard with his muffler... or
> Mottard (p. 217).

In addition, as in *La Maison de rendez-vous*, a dense network
of analogies tends to dissolve the possession of proper names in
the mobile substance of the narrative. Invoked by the fiction, the
surname reflects it; preceding the fiction, it announces it: such
are its common roles. A very visible occurrence at the end of
the book:

> Either Mortin at his window...
> Or *la mort* (death) under the sycamore (p. 221)

provides an emblem for retrospective use. Thus the Crottards
[whose name could be translated: Shitters] suffer from a chronic
malady: dysentery. Mademoiselle Ronzière, page 63, elicits "*onze
heures*" (eleven o'clock) in the following line; Moignon's widow,
page 68, leads to "*pauvre mignon*" (poor dear) eleven lines
later; Maillard provokes "*sur le mail*" (on the mall) twenty-six
lines afterwards, page 92; Biangle, page 108, brings on "*on s'est
mis en branle*" (we got going) seven lines down; Mortin, already
on page 201, is followed by "*la mort qui gagne du terrain*"
(death gaining ground). Another case of a name providing the
fiction with a theme by easy derivation is, page 139:

Or maybe I'm getting mixed up with the Duchemin inheritance, anyway at the intersection of New Street and Casse-Tonnelles [*du chemin* = of the street].

Conversely, a girl taken to the forest is called Sylvie. The arrival of a bird, page 193, precedes that of Serinet (Canary) seventeen lines further on; a certain *Machin* (gadget) on page 221 announces the Marin Marchin affair, mentioned seven lines later. Slightly more complex, the name Latirail is formed by a superposition of the words *portail* (gate) and *attirance* (attraction) from the previous paragraph.

Finally, needless to say, these Lorpailleur, Latirail, Mortin, Apostolos and company, implicated in the complications of *Le Libera*, have already been worked over in the author's earlier books, as a simple glance at the characters of *Mahu, L'Inquisitoire, Autour de Mortin* is sufficient to confirm. We can well imagine that these episodic reappearances are far from conferring any additional solidity to the one or the other. On the contrary, the scores of contradictory anecdotes involving the same names ludicrously increase all those excesses whereby the characters, indefinitely repeated and multiplied, sustain the most severe kinds of deterioration.

## II. ADVENT OF THE GRAMMATICAL PERSON

The reader of *Personnes* or *Nombres*, on the other hand, is immediately struck by the complete absence, in the text and even the epigraphs, of proper names. Mallarmé is not written after "Axioms may be read here, inscribed by no one"; the line *Seminaque innumero numero summaque profunda* does not bear the signature of Lucretius. This banishment notably betrays, on the fictional level, the total effacement of the character. As early as 1961, in order to account for certain techniques in Sollers' second novel, *The Park*, we had to resort to the notion of pronominal characters [see "Writing Between the Lines" in this volume]. Since then, the further evolution of certain authors has so greatly amplified the phenomenon that today we seem to have entered a pronominal era.

In this perspective, several articles by Emile Benveniste, since republished in his *Problems of General Linguistics*, deserve attention. Devoted to the analysis of personal pronouns, they enable us to elucidate the problem. From "Of Subjectivity in Language":

> Now, these pronouns may be distinguished from all the designations that language articulates by this fact: *they contain no reference either to a concept or to an individual.* There is no concept "I" to encompass all the *I*'s pronounced every second by every speaker, in the sense that there is a concept "tree" to which all individual uses of TREE refer. "I', therefore, does not name any lexical entity. Does this mean we could say that *I* refers to a particular individual? If that were so, it would be a permanent contradiction accepted by language, and, in practical application, total anarchy: how could the same term refer indifferently to any and all individuals and, at the same time, identify one of them in his particularity?

And, from "The Nature of Pronouns":

> *I* means "the person pronouncing the present instance of speech containing *I*"... We should therefore stress the following point: *I* can only be identified by the instance of speech which contains it, and by that alone.

From these particularities it appears that, depending on the passage containing it, *I* has equal power to establish a character or to abolish him entirely. Imagine for instance a text accumulating all kinds of determinations concerning that first person. Vacant at first, *I* would gradually take on an ever more precise identity. Little by little, this narrator would acquire all the traditional characteristics of a fictional identity. This is the kind of operation that Benjamin Constant performs in the first paragraph of *Adolph*:

> At twenty-two, I had just finished my studies at the University of Göttingen. My father, minister of the elector of

xxx, intended for me to visit the most remarkable European countries. After that, he wished to have me return and work in the department he directed, to prepare me for the day I would take over his job. By working doggedly, while at the same time leading a very dissolute life, I had obtained a certain amount of success that had distinguished me from my schoolmates, and which had led my father to found some extremely exaggerated hopes on me.

If, on the other hand, the text is structured in such a way as to prevent a coherent determinative identity from coagulating, *I* remains a constant vacancy. This can of course also apply to the second person, but also to the third person. No doubt, as Benveniste points out, the latter is entirely different from *I* and *you*. Nevertheless, insofar as it functions as an abbreviatory substitute, it is sufficient to use it without the element it should be serving to relay. As we might expect, the traditional use of the third person is far too consistently convenient for this new one to abolish it altogether.

A. The Impersonal Pronoun She

As its title suggests, *Personnes* is notably the fruit of such operations. Their difficulty is extreme: no matter how variable or even incompatible they may be, the determinations always tend to consolidate to describe the absent figure of the person. Accordingly, any irrefutable rupture requires that strictly antinomic levels be brought into play. Since, in French, all nouns have gender, with *he*, at the price of some rather curious metamorphoses, it is naturally possible to travel through all the fiction's masculine elements; through all the feminine ones, with *she*. But that is precisely just one more way of adhering to the relative uniformity of the fictional space. In order to discover a radically foreign space and thereby to obtain the possibility of decisive ruptures, it is sufficient to shift the plot back and forth between the two levels of which every text is composed: fiction, but also narration.

That operation requires a preliminary treatment: the programing of a maximum number of similarities between the two

levels. In an essay nominally inspired by Marcelin Pleynet's
*Comme* (*Comme un livre*, in *Tel Quel* n° 24), but which is
equally well suited to various other works, Jean-Louis Baudry
makes this point explicit:

> So the point will be to establish, between the space of the
> book (book, page, sentence, word, etc.) and the space of
> the fiction, the smallest common significant units.

If this is easy enough to do as far as the characters are concerned, the systematic organization of ambiguities on the lexical
level is rather more complex, bringing into play as it does, from
polysemy (*feuille*: leaf—of book or tree) to paronym (*page*/
*plage*: page/beach), the entire range of linguistic proximities.
Thus the fact mentioned above, i.e. that all French nouns have
gender, allows Baudry to use "he" to designate, on the fictional
level, "man", but on the narrational level, "book" (a masculine
noun); "her" for "woman" on the fictional level, for "sentence"
(feminine) on the narrational level, and, by virtue of their
double meanings, to use *"feuille"* as a synecdoche for "tree" in
the fiction, for "book" in the narration; to use *"plage"* (beach,
but also area, expanse, delimited space) for a page of the book
on the narrational level, and to invoke a beach in the fiction.
Once the reader accepts that activity, which the novel itself
states in relatively plain language:

> It's the same sentence that at least is sure. But sometimes
> it comes up tails [no pun in French—Trans. note] (then
> it evokes the visible, all the faces), sometimes heads (then
> it sums up a whole vocabulary).

entire sections of the book, which retain their obscurity by traditional reading criteria, are insensibly elucidated. For instance,
let's read in that light the following fragment of Sequence 50,
keeping in mind that "she" and "her" in French may refer
merely to a feminine noun:

> So if I want to speak of her now, I should perhaps have

to awaken all my memories of her escape. Fortunately, with each new word, a meaning shadows forth and fades away and I avoid the overly specific setting which would immobilize it. I just barely want to describe her now, while she advances, lies down beside me, want to recognize that expectation (body exposed to provoke the gesture and the voice that return it to itself). Since by now everything designates her without naming her, since it's here, the moment I begin, that I find her.

We are witness to the transformation of a "woman" into a "sentence", while the "I" occupied by a "man" lets the "text" (masculine) take it over. The first lines announce the principle and method of the conversion: obliteration of the emerging meaning; lack of precision about the setting, conducive to metamorphosis. Then, gradually, we begin to admit, of each sentence that advances, that it lies down beside the text, that its first draft (its expectation) is set in writing (exposed) so as to induce the corrective scriptive gesture, the formative vocal reading; that, finally, it is the sentence that the text encounters the moment it begins. So it is indeed the sentence that everything designates without naming it.

Conversely, in Sequence 58, where a sentence is speaking, addressing the book, the reader discovers the progressive advent of a human body:

A sentence addresses you and through a reversible action that which cancels itself out recognizes its visibility, that of which all trace is lost is here present. As soon as you try to play that person—silhouette, background image of a discursive form against the light of accidents, of brief intrusions of the world—your body is involved, prisoner of a grammatical fabric that encloses it, sets its limits, suggests an overall appearance. Body that has become the opaque target toward which the sustained action of the words and gestures converges. Your body however broken in pieces. That's how you apprehend it—leg and arm, hand. You say a hand.

There is accordingly no possible hypostatization of the grammatical person, no way to personify it by a character. The reader who, by a naturalist reflex, would attempt to elude the movement betrayed by a perpetual vocabulary of transformation (words like displacement, shifting, fading, disappearance, reversal, fall, escape, dissolution, substitution, etc.) and who would endeavor to settle down permanently on one of the two levels between which the story shuttles, would find himself constantly on a tangent banishing him irrevocably from the curve of the text. Rather than clinging to a reductionist phantasm cutting the other side off from view, he would be better advised to remain continuously attentive to the "persistent ground-noise against which the walls, the objects located in space may be set", that irreconcilable duality which immediately bisects any attempt at personification.

B. The Characterless Person

In the complexity of its procedures, *Nombres* has scores of ways of reducing to zero all maneuvers of appropriation and conservation. This is an indication of the extent to which its multiple environment contradicts everything normally attached to the idea of the fictional character. In "Semantic Levels of a Modern Text" (in *Théorie d'ensemble*), Philippe Sollers says as much in no uncertain terms:

It is therefore an understatement to say that the "character" is disappearing from the narrative as well as the proper name: it is the very notion of PROPERTY and for instance of a proper body—closed, complete, its identity assured by the mirror image and the exclusively spoken function implying a limited subject—that is vanishing.

Now, it is true that he has just finished apparently contradicting the rule stipulating the strictly impersonal nature of the personal pronouns by distributing what seem to be some very clear assignments:

The pronoun "I" (in the written text) consequently designates in the first place the text's principle of organization. "We" refers to the groups of sentences and words. Addressing the reader—who is thus called to appear in the textual space—"you" (plural) becomes predominant, but the reader is primarily one grammatical actor among others.

Yet nothing is actually farther from a permanent investment. No doubt the use of a personal pronoun, "I" for instance, presumes, at least while it is being pronounced, an effect of concentration. But that unification is immediately shattered, subjected to a movement of change and dissociation, to the ample blue and white rupture that it is easy enough to identify as writing if we recall the "blue-black ink" in the last lines of *The Park*:

> If I write among you traces of that story, the second I feel the satisfaction of my recomposition and of my being written briefly among you, I simultaneously invoke that ample blue and white rupture that produces us and releases us, attracts us, changes us . . .

That passage alone is sufficient to convince us of the ceaseless mobility of the personal pronoun's content. Momentarily located in the temporary unity of the writer, the text's active organization addresses itself to the readers: "you". The "we" then takes over this "you" and "I", inscribing them within the displacement that produces and changes them. But this "we" also refers to the totality of the words and sentences that are equally produced and changed by writing. A retroactive reversal takes effect here, forcing "you" to refer to the group of words among which "I" is written. Thus, whereas it initially signified the organizational principle of the text in its generality, "I" is subsequently transformed until it no longer designates anything but the simple word it constitutes among others. And the reader himself, reduced to a word, indeed becomes "one grammatical actor among others." Such metamorphoses naturally contaminate other elements of the vocabulary. Initially applied to the pleasure of recomposition, the adverb "briefly" concerns, secondly, the time it takes to write the letter "I". Hence the importance of a clear discrimination between *polysemy*, in which meanings accumulate in a continual enrichment, and *permutation*, where one meaning expels another in an uninterrupted circulation; between property that increases its possessions, and permanent expropriation. In sum, as Lao-Tse wrote, the point is to "produce without appropriating."

Thus the words, sentences, text, and all the fiction's manifold facets whose elaboration begins once they are put in writing, become involved in a continual play of exchange and metamorphosis. Dismemberments, transformations, violence: the reversible passage from the grammatical to the physiological:

> Yet there was a "we". This "we" faded, returned, trembled and returned constantly: I could feel its presence, a presence made of living words. At this point, precisely, there is no longer room for the least word. What you feel right away is your mouth; dark fullness—grass, clay—you're inside. No use moving, turning. Everything's occupied, full, no cleavage, interval, crack...Yet I found my mutilated body and it seemed as if the flesh had been ploughed, and my sex was sewn and erect like a hard closed ear of grain, and I was looking at this first model from before the Fall shut inside a narrow cell, penetrated by the sun...It was me, I was sure...More precisely we were two, now: the one whose intact skin could be shown to everyone, whose envelope wasn't immediately greeted with horror, and the other riddled with pocks and gashes, raw flesh, purple and violet, skinned like a bull...I was beginning to act on the concatenation, on the novel where these figures entered, on the luminous, empty background where they finally disintegrated.

at the opposite extreme from the representation of a "closed, complete" body, "its identity assured", invites instead certain bloody, obscure operations.

III. FORMALIZATION OF THE FICTION

Several authors have shown how, in a narrative, the fiction

may be governed by formal principles: Propp, for instance, in his analysis of Russian folktales. Although they are undeniably at work, such procedures are usually imperceptible. If the "laws that govern the narrated universe . . . reflect the logical constraints that any series of events organized in narrative form must respect in order to be intelligible" (Claude Brémond, "La Logique des possibles narratifs" in *Communications* n° 8), the reader's attention will hardly be aroused. Thus it is often necessary to resort to a corpus of similar texts, that the analyst contrives to superimpose, if the (common) formal factors are to be made to appear:

1.  The king sends Ivan to find the Princess. Ivan leaves.
2.  The king sends Ivan to find a singular object. Ivan leaves.
3.  The sister sends her brother to find a remedy. The brother leaves.
4.  The mother-in-law sends her daughter-in-law to find fire. The daughter-in-law leaves.
5.  The blacksmith sends his apprentice to find the cow. The apprentice leaves.

> Etc. The dispatch and the departure connected with the quest are constants. The dispatcher and the dispatched are variables. (V. Propp: "The Transformations of Fantastic Tales" in *Theory of Literature*).

For the naive consumer, immersed in the exciting flow of the plot, an analysis such as Propp's is practically sacrilegious: it elucidates that which is supposed to remain obscure—the process of production. By writing poems so similar to each other that they obviously constitute a simple set of variants, Paul Valéry managed on occasion to insert that critical instrument within the production itself.

A.  "The rest of the script proceeds mechanically"
By the use of a procedure that is quite visible in *Jealousy*, for instance, *La Maison de rendez-vous* exacerbates that scandalous experiment. Instead of giving us, as Valéry did, a collection

of autonomous variants, Robbe-Grillet's novel integrates them with its plot. Here the superposition, with its aptitude for disclosing formal communities, is inexorably accomplished by the properties of the text itself. We shall call formalization the tendency whereby the activity of these formal principles, instead of being carefully dissimulated, is intensified, and even made the object of an undeniable ostentation. In fact, as the sequences unfold, similarities and divergencies, both equally surprising, gradually appear. Beneath the profuse variety of variables, more general patterns begin to emerge. Thus, for instance, the countless events with connotations of homicide, suicide, accident, or torture reveal the systematic application of a pattern of aggression. Others, complying with the former, signal, through a similar phenomenon of superposition, the models of wandering, visit, or the repetitive number three.

This alignment of the disparate along the coordinating axis of a small number of basic schemas certainly removes us from the everyday world, and plays a decisive anti-naturalist role. Curiously enough, the same effect can be obtained by the opposite procedure. Applied to an eminently unique act (death), the matrix of aggression multiplies it into a collection of contradictory occurrences. Edouard Manneret committed suicide (p. 94), had his neck broken by Lady Ava's dog (p. 159), was the victim of an accident (p. 165), was murdered by a black policeman with a stiletto (p. 175), with the stem of a broken cocktail glass by some strange official (p. 176), by the Communists (p. 202), by Johnson with a revolver (p. 211).

Carried to extremes, that formalization would generate all the possible arrangements of a limited set of elements (characters, places, objects . . .) and models of combinations (attack, wandering, visit). But, as we can easily imagine, the possibilities are far too numerous to be thoroughly exhausted. The fiction is therefore required not only to comply with the order of a logical sequence, but also to operate a selection. It must therefore rely on some principle capable of determining the successive stages of its development. And in fact, beneath the layers of like and conflicting events, such a principle may be perceived: it determines a ballistic trajectory—growth, fall, disappearance. Various series amply confirm this: the statues, the comic-strip illustrations:

> Most of them illustrate the most famous episodes of Princess Azy's imaginary existence: "The Dogs", "The Slave", "The Promise", "The Queen", "The Kidnapping", "The Hunter", "The Murder" (p. 57).
>
> Each illustration is accompanied by a short caption in large Chinese characters that signify, respectively and in order: "Drugs are a companion that betrays you", "Drugs are a tyrant that enslaves you", "Drugs are a poison that will kill you" (p. 82).

The same principle may be detected behind the evolution of Lady Ava (young and adulated, faded and abandoned, on her death-bed), or of Johnson (possessing Lauren, fighting to keep her, losing her). Once the formal principles are clearly established, it is indeed true that "the rest of the script proceeds mechanically."

B. "Setting the mechanism in motion"

Of all Pinget's books, it is doubtless in *Passacaille* that combinatorial techniques are practised the most systematically: less numerous, the elements and situations are effectively more controllable. But *Le Libera's* use of them was already quite analogous to the one we found in *La Maison de rendez-vous*. From the first pages, it is already clear that "the mechanism set in motion" (p. 7) is, among others, that of a pattern of aggression drawing attention to the victim and leaving the aggressor unspecified. Seven people are injured or killed in the first twelve pages, but only one by an identified assailant. The formula's anti-naturalist effect, emphasized by the deliberate clumsiness of several attempts to retrieve by logical explanation a thoroughly illogical function: "Calamities always occur in July—an automobile accident, a drowning, a fire" (p. 20), is further increased, as in *La Maison de rendez-vous*, by the diversification of a supposedly unique event. Already percepti-

ble with the versatile deaths of Louis Ducreux, this phenomenon especially concerns the accident in which La Lorpailleur
is involved. On her bicycle, she is the victim of a truckdriver
(p. 10) or an epileptic attack (p. 11). But perhaps she just
faked the accident (p. 16), or maybe nothing happened at all:
she just passed the truck on the road (p. 12). There is also a
less spectacular version: her falling off a chair (p. 15).

The fast pace at which the scenes materialize and follow one
another in Pinget's book allows an extremely ample actualization of possibilities. This means that the notion of a trajectory
is both more diffuse and less necessary. Yet, from the aggressive
beginning:

If LaLorpailleur is insane, it's not my fault

to the disillusioned and senile ending:

The bunch of old gags, dumb mirages and the rest of the
junk cluttering up our nutty beanbrains.
Botched bewitchments.

we can nonetheless detect the installation of a process of decay
and decrepitude. Prevented by its formalization from proposing a traditional story, the fiction tends instead to stage a production of the idea of its own beginning and ending.

IV. Formalization of the Narration

That curious hybrid, part actor, part reporter, the narrator
is one of the points where fiction and narration strangely inter-
sect. Introduced in these formalized fictions, that role is bound
to suffer some far-reaching consequences. Here, the narrative
function no longer belongs, as it does in a classic story, to one
character or another depending on the requirements of the plot;
instead, it is distributed mechanically and with periodic, violent switches. This procedure gives rise to what we might call
floating narrators. In fact, the relations between narrative and
narrator are known to be commonly univocal: the two are,

literally, as one voice. In Ulysses' tale to Alinoos, for instance, a single narrator offers a single version: it is *the* tale of *Ulysses*. This of course does not prevent a host of narrators from arriving at any point in the story, bringing either the confirmation of a textual repetition or the invalidation of a new version. Yet, if in the latter case an ambiguity is brought to light, it is only on the level of the fiction as a whole, whereas the relation of each individual narrator to his own narrative remains unequivocal. All that occurs is that stable narratives, respectively related by stable narrators, are arranged in some sort of sequence. Equivocal relations, on the other hand, are produced by quite different devices: stable narrator and floating narrative; floating narrator and stable narrative; and, naturally, their product: floating narrator and floating narrative. Robbe-Grillet's *Jealousy* for instance is based on the systematic development of the first case: to a single narrator, the famous "husband", there corresponds a floating narrative consisting of a succession of contradictory versions. Conversely, rather than being the joint property of a corpus of unanimous narrators, a narrative may be captured by an abruptly alien narrator, with the predictable retroactive effects. Here, lacking a specific narrator, the stable narrative is provided with floating narrators instead. *La Maison de rendez-vous* is a case in point, particularly in the shift from *he* (Johnson) to an enigmatic *I*, by the omission of quotation marks:

> Johnson, who had time to prepare for that question, immediately begins his account of the evening: "I arrived at the Villa Bleue around 9:10 by taxi..." I'm also skipping the part about the noise of the insects, already mentioned, and the description of the statues. I'm going right on to the scene where Lauren breaks up with her fiancé (pp. 96-97).

*Le Libera* is another example:

> According to Mademoiselle Ronzière, Etiennette didn't go

by the bakery until eleven, she was on her way back from
town with a big box from Brivance's, a new dress . . . those
women dying of impatience to see her open the box . . . I
can still see those women all excited, feeling the fabric . . .
(pp. 63-64).

With that kind of double shift, any attempt by one of the characters to appropriate the narrative becomes precarious. But
what are the rules that govern that strange rotation of narrators? It seems that, far from obeying some systematic principle
of distribution, the occurrence which, at that particular point
in the novel, is likely to cause the most confusion, is selected
every time. Here, then, the order of narrators is still in a sense
subordinate to the development of the fiction.

It is true that, in *Nombres*, a certain order effectively under-
lies the fiction's distribution: the anonymous citation of the
line from Lucretius, for instance, at the beginning of the book,
is there to provide not the outmoded elegance of a Latin orna-
ment, but rather a precise thematic matrix: each term of that
formula is like a seed replanted indefinitely, maturing, blossom-
ing out, eventually, on a number of pages according to a profound sum. Nevertheless, the formalization in *Nombres* works
out mainly on the level of the narration. The same is true
for *Personnes*.

A. "The mechanism is in motion"
The reader quickly turning the pages of Baudry's novel is
immediately struck by the material evidence of a "mechanism
in motion" (p. 46). Unorganized in most novels, here the grays
and blanks of the printed page alternate with a regularity that
betrays the calculated nature of their sequence. Better still,
the workings of the mechanism are displayed in a table on the
last page of the novel [reproduced on the following page].

Here, then, we have the exact opposite of a capricious continuity: the narration is allowed to materialize only in obedience
to a rigorous system of fragmentation. It is not a homogeneous
substance that could be poured into the sequential grid of
pronouns as into a mold: it has been strictly ordered to con-

|     | I | She | He | I | He | She | She | I | He |
| --- | --- | --- | --- | --- | --- | --- | --- | --- | --- |
| She | 1 | 5 | 13 | 21 | 29 | 27 | 19 | 11 | 3 |
| He | 9 | 33 | 37 | 45 | 56 | 51 | 43 | 35 | 7 |
| I | 17 | 41 | 57 | 61 | 69 | 67 | 59 | 39 | 16 |
| He | 25 | 49 | 65 | 73 | 77 | 75 | 63 | 47 | 23 |
| I | 32 | 53 | 72 | 80 | 81 | 79 | 71 | 55 | 31 |
| She | 24 | 48 | 64 | 76 | 78 | 74 | 66 | 50 | 26 |
| He | 16 | 40 | 60 | 68 | 70 | 62 | 58 | 42 | 18 |
| She | 8 | 36 | 44 | 52 | 54 | 46 | 38 | 34 | 10 |
| I | 4 | 12 | 20 | 28 | 30 | 22 | 14 | 6 | 2 |

form, in its production, to nothing other than the discontinuity of irreconcilable directives. Defined in this case as noncommutative, the product of the pronouns engenders nine distinct combinations. Five of them are simple: I/I, I/She, I/He, He/He, He/She. Four are complex: He/I (*I* is only possible between quotes), She/I (by a curious reversal, *I* is "interlocuted" into *you*, and *She* becomes *I*), She/She (the whole sequence is then put in quotes). Confronted with the sexed third-person pronouns, *I* is forced to choose between an acrobatic neutrality (censuring, in its attributes, all determinations of gender: since, in French, an unaccented e added to the adjective makes it feminine, the choice would be limited to adjectives which already end in *e* in the masculine, eg. *triste* [sad], and are thus invariable), a determinate sex (masculine or feminine endings), or hermaphrodism (some masculine, some feminine endings). Instead, a fourth solution was selected. *I* does in fact change genders, but never in the course of a single sequence [the book has no chapters, but 81 "sequences", each one-and-a-half pages long—Trans. note]. In its relations with *you*, singular and plural, *I*, as we have seen, derived from *she*, is feminine:

> So now I am standing in front of the mirror, nude (*nue*), and you came to stand next to me.

In the other pairs, it is masculine:

> Masked (*masqué*), I advance through a silent chaos... I see him when he can no longer escape the vast white building...

These inflexible coercive measures avoid the ambiguities that would ensue from a confusion of the sexes. On the other hand, since the order of the very different sequences is determined by the requirement that the combinatorial grid be covered methodically, all attempts to subsume the narrative movement's diversity under a unitary principle are blocked a priori.

B.  "Once the first propositions are put in the mechanism"

In 1965, Sollers' novel, *Drame* (which there are good grounds for mentioning in connection with *Personnes*), organized its sixty-four sequences in checkerboard fashion: a systematic alternation of "he" sequences and "I" sequences. The narration of *Nombres* is engendered by an equally rigorous device: as the title signals from the start, measure is the basis of its formation. The book was assigned one hundred sequences in a cyclic pattern with a period of four. That "predetermined, arbitrary, numerical space" (*Logiques*, by Sollers) does not bother to avoid a certain ostentation. Except, obviously, for the first four, every sequence begins with a double numeric notation. "3.91", for instance, provides a triple indication: this is the ninety-first sequence; it is of type three; it belongs to the twenty-third cycle. In addition, various diagrams inserted in the text give the schemas of this mechanism. The first one, in sequence 4.8, at the end of the second cycle, once the idea of a circuit has been established:

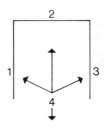

differentiates all the fourth sequences from the other three. This because the grammar and even, tendentiously, the punctuation, according to this partition, follow a mandatory pattern of distribution: the first three sequences are in the imperfect tense; the fourth, in the present, between parentheses and almost always with the second person plural. Since the parenthesis creates an interruption and is concommitantly subject to an inclusion, the present, i.e. the time during which the book is read (by "you", the sequence means the reader), is defined as perfectly equivocal: it breaks with the imperfect of the narration while yet remaining caught in its circuit.

In addition, however they begin (upper or lower case, points of suspension), all the sequences are made to end with a dash of varying length. And, indeed, we soon find that narrational constraint becoming thematic: in 3.23 for instance it is "the line's simple, indestructible force". Thus a kind of symbolic strategy begins to evolve, where phonetic writing as the notation of a language is at grips with the line drawing on which a language may place its own interpretation. With the increasing number of Chinese ideograms at the ends of the sequences, and the permanent presence, at the beginning of each sequence, of Arabic numerals that are independent of the languages in which they can be read, the written word is regularly gripped in the vise of spoken writing.

Within the limits of their common points, no doubt there is still reason to distinguish between *Personnes* and *Nombres*. Thus, whereas the former is content to exhibit *in extremis*, after the last word and, when all is said and done, by way of a table of contents [in France the table of contents is placed at the end of a book instead of the beginning as in the U.S.A. —Trans. note], the programmatic grid of its pronominal encounters, the latter inserts the schema in the text itself, and proposes, now and then (4.8, 4.24, 4.48, 4.52), various successive modifications. In the first case, separable, immutable, fundamental, the formalization prescribes the limits of the enclosure from which the narration cannot escape. In the second, this formalization becomes the plaything of the narration which by its laws it determines to the point of being transformed by that which it produces.

## V. Self-Representation

It is common knowledge that the dogma which would reduce, in Sartre's words, "THE VERBAL MOMENT" to a "secondary structure", separates into two complementary doctrines: expression, representation. For the former, there is a given internal substance which is expressed; for the latter, there is a given external entity which is represented. To the expression of the Self corresponds the representation of the World. The essential, in both cases, is one and the same: the text is but the reflection of something prior to itself. The Stendhalian "mirror taken out for a walk" (*"un miroir qu'on promène le long d'une route"*) is echoed by the Romantic poem-mirror of the soul. It was Victor Hugo, in the preface to his *Contemplations*, who maintained: "If ever there was a mirror of the soul, this book will be it." Not only do the two principles not conflict, then, but in effect they act in perfect concert: anything that obviously disturbs the representation of the World is forthwith ascribed to the expression of the Self. The traditional fantastic tale, for instance, reads that way: it is not the World itself which is represented, but rather a world thoroughly infused with one of the major faculties of the Self: imagination. From the "objective" to the "subjective", the expression-representation creed sweepingly covers a vast field indeed.

The system of productive mechanisms, on the other hand, and directly in proportion to its ostentation, is irreducibly opposed to that comfortable belief. As we have seen (III), the

Russian folktale, in its composition, is the result of a precise matrix. Yet it was only by resorting to a comparison transcending each individual tale that Propp was able to bring this fact to light. It is therefore advisable to discriminate between such purely external expedients, and the internal mechanisms exploited by *La Maison de rendez-vous* and *Le Libera*.

The fiction generated by the latter devices systematically diverges from any kind of reflection of the ordinary world, whose aspects they specifically attack. That which is commonly *unique* (a character, an event) suffers the *dislocation* of contradictory variants; that which is ordinarily *diverse* (several characters, several events) sustains the *assimilation* of strange resemblances. The fiction excludes perfect singularity as well as absolute plurality. In other words, it is ubiquitously invested with mirrors. Deforming mirrors to dislocate the unique; "forming" mirrors to assimilate the diverse.

The novel is thus no longer a mirror taken out for a walk; it is the result of internal mirrors ubiquitously at work within the fiction itself. It is no longer representation, but self-representation. Yet that is not to suppose it divided into two realms, the privileged one which would have the other as its representation. No, the novel is rather, tendentiously, everywhere a representation of itself. This means that, far from being a stable image of the ordinary world, the fiction, in its composition, is perpetually in the process of a double discomposition. The text's proliferation proceeds from the text itself: it writes by imitating what it reads. Whatever be the book containing it, any internal allegory ["*mise en abyme*": a term borrowed from heraldry: marshaling of escutcheons, but here in addition the inset motif is defined as depicting or reinforcing its incorporating emblem—Trans. note] is already, of course, a larval case of these inherent mirror effects. André Gide quite rightly points out, as an instance of this, the tiny convex mirrors in the paintings of Memling and Metsys. Better still, this internal allegory often reflects the constitutive procedures of the text itself. Then if, in addition, it happens to reflect this reflection, it will form, quite literally, a figurative re-duplication. This in fact is probably the way we are intended to read the following

Byzantine allusion dropped on the very threshold of *La Maison
de rendez-vous*:

> On the walls of the Byzantine cathedrals, the bilaterally
> symmetric sawed marble shapes before my eyes into female
> genitals, spread wide open.

where, in this evocation of the maternal orifice, what is stressed
is naturally the productive aptitude proper to self-representation.

## VI. ANTI-REPRESENTATION

If, with self-representation, the stability of the narrative is
constantly undermined by a perpetual threat of fission, it is
even more so, as we have seen in *Personnes* and *Nombres*, by
the systematic disruptions continually inflicted on it by a violent
attempt at anti-representation. In both instances, the fictional
space becomes plural: in the former, by the rapid multiplication of similarities; in the latter, by the inordinate accumulation of differences. "The Way that can be told is not the
constant Way": nothing, perhaps, might better serve as an
emblem of the second activity than the first line of the Tao,
also inscribed in *Nombres*. We have seen that, in order to
achieve the most incisive ruptures, *Personnes* and *Nombres* both
resorted to a very effective device. Since it was sufficient to
bring irreconcilable levels into play and then to shift alternately
from one to the other, their narratives were ordered to travel
back and forth, from fiction to narration, and from the latter
to the former. In this manner the two levels were made to
challenge and engender each other reciprocally, in the course
of a process of production constantly rendered perceptible.
Whereas, in the pursuit of its ideal (to deceive the reader), the
representative effort is aimed at a maximum dissimulation of
the narration so that the fiction, with its illusionist resemblance,
may be confused with that which it pretends to reflect; the
system employed by *Personnes* and *Nombres*, on the other hand,
insofar as it makes conspicuous by turns both fiction and
narration, effectively forms the exact inverse of a representation.
The text's proliferation proceeds from the text itself: it is

written by opposing what it reads. This plurality can be increased. By widening the extent of its multiplicity to include an ever greater number of other texts, *Nombres* accomplished that. This intertextual activity exerts a twofold criticism. Intervention of the text in the texts: reworked by the fabric into which it is received, the formula "the body of real numbers" assumes a volume of meaning which exceeds its strictly mathematical acceptation; torn from any scientific pretention to purity, it ends up inscribed within the semantic constellation that includes it: the previously cited line from the Tao is invested with a precise content (a particular scriptive organization) which deprives it of all appearance of pure paradox. Intervention of the texts in the text: the bringing into play, respectively, of precise references to the semantic activity and to a different civilization. In any anti-representative perspective, the text is written in the plural.

VII. REDUPLICATION, RUPTURE

From the various angles from which we have examined them, the four novels consistently paired off into steady couples. An outline of their typical methods has therefore been established. No doubt the reader of other such books will find them tendentiously characteristic of either the "New Novel" or "Tel Quel". A few short remarks concerning the treatment of the fictional character will confirm this. The similarization of two distinct protagonists, Lassalle and Lessing, is one of the operations accomplished, and initially by the assonance of their surnames, in Claude Ollier's *La Mise en scène* (1958). Conversely, the splitting up of a single entity 0 into irreconcilable characters, now masculine, now feminine, is effected by Claude Simon's *La Bataille de Pharsale* (1969). In *Imaginez la nuit.* by Jean Thibaudeau, a whole long sequence is built on the pronoun *elles* (they, feminine), without its ever receiving a stable identity. And, as we have seen (II, A), it was on the basis of Marcelin Pleynet's *Comme* that Baudry evolved the system allowing for a continual variation of the content of personal pronouns.

Of course, all comparison oscillates between two extremes.

The first has similitude for a principle, unification for an objective, Ecumenism for a name. The second is called sectarianism; its effect is that of dispersion, its agent is difference. According to the former, we may note that, in their common conflict with the representative dogma, the activity of the "New Novel" is reduplicated by that of "Tel Quel". The former subverts the category of character, the latter abolishes it. The former tends to formalize its fiction, the latter, with more violence, its narration. The former turns the process of representation against itself, the latter nullifies it.

According to the other extreme, Tel Quel's action breaks with that of the New Novel. The abolition of character makes its mere subversion look like the misadventure of a survival. Faced with the violent ruptures provoked by narrational formalization, the tendentious formalization of the fiction seems like an ultimate reprieve granted the narrative. For anti-representation, self-representation is still too representative.

All proximity and distance, the radicalization of the New Novel's activity as operated by Tel Quel can thus only be epitomized by a contradictory figure. So, to conclude, we might evoke that paradoxical place where, the greater the weight given to the support, the farther the departure from it: the trampoline.

*Translated from the French*
*by Erica Freiberg*

# robert pynsent

# Contemporary German Fiction: The Dimensions of Experimentation

> *What is great in man is that he is a bridge and not a goal: what is lovable in man is that he is an* over-going *and a* downgoing.
>
> FRIEDRICH NIETZSCHE
> *THUS SPAKE ZARATHUSTRA*

Serious German literature does not set out to entertain the reader. Indeed the Germans have the pejorative expression "entertainment literature". Instead of giving their readers a bit of fun, German writers have given them a great deal of instruction and *Weltanschauung*. It is no longer a joke to talk of German writers as authoritarians; it is no longer a joke to talk of German literature as demonstrating less humor than any other major West European literature. It is a fact. What is striking about contemporary German literature is that its perpetrators realize this fact—with a bit of help from the Austrians and, to a lesser extent, the Swiss. What is more, contemporary German writers are fighting, in their own German way, against this fact. The result is a cult of self-consciousness, a blush before the Muse(s) which sometimes does cover the scars, but sometimes seems to inflame them.

The age of Günther Grass, one-time literary *enfant terrible*, one-time sugar-daddy of politically undernourished students, part-time theorist, is past; the age of Uwe Johnson, personified West-is-better-than-East-myth, investigator of analytical realism, disjointer, is past; the age of Heinrick Böll, darling of the dashing bourgeois, darling of the social pseudocritical, consti-

pated Cologne Catholic, is past. The lower middle-class milieu
which fascinated these men is now irrelevant to literature, but
many of their techniques survive. None of these three writers
is authoritarian; indeed all are pleasantly broad-minded in their
own way. None of these three writers is humorless. All three
are important background reading, and their ideas and techniques, even if here they go unmentioned (together with other
major younger writers like Martin Walser), are often the basis
of the ideas and techniques of the authors I shall meddle with.

Peter Weiss' *The Shadow of the Body of the Coachman*
(1960) starts off in a different direction from the works of
these three writers, though its technique runs along some of
the same lines as Johnson's. The characters in this short novel,
however, are not petit-bourgeois; they are unclassable eccentrics; every one of them is a travesty on the idea of class, a
pleasant insult to the contemporary German's sartorial and
pourboirial social taxonomy. It is easy for Germans to laugh
with, at, and for the heroes of Grass, Böll, and, if they read
him, Johnson, but though Weiss' *Shadow* may spark a social
laugh, many German readers will probably not know why. The
book begins with the sentence: "Through the half-open door
I can see the muddy, well-stamped path and the warped planks
of the pigsty." And so it goes on in the same slowly chiselled
matter-of-fact style. The first sentence is, however, compara-
tively short. Most of the sentences in this "micronovel" are long
and logical. They move with a certain harnessed dynamism.
Both diction and syntax are self-conscious to an extreme; often
we have the impression that Weiss has the objective attitude
of a foreigner towards the German language: after all he is an
"exile", a German living in Stockholm and travelling on a
Swedish passport. We see this in his banalizing word-play and
vaguely archaic constructions. The whole novel is seen through
the eyes of a superficially involved narrative 'I', an 'I' who is
as asocial a companion to the rest of the characters in the book
as they are to each other. At the beginning of the novel the
narrator describes the farm house and its immediate surroundings where the action takes place from the somewhat cold seat
of the outside lavatory, where he has started to write the

*description* of the household, *i.e.* the novel. All the other inhabitants (*vice* guests or employees) in the house are introduced by functional names, the Captain, the Doctor, the Housekeeper, the Father, the Son, except Herr Schnee, the invert who collects stones. The micronovel consists in a description of the absolutely regular customs of the house, and the narrator's attempts at describing them. Otherwise there is a bit of sex in the way of dreams and one or two *events* like a beetle almost scorching itself on the kitchen stove. Given the eccentric situation, all the action of the novel is normal, and the most normal action is the crux of the matter, the final sequence, where, from the farmyard, the narrator watches the shadow of the Coachman copulate with the shadow of the Housekeeper. Weiss intersperses his micronovel with collages which represent: first, the tentative mosaics of the narrator's imaginings; secondly, the narrator's fragmentary contact with the other characters; and thirdly, the way the narrator anatomizes the realities he sees and hears. *The Shadow* is emotionless except for the narrator's compassionate relationship with the Son, and it is Absurd. It is Absurdly funny and socially anarchic. What is more, it was very influential.

If we accept that Weiss is important because he was influential and that influential means germinative, we must consider as equally important, equally germinative, and potentially germinative the nonauthoritarian "Vienna Group." The Vienna Group began, quite ineffectually, in 1952, when Gerhard Rühm met that peripatetic H. C. Artmann, a budding literary innovator whose fads were literary Baroque, Pre-Romanticism, and Surrealism (*à la* Arp). In April 1953, Artmann composed the eight-point manifesto of the Vienna Group, of which the most important are propositions 2) "the creative act is poetry merely for the sake of poetry, free from any ambition of recognition, praise or criticism", 5) "the creative act is pose in its noblest form, free of all vanity and full of jolly humility", and 7) "the creative act is, materialistically, completely worthless and, for this reason, can never contain the germ of prostitution. Its very completion is essentially noble." The first task the Vienna Group accomplished was the "discovery" of dialect as a "pop" component of literature. The Vienna Group was politically and artistically anarchical; capitalization, an intrinsic part of German orthography, was done away with except for emphasis; logical sentence structure *in prose* was done away with except insofar as it served the absurd; humor was as important as content; the joke, visual, verbal, situational, was the seriously fun elixir of fiction.

H. C. Artmann is the oldest, and by far the best known of the Vienna Group. His prose masterpiece is his *diarium, The Search for Yesterday or Snow on a Hot Roll* (1964). Perhaps he meant it to be 100% autobiography, but it reads as if it were at least half-fiction. It is a montage linguistically (apart from German, he uses English, Erse, Welsh, Danish, Swedish, French, Spanish, Czech, and Hungarian—with *misprints*) and *genre*-wise. It blends Proust-like character and emotional impressionism, dreams, scenarios, "poems", inventories, historical and quasi-historical episodes. It is run through with literary, pop-song, and comic-strip allusions, and a sort of snobbery often peeps through the fabric, especially with his popped-up salon-style reminiscences of practically all German avant-garde writers of the early sixties. Some of it is extremely funny, but occasionally it rings somewhat artificial as, for example, in the author's portrait of himself as a "hater of the police, despiser of the authorities, emetic of the left-wing, itching-powder of the right-wing", though at other points he is more self-effacing. There is plenty of word- and sound-play *à la* Weiss, but Artmann whimsies in a way Weiss never does. The social criticism of *The Search for Yesterday* we find again, in a naive form, in his collection of thirty pictures of thirty different occupations in *Hard-Work and Industry* (1967). Each picture is divided into eight short paragraph-scenes written in the style of a seven-year-old's school composition. The performers of the thirty occupations are, on the whole, "petits bourgeois" practicing uprightness for uprightness' sake. Uprightness and pride-in-work are banalized both by Artmann's platitudinal style and the skillful way he reproduces the trite or grotesque elements of the artisans' lives. *Frankenstein in Sussex* (1969) banalizes various modern myths. It is a pastiche of Carrol's Alice, Frankenstein's monster, Frau Holle (the old lady in German fairy-tales who shakes out the beds in heaven and it snows), Mary Wollstonecroft the Godwinite, Mary Shelley, young English gentlemanhood (personified in James Hamilton Bancroft with his plus fours and shooting stick), a hippie *manqué* (going by the name of Wilbur von Frankenstein), and a Sussex village policeman. Quite apart from all this, fun is poked, with elegantly naive zest, at almost the whole Freudian mythology. At the end of the story the frustrated Monster takes Mary Shelley for his mistress having been yearning for a bit of sex for a hundred and fifty years. After *Frankenstein in Sussex* Artmann goes down the drain. His collection of short stories *How much, honey?* (1971) is second-rate. I have the impression that he tried to write a series of parodies of low low-brow literature, but the result is not funny enough to be called anything but low low-brow itself. The way Artmann experiments with the language of invective in the title story and in "airman, say hello to the sun from me" (with its hero Krchpfrrchpfrz) is great fun but not great literature.

Gerhard Rühm is primarily a poet, of the concrete and dialect variety. He writes concrete prose, prose montage, its content similar to what we expect from concrete poetry but with little room for visual effects, if it is not totally visual like the "text-pictures" (1955-64). In 1970 he published *DA, a letter game for children*, which is a sort of morphological fiction, or, perhaps more exactly, a biography of the two letters D and A and their permanent juxtaposition in the word *da* ("here" rather than "there"). It is a visual pun which takes one minute to read. His collection of fairy tales and fables *Bone-Toy* (1970) is written in the style of Artmann's *Frankenstein*: true fairy-tale style, the "naive realism" the Vienna Group aimed at. It is a book of myths and a breath of fresh air, like most of the work of the Vienna Group, after the general obsession for *littérature engagée*. Where he, or the others, are "committed", they are amusing, irreproachably broad-minded. Rühm's attitude to language, like his commitment, is anti-authoritarian, anarchic.

Friedrich Achleitner, like Rühm, writes primarily concrete and dialect poetry, but his prose is more important. He was one of the first to make prose-montage into nearly traditional fiction. His story, "the man without a moustache" (1957), is partly amusingly grotesque social criticism and partly straightforward jinks. The achromatic style and persuasive illogicality and the eternal puns lend Achleitner's stories an attractive absurdity. His "preparations for an execution" (1957) has most of the same qualities, but if anything it is even more grotesquely simple in its descriptions of regimental P.T. movements. Achleitner's technique in this montage, and perhaps more so in "the good soup" (1958), is similar to Weiss' in *The Shadow*; the thought behind it seems to be: reality is only reality after a detailed analysis. In Artmann's, Rühm's, and Achleitner's prose we find the inventory technique, naked lists of objects, notions, characteristics, which banalize the situations described; we find this in Weiss too.

Possibly in twenty years' time no one will be reading Artmann, Rühm, and Achleitner, but the two posthumous novels of another member of the Vienna Group, Konrad Bayer, are already classics, classics in almost every sense T.S. Eliot would allow the word. The first, *The Head of Vitus Bering* (1965), is a macabre short novel about the epileptic Bering's life in St. Petersburg and his voyage to the Arctic. Historical facts blend with projections of Bayer's own philosophy both in the novel proper and the "index", which is very much a component part of the novel. The result: very funny and very disturbing. Bayer uses various techniques to effect alienation. These may be typographical:

> and the ship went through a sea of fire
> ?
> is this how day and night come about?
> ah.

It may be by means of a grotesque anti-situation: "in china the ear was the most sought after trophy, whereupon Beethoven appeared." It may be through carefully grotesque syntax: "the and czar his sank poet in could a think a deep of depressed nothing mood better than to order the alphabet according to

the national anthem." Some of these techniques appear in
Bayer's second novel, *the sixth sense* (1966), which is, at first
sight, a less objective work because of the first-person narrator,
though he is more important as an observer than as a friend
of one of the characters of the montage, franz goldenberg. *The
sixth sense* is anarchic both in language and content. The unity
of the novel does not lie in any plot in the conventional sense
of the word, but derives from verbal and situational refrains
like "when life and property are threatened, all distinctions
disappear," or postures: a variety of characters do what another
character has done before: lie on the dressing table, dance on
the bar of a night club. The novel begins with four photographs:
woman semi-silhouette, negative version, same woman full-face,
negative version. Then come the first words, "thus began the
evening which completely disappeared in flowers", which become a verbal refrain, and then can be taken either as a contrast or a parallel to the theme of violence combined with anti-
authoritarianism: "behind the bar two red indian policemen
were still burning." There is always a non-participant mob
watching the actions and revolutions of the novel, and the mis-
anthropic narrator fuses now with this mob, now with the
actors: he judges the action only insofar as his descriptions are
sometimes loaded. The language of the novel reflects the anarchic action: grotesque oxymorons, massive baroque sentences,
and, at one point, a forty-three word paragraph of words beginning with 'd'. The indirect characterization through action
is grotesque: "nina bit gently into my large dream eyes." Sex
is grotesque: goldenberg masturbates underwater in a hole
he drills into the sand. Clichés are perverted (a device used by
the Moderns consistently since Eliot and Stevens, but only
coming to a head in German literature in the early sixties) and
thus banalize the situations in which they arise: "the light of
evening switches on its red bulbs, the tree-tops their golden
ones." At one point the ordered chaos of the novel is given typographical representation. Verbal and situational refrains are
twisted round each other by double overprinting; nightmare,
illusion, confusion, and violence are mixed, but the print remains legible.

Another member of the Vienna Group is Oswald Wiener, who has dissociated himself from the others and the work he produced while in the group. He has published one "novel", *The Improvement of Central Europe* (1969). It was popular among the intellectual snobs when it came out, for it is a work of absolute snobbery (much worse than *Finnegans Wake*), on the whole deadly serious, but sometimes flying out of cynicism and misanthropy into a certain humor. It begins with an index to the people and subjects mentioned in the novel, followed by an authoritarian manifesto in the form of a long preface (however much the author castigates artistic manifestoes). The novel proper is a nice piece of *genre*-mixing and technical expertise. Some "remarks" serve as an afterword, which is followed by three appendices and a formidable bibliography. The pages are, strangely enough, numbered, but in Roman numerals, all CCVII of them. It is a novel in that it shows the development, by means of static rather than dynamic situations, of an ego. Its situations are built up on authoritarian and anarchic apophthegms: "what exists is out of date"; "the world belongs to me, the world is an extension of my continuity." Semantic, ontological, and aesthetic theories are expressed in paradoxes, puns, and pubic cantankerousness. The vocabulary is rich, precise, and demanding. *The Improvement of Western Europe* is a novel about writing a novel: it could be called a mod version of *Tristram Shandy*. Wiener gives us much less of a story than Sterne; for Wiener story is a disgustingly bourgeois concept. However this book may exhaust its readers, it is not without self-ironization; Wiener states his ideal thus: "I write for the intellectual shits of the future."

Weiss' *Shadow* and the Vienna Group are important because much of contemporary German literature might not have been written without them; indeed their ideas should and will be exploited further. On the other hand Thomas Bernhard, another Austrian, is interesting because he fits into no scheme. He is probably influential because of his psychology; he has no deep relationship with any other living or dead author. The elements of Kafka and Broch are certainly there, but only in the background, as part of the victuals of the cultural tradition which nourished Bernhard. He is the most depressing and most consistent modern German writer. He aims at destroying the idyllic mythology of Austrian life, especially life in the mountains, and creating a new demonology. His first novel, *Frost* (1963), begins this development, followed by the short semi-epistolary tale, *Amras* (1964). The latter traces the physical and intellectual disintegration of an Innsbruck family of intellectuals. The starting point is a family suicide attempt; the parents are successful, but not the two sons, who are rescued from judicial revenge by their uncle who confines them in a medieval tower on his estate. One of the brothers, the epileptic Walter, finally throws himself out of the window and the other, the narrator, escapes from Austria and the threat of a mental hospital "to find *himself.*" The style of the novel with its sometimes analytical sentence formations, sometimes baroque convolutions, reflects the fragmentariness of related experience. Sentences are long and separated by three dots rather than a full stop. The tale is socially relevant in that the brothers are attracted by the bohemian circus artists and, with them, attack the "petit bourgeois" narrow-mindedness of the citizens of Innsbruck. The seven short stories in Bernhard's *Prose* (1967) pick up the themes of *Amras*: hopeless family relationships, sickness, suicide, and insomnia. The underlying theme of these stories is the same: people cannot come to terms with the past which persecutes them. The characters, like those of *Amras*, are upper middle class, with the exception of the criminal, Winkler, in the last story. The impossibility of efficient communication between human beings is a central theme of these stories and arises again and again in Bernhard's later work. His second novel, *Distraction* (1967), again deals with family relationships, sickness, and suicide. The narrator is the son of a country doctor and goes one day with his father on his round. The first half of the novel is taken up by visits to the bourgeois, and describes the violence, antisemitism, egotism and middle-class prejudices of Austrian country people. The second half consists almost entirely of the philosophical, autobiographical and self-analytical monologue of Prince Saurau, a distraught (*i.e.* in the eyes of Austrian society: mad) patient of the nar-

rator's father. In *Watten* (1969) (*Watten* is a card-game) the
central character and narrator is an aristocratic doctor, who
has been deprived of his practice by the State. Four men, including the doctor, had always played *Watten* in the local pub,
but since the suicide of one of the four, the doctor cannot be
persuaded to play any more. The constant repetition of the
word *Watten* gives a strong element of the Absurd to the whole
story. *Watten* is as anti-authoritarian as Bernhard's previous
works, but there is more humor here than we have seen before,
however sardonic it may be. His third novel, *The Limepit*
(1970), is as depressing as most of his works: it is a deliberately
boring masterpiece. The narrator is an insurance agent and the
central character, Konrad, is, once more, an intellectual. He
is married to a cripple who was once a great beauty and whom
he murders early on Christmas morning. The novel shows in
retrospect the way Konrad and his wife tortured each other
intellectually. Konrad is dotty and his life-work, a dissertation
on Hearing, is dotty. He is even more distraught than Prince
Saurau. The novel contains clever attacks on rumor, the self-
righteous perversions of an event in the months of the bourgeois. Technically the novel is beautiful: the sentences are well-
balanced and the weird atmosphere is enhanced by the dialectical idea-destruction inherent in these sentences. Most of the
novel (pp. 16-270) takes up one paragraph, which reinforces
the inevitability and indurate pessimism of the whole. Bernhard's latest work, a collection of short stories called *Midland in
Stilfs* (1971), is consistently depressing and restless. The title
story has a certain kinship with *The Limepit*: the narrator
says, "Our existence is a fatal existence. Stilfs [a mountain
hamlet] is the end of life." Suicide, madness, hopelessness, and
the macabre are the central themes of these stories. One phrase
in the third is an elegant summary of Bernhard's art: "the refinement of despair."

The first true German I shall deal with in this essay is
Jürgen Becker. His first work, *Fields* (1964), is a programme-
novel or novel-programme like Wiener's *Improvement*. The
subject of the book is the author-narrator and his environment:
Cologne and its environment. Heissenbüttel has called him a

writer of "topographical narratives". The topography of *Fields* is centered on the narrator's ego, who has conversations sometimes with himself, sometimes with the reader. It demonstrates the narrator's self-conscious awareness of Time, Experience, and Memory, and the discontinuity of Time, Experience, and Memory. Everything in the book is in flux: history, places, people, language, the ego. *Fields* begins with waking up, an awareness description:

> has the moon risen now (?)        I start
> up in bed sitting and I scratch myself
> to death straight away . . .

And so it goes. The style is a refinement of baroque. Apart from melodiously baroque accumulations like "still cold still gloomy still chewing" and rather forced colloquialisms like "although you couldn't care a fuck about the pickle you can see I'm in, I've been a good long time on my way", we have Decadent-baroque synaesthesia like "a green smell" or "the sour breeze". We also have the logical realism of banalization in, for instance, his alienating definition of a point near Cologne: "about at the position point p right (y) $77 + 0.80 = 77.80$ to the power of (x) $56 + 0.95 = 56.95$; ordnance survey map 2844 (Burscheid)." He uses dialect, word- and sound-play, and typographical devices such as word-spaces, lines of dots, and curious vowel-less words to convey the fragmentation of memory and experience. The book ends: "in front is three years ago; behind is now; fields." Of course there has to be a spot of philosophy in the book. The Pragmatist pluralism we find is elderly hat in the extreme. Becker's second work, *Edges* (1968), is more ordered, though the ordering is a bit of a gimmick. The book is divided up into eleven parts, the first and last being the most conventional as far as prose technique is concerned; two and ten are less conventional, three and nine still less, four and eight less still, five and seven even less still; six is a blank like "Field 25" in *Fields*. In *Edges* Cologne and its environment are the background rather than the foreground as in *Fields*. In neither is there a story in the traditional sense of the word; in both the author deals with language in a self-conscious manner; *e.g.* in *Edges*, the author-narrator, looking at the map which is a *leitmotiv* of the book, says "this is the Mississippi, that is a word which designates a river." *Edges* deals, off and on, fairly thoroughly with the problem of story-telling; the result is: "A glance at the paper would again produce a novel about what was not in the paper, and in a novel like that one could, in three years' time, read about things that do not matter any more." Time and memory are as important as in *Fields*; they are the "edges of darkness." Becker's third work, *Surroundings* (1970), is again founded on associations, though there are more tiny, logically formed anecdotes here than in *Fields* or *Edges*. The theme of the book is everything that surrounds us and the significance of individual elements of that everything. The few characters (who are names rather than persons) we found in the previous works turn up again here. He exploits a technique in *Surroundings* which he seems to have been working towards: words are defined by their environment, for instance "soon": "But soon is really soon. This moment will soon be a moment in the past. When we hear the keys jangling, we know that we shall soon be let out. Soon you too will overcome your last scruples," and so on; he creates a mythology of words. Becker is quite funny, but I feel he is authoritarian, and this is backed up by the amount of didactic apophthegms we find in his works; the most relevant (for this essay) is: "In the future art will only consist of ideas."

The funniest (linguistically), the most macabre, *the* baroque writer of contemporary German literature is Ror Wolf. He is a greater writer than Becker and most of his contemporaries because he does not take himself as seriously as they do. The central theme of Wolf's first book, *Continuation of the Report* (1964), is food, eating, peasants, farms, the slaughtering of animals for food. The novel describes in orgiastic baroque language and imagery meals, people, and the first-person narrator. It mixes the grotesque, naive realism, and a decadent impressionism built up on "landscapes" and "pictures", which blend into the central food theme. Conversations, actions, and physiognomies blend with the noise, smell, and action of eating.

Mealtimes were important in Weiss' *Shadow*, but Wolf's auditory visual, and tactile analyses of eating go much further than Weiss'. The disease, wounds, blood, pus, and deformations that we find in *The Shadow* are in evidence in even greater detail in *Continuation*; sickness is an obsession. If Pound ever imagined such a thing as Imagist prose, this would be it. The style is a careful confusion of the lyrical and the grotesque. Phrasal and situational themes recur as do the author's ironizing comments on his own writing like "I don't know", "yes", "no, not quite", "or perhaps", "why not", and descriptive statements like "I can hear a clapping stamping clanking pouring tinkling, no I would not like to swear it is really a clapping stamping clanking pouring tinkling." His use of inventory also goes far beyond Weiss or Achleitner. Wolf's second work, *Pilzer and Pelzer* (1967), a novel or "adventure series", is a beautifully chaotic burlesque of detective fiction, sea fiction, boys' adventure stories in general; *Ivanhoe* is not a patch on it. The story of *Pilzer and Pelzer* is very simple: the first-person narrator goes to Pilzer and Pelzer's flat to condole a widow. This is always an embarrassing situation, but in place of embarrassment the narrator has fantastic hallucinations. He uses the same techniques as in *Continuation* but, though the language is not as contorted, the situations are; hence it is more comic. Sex-and-violence was animal and grotesque in *Continuation* and so it is here; it is a parody of the ughish sexploitation of lesser Olympia Pressists. The landscapes we had in *Continuation* are re-emphasized by the refrain "I was standing by the window and..." Wolf's third work, *my family, twelve murderers' songs* (published in 1968 under the punning pseudonym: Raoul Tranchirer) is verse and so does not belong in this essay, but it is worth pointing out simply because here we see the lyrical vocabulary and rhythm of Wolf's prose put into verse form. It is great fun and quite as elegantly grotesque as his previous writing. His next work is a collection of prose pieces written between 1957 and 1969, *Thank you. Don't mention it* (1969). As in his previous works Wolf composes his stories by molding his paragraphs into word-sound-idea patterns rather than describing consecutive actions. The montage technique *à la* Vienna Group reveals itself here in a clearer and less polished form than in his previous works. There is plenty of the *grotesque* in these stories, but they are not as *macabre* as we expect, and the comedy does not succeed as well as it does in *Pilzer and Pelzer.* We do, however, have some more striking examples of his pleonastic technique here than we have had before: "the medical check-up, you know what I mean, the diagnosis, the examination, you see, the results, the complete picture of your state of health, your complaints, your infirmities . . .", and also more explicit pornoparody: "The Marquise undressed and was dragged off by the satyrs." Ror Wolf's latest work, *A Point is a Point* (two versions, 1970 and 1971), is a photoverbal montage of the world of soccer: artistic reportage rather than fiction. But then reportage is the way a lot of German literature is going. Wolf plays about with the clichéd jargon of soccer and soccer-reporting; his attitude hovers between irony and fanship. Photographs from "historic moments" in soccer matches are mingled with the text to create a mixture of grotesque persiflage and Carlylean eulogy. It is great fun but not great literature in the way *Continuation* is. It sadly parallels Artmann's development down to *How much, honey?*, although Wolf has not lost *all* his originality in *A Point is a Point*, and his use of photographs is almost new.

Hermann Peter Piwitt is well known as a writer, but his one book of creative (imaginary) literature, the collection of prose pieces, *Landscape Full of Herds* (1965), is unknown or forgotten. The grotesque and animal/insect aspects of these stories are comparable with Wolf and the analytical treatment of awareness comparable with Becker. The first six stories are jigsaw puzzles of awareness and self-analysis; the last four are a mixture of awareness fragments and almost conventional excursions into the Absurd. The style is similar in all the pieces and a certain thematic unity is lent them not only by the peasant setting but also by the frequent appearances of Uncle Rasha with his ridiculous aphorismic sayings. We find the emphatically self-conscious use of language we have seen in other writers: "Possibilities of escape diminish with the waning of the moon. Sentences like this, which, incidentally, are very suitable for recitation in and out of schools, constantly take the reader unaware because of their verbal elegance, a quality which even I save up for emergencies like this." Piwitt combines thematic refrains with mock-lyrical style and deliberate tripe, a technique of Wolf and Becker, though Piwitt has developed it independently.

Perhaps one cannot be so sure of the independence of Guntram Vesper in his use of these techniques, but he shows enough originality otherwise to persuade me he has arisen uninfluenced by Wolf and Becker. His anti-militaristic novel of primitive village life, *War Memorial Right in the Distance* (1970), is divided into tenuously connected chapters, each of which presents a precise fragment or, occasionally, a complete history. These fragments study the primitive and special aspects of primitive society: crime, incest, macabre rural superstitions. Vesper's use of the grotesque, verbal and situational refrains, his anti-authoritarian attitude to government and sardonic humor, all link him up with the Vienna Group/Ror Wolf tradition. Piwitt, Wolf, the Vienna Group deflated sex, but they deflated it by ironical vulgarization; Vesper deflates it by scientific irony: "The pointed end of the spermatic duct, I mean the ejaculation-channel, penetrates the prostate gland and emerges on the spermatic protuberance." The anti-nationalism of *War Memorial* is a trait which we find in much of German literature since the second World War; Vesper's is somewhat more acid than most.

Peter Handke, an Austrian, is younger and better known than any of the writers we have looked at so far, though his drama rather than his prose fiction made him famous. His plays are closer analyses of the linguistic and existential problems which arise in his prose. In both he deals with the way language controls our perception, and the way meanings can be twisted by both verbal and physical situations. *Prediction* (1966), for example, is a string of perverted clichés, a warped analysis of reality through clichés which could be seen as the logical development of the prose of the Vienna Group and of Ror Wolf. *Kasper* (1967) reduces language and reality to phonemes and then brainwashes the central character into a false perception of reality by teaching him conventional verbal reactions to reality. *Quodlibet* (1970) reduces the language of society to a state of permanently absurd ambiguity, and *Ride over Lake Constance* (1970) does the same to social behavior. Handke's first novel, *The Hornets* (1966), has the same theme as his first published play, *Insults for the Audience* (1966): "You will hear what you have otherwise seen." *The Hornets* is a village novel and its narrator is Gregor, the blind son of a small farmer. The novel is centered on the day he went blind and built up on awareness analysis (cf. Becker, Piwitt), memories, dreams, and word-environments. The atmosphere is gloomy but not as gloomy as in Bernhard's villages; there are deaths but no suicides. Like Bernhard, Handke has an aversion to the police. Gregor's relationship with the rest of his family is as negative as a Bernhard hero's. Where Bernhard is intellectual in the treatment of his characters, Handke is sensual. Handke's language is not relentlessly elegant, grinding like Bernhard's; it is often almost light or playful, sometimes, as in the food scene, baroque: sometimes he manages to alienate the reader to the extent that he does not know whether he is meant to feel tension or to laugh:

> And suddenly, he said, suddenly, suddenly the water rises, the water rises, suddenly the water rises, the water rises, suddenly the water rises the water suddenly rises, the water rises and
> and    and    and    and and and    andandandand
> No!    I said
> And    now, he said.

Handke's second novel, *The Hawker* (1967), is a clever pastiche of all varieties of detective stories, but disappointing. Each chapter is prefaced by an analytical theory of how the chapter should develop the plot according to the traditions of the thriller, so we might speak of an inherent irony of authorial self-destruction in the novel. This is enhanced by the author's ironic detachment in the novel proper. (We found this in *The Hornets* and, of course, in Ror Wolf.) The characters of the

novel are nameless; thus the aura of names, which is an intrinsic part of a thriller, is deflated, and the idea of a hawker
as an amateur detective is pleasantly cynical. Somehow, however, the reader gets annoyed with the clichés and the pre-
dictability of everything. The deadpan humor is too deadpan
and lacks the flashes of wit which would give critical weight
to the deadpanness. The collection of short stories, *A Welcome
for the Board of Directors* (1967), is amusing but not particularly significant anti-Establishment stuff. These stories up-
hold and deflate the Kafka heritage in modern German literature; one of them is simply a paraphrase of *The Trial*: one waits
for the twist and it never comes. There is one piece of elegant
syntactic grotesque in "The Intrusion of a Woodman on a
Peaceful Family", where sixty-two words intervene between the
verb and its separable prefix. The subject of Handke's collection
of sociocritical experimental prose texts and stories, *The Inner
World of the Outer World of the Inner World* (1969), is
language and semantic, syntactic, orthographical and emotional
aspects of language. Microsituations are represented by sentences, words, sounds, or letters of the alphabet; and macro-
situations by the blurred photographic and newsprint collages
inserted between the texts. One of the stories, "Three Readings
of the Law", is a sort of register analysis: the first reading consists in a list of naked words, slogans—and the audience claps
after each one; the second is an objective explanation of what
the slogans mean in plain language—the audience grows uneasy
and at the end boos and hisses; the third is a list of slogans
with an explanation of their meanings hidden behind officialese
and earns storms of applause from the audience. There are
plenty of concrete jokes in his book, like "text 31", which consists in the following sentence in large print. "THERE IS
SOMETHING LYING ON THE PAPƒR". Handke's third
novel, *The Anxiety of the Goal-Keeper at the Penalty Kick*
(1970), is very nearly a conventional novel. Josef Bloch, a
former goalie, is (he assumes) given his notice and goes to
Vienna. He meets a cashier at a cinema and, one night, follows
her home, sleeps with her, throttles her the next morning and
takes a bus to the frontier. He stays in this frontier village

while the police are hunting him. The novel ends with Bloch at a local football match seeing an unsuccessful penalty kick. So much for the plot, but the novel is essentially, like *The Hornets*, a study in awareness and the problem of communication. The novel's humor is as quiet as Bloch's quiet anarchism: "Bloch could not think of anything suitable. He said something obscene. She sent the child straight out of the room." The problems of language and reality of *The Inner World* and of his plays, are taken up again in *The Anxiety of the Goal-Keeper*. Handke explains the linguistic riddle of sign and symbol to the laymen in one paragraph where I. A. Richards took a couple of hundred pages:

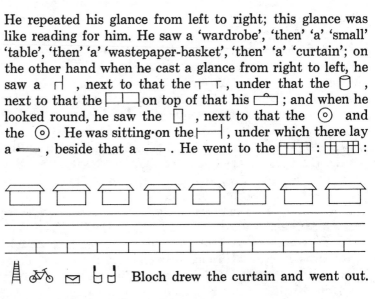

He repeated his glance from left to right; this glance was like reading for him. He saw a 'wardrobe', 'then' 'a' 'small' 'table', 'then' 'a' 'wastepaper-basket', 'then' 'a' 'curtain'; on the other hand when he cast a glance from right to left, he saw a ⊓ , next to that the ⊤⊤ , under that the ⊖ , next to that the ⊏⊐ on top of that his ⊏⌒⊐ ; and when he looked round, he saw the ⊓ , next to that the ⊙ and the ⊙ . He was sitting·on the ⊢─┤ , under which there lay a ◖═ , beside that a ═ . He went to the ▦ : ⊞⊞ :

Bloch drew the curtain and went out.

G. F. Jonke, four years younger than Handke, from southern Austria like Handke, begins, like Handke, with an Austrian village novel, *Geometrical Village Novel* (1969). Its subject is everyday life, its method fabulous reportage. We have a social survey, a history of some of the families in the community, a description of the countryside around and its bulls. We also have a depiction of the perennial village disaster, strange bird-like animals that devour mortar. The geometry of the novel is both verbal and visual (maps, the itinerant artistes' tent, etc.) and represents the banal regularity of life there. It is an immensely funny book hovering between social or human satire and burlesque. We find also self-ironization of the narrator as in Wolf and Handke: "No, that is not true, that is a mistake, that is wrong, that is not so, that is a lie." Jonke uses half-serious typographical techniques:

> ... through the cracks of the doors I got an impression of the inside of the houses and yards
>
> fire
>
> bush
>
> fan
>
> then the doors
>
> shut again...

The stranger who comes to the village speaks an extraordinary language which a professor eventually decides is a phonetic poem. The mayor always gets the testicles of the bull ritually roasted on the village square. One of the rules learned by the children in primary school is "we always follow the instruction laid down in the encyclical 'humanae vitae' Papi Pauli Sixti." And so it goes on. Jonke's *Viewing of the Glasshouse* (1970) is a parody diary again set in a banal rural setting; the basic story, printed in italics, is of two people inspecting the outside of a glasshouse and their discussions with the owner about when they will have gained enough knowledge about the outside to go inside. The sub-themes, that is most of the book, in normal print, are a naive realist description of the building of a house, a canal, and a bridge, and the mysterious inaudible conversations inside the local pub. The techniques are fundamentally the same as in *Geometrical Village Novel*, but here the burlesque mythopoeic aspects of rural life are more important, for instance, the large wooden boxes that appear at the roadside and which are supposed to conceal some sort of statues to be unveiled at some rural festivities:

Persons who endeavor to open or misplace the boxes will,
even when the sky is blue, be struck by lightning,
carbonized,
and
will fall to the ground.

Among other grotesque situations in this novel is the crane
driver who is paid by the unemployed to drop his load on
workers at the building site. A nightmare scene where fisher-
men are devoured by barracudas is reminiscent of a scene in
Wolf's *Pilzer and Pelzer*. Jonke has great fun too with language
and, especially, ridiculous, long words like *Abendspaziergangs-
verständigungssysteme*, a joke he begins to exploit in his geometrical novel and continues to play with in his collection of
conventional funny short stories, *Beginning of a Despair* (1970).
There are some good moments in these stories, but they do not
succeed as his novels do. He satirizes Austrian provincialism as
strongly as ever. His latest novel, *The Increase of the Lighthouses* (1971), is constructed in a similar way to *Viewing of
the Glasshouse*, but both his technique and his humor give a
more polished impression. The main themes are the construction
of inland lighthouses in Austria, a reds-under-the-beds-type
enemy, a lighthouse superintendent's inspections of the lighthouses. It has a preface complete with mock academic footnotes,
an afterword, and some banalizing concluding remarks. He plays
with syntax, words, and sounds in the language-bound tradition
of contemporary German literature.

Rolf Dieter Brinkmann is quite a different sort of writer from
those we have so far treated. At the moment he is best known
for his uninspiredly vulgar verse and as a translator of American
underground literature, but his best work lies in his prose. His
collection of five realist-cum-impressionist prose pieces, *Whirligig* (1966), have something technically in common with Piwitt's
*Landscapes*, but Brinkmann's themes are urban. In each piece
in *Whirligig* there are a series of little stories reflected by the
physical appearance, movements, or dress of the nameless
people described, but more important than the little stories
themselves is the overall experience of which they are part.

The first piece, "In a Side Street", eloquently describes things seen in and through a grocer's window; the man looking through the window connects what he sees with pubertal reminiscences and existential divagations, all of which are periodically interrupted by the external reality of the cars whishing past him on the streets, or the objects his wife is buying in the shop. The style of these prose pieces is elegant, rich in imagery and sensual description. Brinkmann's best known prose work, the novel *No-one Knows More* (1968), is different: "Angry Young Man stuff come a bit later, or, looking at it from another angle, come in time to use the real fucking language of real fucking anger." This depressing, static novel describes the violent discontent of a young student *manqué* and his wife; it is absolutely humorless. It depicts the frustration of modern young men with their idyllic memories of the drag shows and supersex of Swinging London. The touches of lyricism we do find in *No-one Knows More* are never as effective as they were in *Whirligig*.

As a social realist novel Hubert Fichte's The '*Palette*' (1968) is much more effective than *No-one Knows More*. It depicts a group of beat lay-abouts and petty criminals, most of them homosexual (male and female) or bisexual, who gather in a Hamburg bar called the Palette. The novel's narrator-observer is Jäcki, an intelligent half-Jewish illegitimate child. The prose flickers like a film; memories of conversations, actions, sensations dovetail to evoke a thoroughly convincing picture of the staccato life of German beat generation youth. Beckeresque topographical descriptions, Wolfian inventory technique, wry humor, and the connecting serious theme of the passing of time and friendships help to make The '*Palette*' more than a sociological document, and prevent it from being a manifesto of social anti-authoritarianism.

Other important committed writers are Günter Herburger, Martin Sperr, Uwe Brandner, and Wolf Wondratschek. Herburger is at his best in his post-beat verse; his two new volumes of committed children's stories, *Bulb Can Do Everything* and *Bulb Can Do More* (both 1971), are about a light bulb going by the name of Bulb, and his evaluations of society are very clever; it is a new sort of children's book, different from Soviet bloc books of the same type, because there is no Party line. Sperr is a dramatist and his novel *Hunt for Outsiders* (1971) is based on his dramatic ideas. It is an almost conventional novel set in a Bavarian village just after the Monetary Reform, and a historical novel with constant references to historical events and footnotes very much *à la* Walter Scott. The central character is a Woyzeckian homosexual called Abram. He is caught fiddling with another social outcast, the idiot Rovo; he murders his betrothed; his mother escapes; Abram cannot. The Bavarian village of Einöd is demonized in much the same way that Bernhard demonizes his Austrian villages and, as with Bernhard, the characters of the 'abnormal' personages contrast very favorably with those of the 'normal'. Sperr is subtle and bitter. Brandner's latest work, *Mutation Milieu* (1971), his fourth novel, is very much committed, sociopolitically and philosophically. It is an episodical, plotless social panopticon, belly-socialist and at the same time elegant and quietly amusing. It moves from grim realism to rococco, from self-conscious word-play to political verbal association, from the debunking of the micro-myths of cliché to sceptical cocacolaism. *Mutation Milieu* has something in common, technically, with Wondratschek's first prose work, *The Day Used to Begin with a Bullet Wound* (1969), a collection of short stories where a verbal or situational theme is developed rather than a plot; it is the same sort of panopticon, but Wondratschek is artistically more self-conscious than Brandner. His self-consciousness is not only linguistic, as with Brandner, but seems to penetrate his whole outlook; he goes further than Wolf or Handke with his ironization of the narrator's job in sentences like "In Munich or somewhere a man or someone has killed or something his wife or someone". He has his own little semi-authoritarian artistic manifesto: "Only the sentences count. Stories do not interest anyone any more. A story is the memory of a sentence. I shall tell a sentence to its end." His second collection, *A Peasant and a Peasant-Woman Beget a Peasant-Boy Who Definitely Wants to Become a Farmhand* (1970), is even less of a collection of stories than *The Day Used to Begin*, where there were, at least, recurrent themes. Although *A Peasant* is often amusing and technically persuasive, here one feels the author has become a bit too big for his boots. He seems to have sat down and jotted down a few vaguely associated thoughts, pruned them a little, and published them because his first book was such a success. The trouble is that, in *A Peasant*, the thoughts do not express anything but themselves; the result is really trash which hopes to be taken seriously.

Christian Enzensberger, younger brother of the poet Hans Magnus and Reader in English at the University of Munich, has, apart from his translation of *Alice in Wonderland* and a book on the Victorian poets, done a bit of serious and witty *littérature engagée* with his *Excursion on Dirt* (1968); it is a pastiche; it is a satire; it is politics; it is literature—and ecology. The *Excursion* is a socio-political examination of the taboos of dirt worked out on basically Beckeresque principles; it is a topographical analysis of the word "dirt." It is a linguistic game, an adventure story, and a piece of excellent style spun out with relentless humor. Apart from impressionist views of major cities (especially London) he quotes in a scholarly fashion from authentic sources and from the (nonexistent) great English novel *Cranley*. Much of the work is in reported speech purporting to come from the pen of some sociopolitician of dirt. Like some of the work of the Vienna Group the *Excursion on Dirt* has a bibliography and index.

Helmut Heissenbüttel, though he belongs to the generation of Weiss and H. C. Artmann, is the doyen of the German avantgarde, indeed so much so that, according to Piwitt, no critic has even dared say anything against him because everyone in the German literary world is under some sort of obligation to him. Heissenbüttel's *Textbooks* (1960-67), storyless prose pieces, are, generally, either constructions of word associations or descriptions of the Typical in the looks, thoughts, and behavior of man and woman. The *Textbooks* are divided into straight prose (fiction?) "Quasinovels" and more metaphorical prose and would-be poetry "pamphlets". Some of the texts written in the fifties, like the "Psychological Process", anticipate Weiss' analytical realism; in many of them he exploits the possibilities of the verb, a very un-German part of speech until Wolf and

Handke came along. Heissenbüttel is a great master of the aphorism, but his aphorisms are not in the last month of pregnancy like the traditional Lichtenberg-Nietzsche aphorisms; they are purely verbal philosophy, and meant seriously, which makes them banal. We do find in Heissenbüttel the techniques, like extensive word-play, inventory, syntactic grotesque, and multilingual montage, that we expect from the Vienna Group, but he does not have their "oomph." Most of the texts simply go on for too long; the ideas in the first few sentences are often good but, expanded, they get boring. On the whole these texts are just too clever-clever. His *D'Alembert's End* (1970) is an unreadable macrobiblion of literary tittle-tattle; again, it does not move with the necessary panache to come off in the way Artmann's *Search for Yesterday* does.

Franz Mon, a member of Heissenbüttel's *cénacle*, has produced one major work of experimental prose-fiction, *herzzero* (untranslatable = heart zero) (1968), in which two parallel texts tell roughly the same story. The story lies in recurrent words, phrases, clichés, more than in the two (almost) straightforward fairy tales or in the six re-emergent episodes: a fire, people hiding in the latrines and falling into the boggy earth around them; the lascivious huntsman; heart disease and some extremely virulent form of gastroenteritis; the moving of the tribes of "Israel" from place to place; a man chasing his sweetheart; brainwashing in a lunatic asylum for undesirables. Other *immanent* stories are contained in the context in which Bismarck, Hindenburg, Hitler, cats and mice, buying shelves, the death of a thoughful old man, sunbathing, sodomy, masturbation, copulation, and so on, come up. The style is an elegant confusion of dialogue, baroque-lyrical passages, quasi-concrete poetry, and conventional narrative. Parallels to the technique of Wolf and Handke abound; on the whole *heart zero* is an amusing work, but too long.

The Austrian, Michael Scharang, is another, younger, scion of the Heissenbüttel *cénacle*, and he sports a Ph.D. behind his name. His first work, *Proceeding of a Proceeding* (1969), is a collection of fifteen short stories about eccentric situations and eccentrics in eccentrically normal situations; they are told with superb elegance. The stories, full of banalizations, ironical linguistic self-consciousness, word-play, the grotesque, the surrealist, and the macabre, usually have social or political implications. The figures in these stories are mostly "petits bourgeois" or "respectable" working class. *Proceeding of a Proceeding* is rich in anti-situations and semantic grotesque: "This cello has more calories." Scharang's second collection, *An End to Story-Telling and Other Stories* (1970), is more politically committed (committed = left-wing socialist) than *Proceeding of a Proceeding*. The motif is disillusionment, no hope for Western society so long as there is a capitalist régime. His stance is not narrow-minded; he does see the fence-sitting indolence of the workers, a view rare among committed writers of East and West. His style is simpler here, but he still dollops a good deal of healthy humor into his narrative soup. Scharang has recently published a collection of rather conservative Marxist essays, *Towards the Emancipation of Art* (1971), but, with the exception of the essay on radio drama (radio plays are *the* "in" genre in German-speaking countries), they are benevolently free of new ideas. He does, however, write in an unusually lucid style for a German Marxist.

Friederike Mayröcker is a much more radically experimental prose writer than the Luchterhand-Heissenbüttel school, whose deadly dull linguistic experimentation her texts often seem to parody. She is a close friend (whatever that may mean) of the Austrian phonetic poet and fellow English teacher, Ernst Jandl. Her *Minimonster's Dream Lexicon* (1968) exploits the metaphorical possibilities of language as sign and symbol with anarchical verve. Where with the Vienna Group, even in the concretest of their concrete poems, we can usually bend our minds and produce some philosophical or ideological interpretation, with this Mayröcker collection we can only try linguistic-esthetic interpretations, if we believe that literature *must* be interpreted. This collection is pure linguistic fiction. An example, the text "Minimonster's Dream Lexicon.1." will demonstrate what I mean: "At Emmerich terrarium (north-tele) should came off well. and the assimilation of 'pinmoney' of James Rosenquist/F III. This conquest should dying. as a result. Pot (balls), esp. with the phoenic, aiming as shortly . . ." Her visual technique is a forewarning of Handke's *Anxiety of the Goal-Keeper*: "A 〰 (swan) in the ⊞ (window)." in the text "RADIATIORS cum true decorative footnote". Her second collection of prose texts, *Phantom Fan* (1971), is technically, but not linguistically, yet more sophisticated than the *Dream Lexicon*, but it is quite as funny. The word-play, use of dialect and the grotesque, and the admirably iconoclastic attitude to language strike us even more than in *Dream Lexicon*. There are no real stories here, but plenty of mini-anecdotes.

Three young Swiss writers promise great things, even if what they have produced so far is nothing exceptionally exceptional. Margrit Baur's volume in three novels, *On Streets, Squares and Other Circumstances / The Simple Senses and What Remains to be Said / A Continuously Continuing Story* (1971), is, all three of it, based on environmental association, peppered with social satire *à la* Robert Walser's burlesques on Swiss regularity. This three-novel uses banalization, inventory, puns, and perverted clichés, with a spark of women's lib for good measure, without gripping any particular theme. Werner Schmidli's collection of prose pieces, *Don't Say: The Fun Ends with Money* (1971), sets out to dun verbal and situational clichés in as many ways as the author can think of. It is a very successful collection; "We Know Our Way About", a pastiche of the clichés of holiday and *après*(sic!)-holiday conversations and postcard greetings, is perhaps the best of all. Rolf Geissbühler's *33 1/3* (1971) is a circular novel made up of recurrent words, phrases, and sentences. The central character is a young secretary, Miss Silberstein, who has a pash on everyone she meets. Geissbühler uses pun, zeugma, or even rhyme as a banalization technique. He is 100% anti-authoritarian, but his anti-authoritarianism is not as amusing as Schmidli's.

No survey of contemporary German fiction is complete if it does not mention an apparently ephemeral trend which goes against the political realism of mainstream new German literature. This is the literature which has arisen in the wash of the pop culture of the sixties. Pop literature, like pop painting, is a contradiction, as the basis of pop is the glorification of the moment, a revolt against the permanence of bourgeois values. Let us call this literature "popwash", bearing in mind all the possible connotations of such a word. Jürgen Ploog's *Coca Cola Hinterland* (1969) is Germany's answer to the American underground popwash; in fact it is American popwash written in German, though it does fit into the contemporary German tradition in that linguistic themes and variations on linguistic themes form its basis. If this book comes near any writer of the more conventional brand, Ror Wolf is the first to come to mind. *Coca Cola Hinterland* is an impressive aleatory storm of sexual contortion, muscular violence, science fiction, Donald Duck, Superman, and Frank Zappa. Pictures like "every evening the grey-green Chelsea girl shoved with throttled motor through the docks and showed her celluloid tissue of time pores scars nipples" are thrown together with strings of sexual and astronautical patois. *Coca Cola Hinterland* is an achievement simply because it is *not* boring and because it does evoke the polychromatic chaos of acid society. Nothing else in German popwash literature comes up to it. Michael M. Czernich's *The Thousand Eyes of Dr. Fiddle* (1970), a mixture of straight prose and scenario, only succeeds, if it succeeds at all, in preaching the religion of sex-and-violence for the sake of sex-and-violence. Peter Matejka's *Kuby* (1970), "translated from the esperanto by budak budala", is as immature as *Dr. Fiddle*. It differs from the rest because there is a story, even literary allusion, and sex and violence are largely irrelevant to it; it attempts a comic strip in many words and a few pictures. Tiny Stricker's *Trip Generation* (1970) is an attempt at a popwash travelogue, pop-vamped reminiscences of Turkey, Persia, India, and Pakistan spiced with the drug-taking and bisexual experiences of the author-narrator. Last and least comes R. D. Wulff's *Keep it Clean, People* (1971), a boring popwash plaid of sex, violence, primitive sententiousness and general verbal chaos. The trouble with popwash literature is that its writers set out to shock in full knowledge of the fact that the only people who read their stuff will be other would-be shockers. German popwash writers have something of the artistic hubris and little of the skill of the esthete pornographers of the nineties. Popwash is a dead end.

# Who now?

## jerome klinkowitz

# Literary Disruptions; or, What's Become of American Fiction?

*It is a curiosity of writing about angels that, very often, one turns out to be writing about men.*

DONALD BARTHELME
*CITY LIFE*

*I think there are two separate things. There are, you know, wise people around who can't write for shit. I mean, they're just not artists. . . . And there're probably idiots around who can write good books.*

RONALD SUKENICK
"Interview,"
*THE FALCON* (1971)

People at large no longer believe in fiction as a medium that expresses the truth of their lives. "Successful novels" present data, yes, but in terms of fraudulent ideals, and it is not long before readers begin despising these works for the lies they present as real life stories. Our persistent old-fashioned story tellers would make us believe as fact that life has leading characters, plots, morals to be pointed, lessons to be learned, and most of all beginnings, middles, and ends. A provocateur such as Kurt Vonnegut, Jr., can play with the cynical farce of all this, when in *Breakfast of Champions* he ponders the abominable behavior of his countrymen and concludes that "They were doing their best to live like people invented in story books. This was the reason Americans shot each other so often: It was a convenient literary device for ending short stories and books." Vonnegut adds that others suffer disappointing lives which fail to be perfect fictions, but year by year we learn that still more readers despair of the whole mess and abandon fiction altogether for history, biography, or even television. The more instant and accurate the replay, the more truthful seem the facts, although in the process the organizing and clarifying process of art is forgone, and fiction no longer exists.

"Television can give us the news, fiction can best express our response to the news," says Ronald Sukenick, whose novel *Up* and collection *The Death of the Novel and Other Stories* were among the first works to face the problem of fiction in a world which claimed its possibilities were exhausted. Despite the American novel's conservative stability of form since the experiments of the 1920's, Sukenick and his contemporaries—including such wide-ranging innovators as Donald Barthelme, Jerzy Kosinski, and Raymond Federman—have made progress in clearing the way for a new sense of life in fiction, at the same time grounding it in the proper realm of art: not just the data of experience, but our reaction to it, which is where we really live and where any truth is likely to reside. Sukenick's latest work may be the climax of this movement, as the new methods of fiction finally establish themselves in a useable tradition. His novel *Out* is a study of connections, not resolved in any rational solution but rather as a spatial entity: only the feelings are "ordered and refined." Sukenick's object of art replaces "abstraction, reduction, essentials, separation, and stillness" with "inclusion, addition, the random, union, and movement." One of his models in the story is the American Indian medicine man, Empty Fox, who shows him how his rational culture, with its shabby pretense of signs—both linguistic and physical—has despoiled the West. "The Wasichus make Disneyland of all this so they can sell it they get the Indians to pretend they're Indians they make believe these beautiful mountains are beautiful they pretend that magic is magic they make believe the truth is the truth otherwise they can't believe anything. There is a place with a billboard of a mountain in front of the mountain you Wasichus can't see without pretending to see anyway you don't believe it. Anyway that's why you all have cameras you're not friends with your eyes only with your minds you can't understand this." Sukenick's literary ambition, "I want to write a book like a cloud that changes as it goes," complements Empty Fox's tribal role: "I want to erase all the books. My ambition is to unlearn everything I can't read or write that's a start. I want to unlearn and unlearn till I get to the place where the ocean of the unknown begins where my fathers live. Then I want to go back and bring my people to live beside that ocean where they can be whole again as they were before the Wasichus came. That's why I like to travel this way."

*Out* follows two lines, tracing connections through a series of "meets" to some final satiability, at the same time that a narrator-character keeps talking to sustain a narrative. The messages he receives define his story: data accumulates obscurity persists, meaning disintegrates connection proliferates, speed increases space expands, enlightenment grows. He fears the desert, his own emptiness, the silence which resists the desperate need for connections, for words ("I love you"). He must keep talking, moving, crossing the Continental Divide and posing new identities, true fictional constructs which synthesize experience without becoming it. "Red Desert for example that's where Roland Sycamore is staying now Roland Sycamore you don't know this yet peeled off from the Sukenick character after the karate fight and the latter is no longer a character at all but the real me if that's possible I'm getting out of this novel. When you fly too far you don't come back."

But things do come together. The two lines of the novel merge as the count-down of chapters decreases from numbers of lines versus lines of space (10-0, 9-1, 8-2, 7-3, etc.) until section 0: no lines, all space, and the book disappears in a conclusive silence. Ronald Sukenick has moved beyond the impasse of conventional fiction, where objective realism (whether photographic, sociological, or psychological) and subjective lyricism debated each other's claim to the real thing, to fiction at its most simple best. *Out* gives us action, adventure, humor, and wisdom without the pitiful lie that it has all really happened, or that it signifies anything other than what it most apparently is. Viewed from the complexities of theory or the most basic of constituents, *Out* is pure fiction, free from the representational burdens which of all the arts seem to have prejudiced fiction the most, and which have kept the American novel within such close bounds so long.

Because of his regular *New Yorker* publication and remarkably well organized story collections, Donald Barthelme is the most popular and the most apparent writer in the new style. One of his first national publications, a review of the *39th Annual of Advertising and Editorial Art Design* for *Harper's* in October of 1961, found him looking over the year's best ads and noting that many "give not so much as a clue to what is being advertised." The award-winning spreads were nothing but form, with content "typically nowhere in sight." Barthelme could understand how these ads were making millions, for they were striking to the core of a new-found sensibility he was exploring in his own fiction at the same time.

In his earliest work Barthelme's basic concern was with the forms of language, even the sounds of words, and he practiced clever disruptions to make people see what was really happening before their eyes and ears. Many stories played with puns, while others were suggestively disconcerting, but in all cases readers were forced to think deeper of the "poppycock" they were accustomed to hear. "We have rots, blights, and rusts capable of attacking [the enemy's] alphabet," boasts an engineer in "Report," who has also studied "the area of realtime online computer-controlled wish evaporation," for the simple reason that "Wish evaporation is going to be crucial in meeting the rising expectations of the world's peoples, which are as you know rising entirely too fast." Some of Barthelme's first *New Yorker* works, never collected, were parodistic exercises in the uses of language. In these early pieces he would seize a conventional, accepted structure, and inject it with a dose of absurdity, such as using the familiar form of *TV Guide* to compose a single page, forty-chapter novel ("On a field trip, Timmy finds a rock," announces one program note-chapter; Chapter XVI reads, "Sandy Koufax and Sen. Hubert H. Humphrey discuss ambergris").

With an absolute sense of the shape of sentences and even

words, Barthelme found that he could shock readers into a new awareness of the world. For this subject his novel *Snow White* is a thematic *tour de force*. The foremost theme of the book is words. "OH I wish there were some words in the world that were not the words I always hear!" Snow White laments, but she hears only the same old ones, because "I have not been able to imagine anything better." She needs, of course, her prince, but her world is essentially prince-less. It prizes, instead, "equanimity," for anything else would be "bad for business." Its language, we learn, is ninety-nine percent "blanketing," the part of language which "fills in" between the other parts. " 'That part,' " we are told, " 'the "filling" you might say, of which the expression "you might say" is a good example, is to me the most interesting part.' " Of particular importance are " 'those aspects of language that may be seen as a model of the trash phenomenon,' " aspects which are largely the substance of *Snow White*. Hers is a world of "dreck," of unimaginative life where no one responds to her "hair initiative" because "Americans will not or cannot see themselves as princely."

In a world of 100 percent trash, its imagination dead and its language simply "blanketing," how does one break through all the blanketing, trash, and *dreck* to a happier reality one hopes would remain beneath? Barthelme's form provides the answer, and in several self-consciously experimental stories written after *Snow White* he plans an epistemological strategy to get at the heart of things. His widely reprinted "Robert Kennedy Saved From Drowning" demonstrates the problem. It is an attempt to understand one of the most "blanketed" and obscured events in our recent history, the substance and appeal of the most enigmatic of politicians, and Barthelme's form expresses the near impossibility of the task. Gathering notes from all available sources, the story tries to tell what the man was. In individually subtitled paragraphs, K., as he is called, is observed at his Justice Department desk, in public affairs, and at his home, but his behavior seems totally ambiguous. Reports are taken from others, as K. is described by secretaries, assistants, a former teacher, and a friend; but they are just glimpses, hard to pin down, and often contradictory. When K. himself speaks,

we hear only *dreck*: " 'It's an expedient in terms of how not to
destroy a situation which has been a long time gestating, or
again how to break it up if it appears that the situation has
changed during the gestation period, into one whose implications are not quite what they were at the beginning.' " Caught
in moments of reflection, he is no more helpful, speaking
vaguely of "an insurmountable obstacle," hurling himself "into
the midst of it," and proceeding "mechanically." He has his
"dream," composed of lyrical orange trees and a farm in the
hills, but also with "a steady stream of strange aircraft which
resemble kitchen implements, bread boards, cookie sheets, co-
landers . . . on their way to complete the bombing of Sidi-
Madani." Finally the writer performs the act of an actual reporter on a California beach—he saves Kennedy from drowning.
For once, "His flat black hat, his black cape, his sword are on
the shore"; but the modern Ahab cannot strike through, for
Kennedy "retains his mask." His ultimate words, on so crucial
an occasion, are a simple " 'Thank you,' " even less than expressed to the waiters who brought him his lunch. "Robert
Kennedy Saved From Drowning" stands, intentionally, as a
formalistic example of a world of *dreck*. The random juxtaposition of media accounts, documentaries, and personal reports—
the raw materials of our own history— add up to nothing conclusive: they are the spatial reality of our age, and a new way
is needed to count their meaning.

Knowing the world is, for Barthelme, ultimately an achievement of the imagination. His stories are formed on one level
by the clever manipulation of words and phrases, and on another by the introduction of startling conceptions, both of which
are then worked out in a deft parody of conventional structures.
Barthelme's harshest critique of a fellow novelist, in a review
for *Holiday* in April of 1966, is that he is "tired," that "the
feeling of terror Mr. [Graham] Greene could once produce from
these materials has leaked away," and that "we are left with
the manner." It is a case of "exhaustion at the deepest level, at
the level of feeling." Barthelme does not exempt himself; his
agent reported in the *New York Times Book Review* that his
own "central obsession is not to be boring, because he is so

easily bored himself." Barthelme's measure against boredom is a revitalization of material by imaginatively exploiting it within unlikely contexts. He dismisses old and irrelevant forms which no longer fit the reality we experience, and by clever juxtapositions (in words, in conceptions, and lately in pictures for his collage stories) shocks us into an understanding of what is really going on. Barthelme's vignettes are not simply arguments in the dialectics of form, but are rather imaginative volcanoes, revitalizing our language, our conceptions, and our experience itself. "The Balloon," "Views of My Father Weeping," and particularly the novel-like synthesis of stories in his latest collection, *Sadness*, offer a truly enlightening critique of the quotidian lives we lead and which, for us to survive, we cannot let fiction desert.

Barthelme's innovative techniques could be seen in other writing tending away from the mainstream: in W. S. Merwin's vignettes (which joined Barthelme's in the pages of *The New Yorker*), and in Richard Brautigan's novels, particularly *Trout Fishing in America*, where by a similar method of unconventional juxtapositions the banal facts of America could be better seen and imaginatively transcended. An indication that such style might be winning larger acceptance was the selection of *Steps*, a novel by Jerzy Kosinski, for the 1968 National Book Award. *Steps* has as many short chapters as *Snow White* in even fewer pages; plot is replaced by more inventive associations; and its entire thrust is as an imaginative transcendence of otherwise documentary material. Moreover, Kosinski works from an esthetic which turns away from the craft of such earlier modernists as James Joyce and Vladimir Nabokov. These writers "stretched language into new forms," Kosinski noted in *Tijd van leven— tijd van kunst* (Uitgeverij de Bezige Bij: Amsterdam, 1970, my translation). For modern, sophisticated times they offered "an explosion of words" to compensate for the sensory limitations of printed characters. Kosinski prefers instead to write the bare minimum, so that "the reader is forced to imagine what the novel merely suggests." He feels he can trust this minimal expression because he writes in an adopted language, with complete confidence that no subconscious motivations or traumas interfere with his artistic selection of words. "A writer who writes in an accepted language which he has learned as an adult," Kosinski concludes, "has in that language *one more curtain* that separates him from spontaneous [or otherwise un-controlled] expression."

Kosinski's theme is the self versus society; but rather than lament the loss of self and accuse society for its repressive force, as mainstream modernists might, Kosinski explores the self's survival, and just how terrible its surviving power may be. His first novel, *The Painted Bird*, tells of a self enduring incredible and grotesque trials: a little boy from Warsaw is lost for six years in the war-torn countryside, and is gruesomely brutalized by the backward peasants, who fear he is a Gypsy, a Jew, or a devil straight from hell. *The Painted Bird* is a ghastly involu-tion of the picaresque novel and *bildungsroman*, as the boy proceeds from one horror to another, experiencing an education to the darker side of life. It is his strategy of survival, however, that is the darkest element of the book. The most lyrical events in his young life are those of death: the panorama of a bombed building, the imposing stature of a Nazi officer dispatching "un-desirables," or the startling beauty of a living body stripped to the bones by rats. If the lighter side of life should surface, such as in the boy's idyllic love for the pastoral Ewka, it is quickly blasted away by such sights as her forced copulation with a goat. To survive, he must plot revenge, and is ultimately satis-fied when the barbarian Kalmuks ravage his village. "For a moment, as I looked at them," the boy admits, "I felt a great pride and satisfaction. After all, these proud horsemen were black-haired, black-eyed, and black-skinned," like himself. "They differed from the people of the village as night from day. The arrival of these dark Kalmuks drove the fair-haired village people almost insane with fear." There follows the most extravagant cruelty and horror in this already horror-filled book. Most of it was censored by the publishers of the first edition, and is available only in the paperback and Modern Library printings: men are not only slaughtered, but castrated in front of their wives and daughters, who are in turn forced to eat the bloody parts. Girls are gang-raped in all bizarre fashions, and the entire village is destroyed in a frenzy of hate. If there was any doubt as to what may be the truth of life, *The Painted Bird* resolves it on the side of darkness. The simple act of existence as one's self puts one at odds with society, and even one's fellows are safest when kept at bay.

The perils of the self continue through Kosinski's second novel, *Steps*, and its form expresses Kosinski's extended theme. In less than one hundred and fifty pages we see over forty episodes in apparently random juxtaposition, but all eventually focused on "the protagonist," as Kosinski calls him, and his search "back through a particularly painful past for an age of innocence, for the self which, he feels, is waiting for discovery behind the blacked memories preceding his traumas." The strategy is an immersion "in the heart of the trauma itself." Both the protagonist's action and the author's method are indicated in the title of Kosinski's critical essay, *The Art of the Self* (New York: Scientia Factum, 1968): through many scenes rehearsed from *The Painted Bird* and his earlier sociological works —copulation with beasts, castration, the power of the collective, the cool revenge of homicide—Kosinski describes a hero exploring his own reality and ability to relate to others. But "to him the most meaningful and fulfilling gesture is negative: it is aimed against the collective and is a movement towards the solitude within which the self can display its reality."

In the last pages of *Steps* Kosinski transposes his hero to the United States, where he lives an underground existence for a time, learning the structures of power in this new society. His third novel, *Being There*, moves the action above ground, to the very heights of public attention and importance. In this latter work Kosinski applies his theories of collectivity and self to the very contemporary American life, where television, as he himself has said on TV, "makes us victims of a collective image which . . . engulfs us." His central figure for *Being There* is a person entirely defined by the medium. Named, as if by chance, "Chance," he has spent his entire life secluded in a rich man's garden, his sole device of communication being a television set, which "created its own light, its own color, its own time." By changing channels, Chance finds, "he could change himself," and "Thus he came to believe that it was he, Chance, and no one else, who made himself be." But Chance is the farthest thing from a personally-created self, the dominating creature we saw described in *Steps*. Rather he is an absolute blank, drawing his reality from forms he sees on television. Hence he can serve as mirror to other dominating selves, and be universally appreciated. His genius is his total lack of substance; in conversation he can only repeat parts of sentences, "a practice he had observed on TV," and speak in simple terms of his garden, which his imposing listeners take for metaphors of their own ideas. Because of the high connections of the people he accidentally meets, the peculiar mania of the American collective is allowed to take over. Chance is thrown up as a national figure, an "adviser to the President," and is lionized by the press, radio, and of course television. Most recently Kosinski's *The Devil Tree* complements this public view with America's private collective, the family trust. Its young inheritor, Jonathan Whalen, lives a schizoid existence in a world his own history won't allow him to create. "I do everything to get a reaction," a prostitute tells him; and so does Whalen to survive, quite powerfully.

Kosinski's theme radically departs from the conclusions of mainstream writers, such as Bellow, Malamud, and Updike, and critics, among them Wylie Sypher and Charles M. Fair, who lament the loss of the self. Instead Kosinski is joined by a new group who stand in awe of the surviving self, whether that self be liberated by drugs (Hunter Thompson, *Fear and Loathing in Las Vegas*), psychosis (Roman Polanski, *Repulsion*), or sociopolitical environment (LeRoi Jones/Imamu Amiri Baraka, *Tales*). In technique Kosinski and many of these other writers seize Barthelme's imaginative freedom to transcend historical limitations (in Kosinski's case, the matters of his own experience); but their redirection of these is no less crucial to the course of fiction.

The disruption of American fiction is substantial: Barthelme's comic disabuse has made it uneasy for writers to write, or readers to read, in the insipid forms of the past; and Kosinski and others have discredited that noble theme, the loss of the self, which had fueled so many novels before. But the most complete disruption goes beyond theme or form: as practiced by such writers as Raymond Federman (*Double Or Nothing*), Steve Katz (*The Exagggerations of Peter Prince*), Eugene Wildman (*Montezuma's Ball*), Gilbert Sorrentino (*Imaginative Qualities of Actual Things*), and of late by William H. Gass (*Willie Master's Lonesome Wife*), it questions the entire premise of traditional fiction. As Ronald Sukenick told interviewer Joe David Bellamy for the *Chicago Review*:

> one of the reasons people have lost faith in the novel is that they don't believe it tells the truth anymore, which is another way of saying that they don't believe in the conventions of the novel. They pick up a novel and they know it's make-believe. So, who needs it—go listen to the television news, right? Or read a biography. Okay, if you could forget that business about illusion, you'd be more honest. Nobody is willing to suspend disbelief in that particular way anymore, including me. So once you get to the point where you admit that you are writing a book and it *is* a book, there really is no difference between fantasy and realistic action. It's completely continuous—it's all made up.

Raymond Federman, joining Sukenick and the other disruptionists in a search for viable forms of fiction, brings with him the authority of the modern French experience. He left France for America in 1947, the year Camus was depicting Joseph Grand's novel-length effort to write a single opening sentence and the discovery of how inadequate was any language at all: "the attempt to communicate had to be given up. This was true of those at least for whom silence was unbearable, and since the others could not find the truly expressive word, they resigned themselves to using the current coin of language, the commonplace of plain narrative, of anecdote, and of their daily paper. So in these cases, too, even the sincerest grief had to make do with the set phrases of ordinary conversation." Moreover, his extensive studies of Samuel Beckett taught Federman not to settle for the set phrases or stock form of ordinary fiction: "The novel cannot truly pass for reality, the theatre is unable to create believable illusion, and the cinema, which essentially should communicate with the viewer simply through a series of moving images, must rely on sound or other devices to achieve its primary goal."

Unlike the French new novelists, who write at least in part from the philosophical imperative of phenomenology, Federman is closer to his fellow Americans—Sukenick, Barthelme, and even Richard Brautigan—who face the concretely social problem of an unreal reality and the irrelevancy of forms which depict it. Thematically, his novel *Double or Nothing* handles the now familiar story of adjusting to the incredible presence of contemporary American life. The solution, however, is in his technique, which foregoes the French approach of describing a phenomenologically real world in favor of making a reality more real: that of the book itself. His "real fictitious discourse" (the book's subtitle) is not a sham illusion of some other life but rather just what it says, so many words on so many pages, bound together as a book the reader holds. Federman's bet is a sure thing; of all possibilities, the book is certainly the most immediately real thing at hand, and from this point reader and author may together move in the positive direction from degree zero.

The writer, who through fictional persona or third person omniscience makes a representation of the outside world, has been degraded by the French novelists back to this zero point. To reestablish a fictional voice, Federman divides its role into thirds: a third person, the protagonist, whose life becomes the accumulation of historical data in the usual sense, but also a second and first—respectively the "inventor" who quite honestly creates these fake historical events, and the "recorder" who transcribes the inventor inventing. "Imagine the imagination imagining," as William H. Gass would say. Or look at these *three* things happening, which according to Federman together make a real story.

The story: a protagonist, occasionally named Boris, emigrates to America and is through great labor initiated into a strange new world, simultaneously with the inventor's creation of these

"events"—a very immediate task, attended by concrete preparations for writing (so many days alone for work, so many boxes
of noodles for food, so many squeezes of toothpaste), all watched
over by the recorder, who gives us the complete, eminently real
fiction. As we learn from the preface (or, rather, from the
"THIS IS NOT THE BEGINNING"):

> this is then how it all started at the beginning just like
> that once upon a time two or three weeks ago with the first
> person recording what the second person was doing as he
> planned the way he was going to lock himself for one year
> in a room to write the story of the third person all of them
> ready anxious to be to go to exist to invent to write to
> record to survive to become

Two hundred and two pages of concrete typescript, without
even its margins typographically "justified," the book is its
own becoming, and hence makes a uniquely personal claim to
legitimacy. Federman is covered: no shoddy tricks or trumped-
up illusions of reality, just so much writing. But as he redeems
the method of fiction, he saves its substance, too. Granted that
fiction is not history, but rather something made up; what then
is more real, one phoney "thing" the writer decides has "happened," or rather all the possibilities he *could* contrive, given
his situation? When you read a conventional story, says Feder-
man-the-recorder, "what you are really reading are the answers
to unformulated questions"—the story of the protagonist. But
the inventor is as real a part of the action, so the recorder must
note the "questions" as well, "to give the questions as the substance of his fiction rather than give the answers." The bet is
double or nothing, since "If the questions are given first on
paper then the reader can formulate the answers in his mind."
The full reality of the writer's fictional construct is effectively
transcribed, and the reader is given the chance to receive a truly
unexpurgated text. Federman weighs the possibilities, shares
them with the reader, and occasionally adds extra pages (p. 63,
p. 63.0, etc.) to accommodate variations as he runs through
Boris' life: such a novel can never die; another two hundred

pages can be sustained anytime, if you wish to refigure on the basis of a dollar more or less a week for the room. "IMAGINE THAT!"

Phenomenologists, including Maurice Merleau-Ponty, and many critics of the French structuralists as well have regretted that we must deal with a second-order language, divorced from the thing signified but living only insomuch as it points back to that thing. System replaces essence, which can be bad if the latter is what one searches for. From his studies of Beckett, Federman knows that literature fails when it claims to represent the other, so in his own novel he simply lets it represent itself. As such it is a system, an esthetic one, but by claiming to be nothing else it becomes a real entity. The novel's substance is more vital because it reflects man's imagination, instead of a secondhand lie about the world. The experience of life can of course be selected, shaped, and organizd by art, and so may be best known; that was the battle fought over half a century ago by James and Wells. But once it is shaped by the imagination, the product is no longer life, nor even a sham illusory representation. It is simply itself—and that recognition may be as great an advance as were Henry James' principles of selection so many years ago.

To maintain a sense of life within the sense of art is fiction's greatest challenge, and it is by these terms that the achievement of Sukenick, Barthelme, Kosinski, Federman, and their contemporaries is best measured. They don't write about actual things—who except journalists can, or would want to?—but rather, as Gilbert Sorrentino promises, about the imaginative qualities of actual things. Making a sensible shape of life was something Ronald Sukenick saw not only as a task for his own fiction, but as the obvious element in all literary art. "With what tenable attitude may one confront the difficult circumstances of contemporary American secular life," he asked in his *Wallace Stevens: Musing the Obscure*, "and avail oneself of the good possible in it? How, in short, does one get along?" That's even more accurately the challenge of a fictionist, and the answer is the same: "When, through the imagination, the ego manages to reconcile reality with its own needs, the formerly insipid landscape is infused with the ego's emotion, and reality, since it now seems intensely relevant to the ego, suddenly seems more real." Sukenick's subsequent fiction exploded the full range of outdated creativity, mere fantasy reactions to a world demanding a new approach, and reestablished a role for art which would not drive the life out of fiction. Together with Donald Barthelme's recreation of technique, Jerzy Kosinski's redirection of an apparently exhausted theme, and Raymond Federman's rebuilding of a narrative aesthetic, we are seeing a small renaissance in American fiction. Their work should not be surprising; the true shock is not how far their new novels have gone, but rather how far we let the old novel desert the true ideals of artistic representation in favor of a wholly unreal documentation, which was satisfactory to neither reader nor writer and potentially destructive of the genre itself.

## neal oxenhandler

# Listening to
# Burroughs' Voice

*The artist's privilege is to liberate him-
self from his personal obsessions by incorporating them into the fabric of life,
by blending them so thoroughly with
other objects that we too are forced to
become aware of them, so that he is no
longer alone, shut up with his anguish in
a horrible tête-à-tête.*

CLAUDE-EDMONDE MAGNY

*The* 'grumus merdae' *(heap of feces) left
behind by criminals upon the scene of
their misdeeds seems to have both these
meanings: contumely, and a regressive
expression of making amends.*

SIGMUND FREUD

William Burroughs' five major novels[1]
overwhelm us with a chaos of metamorphosing shapes and forms
which constantly destroy themselves and rise anew. The novels
pulse and glow weirdly with hallucinating lights, they emit
strange electronic hums and shrieks. The first impression is of
a chaos in eruption, but slowly a sense of design emerges.
Burroughs is a poet who knows something about language he
can never forget, something about form that he can never
eradicate. And he *tries.* He tries to wipe out order which ap-

[1] *Junkie* (New York: Ace Books, 1953); the following published by
Grove Press: *Naked Lunch* (1959); *The Soft Machine* (1961); *The
Ticket That Exploded* (1962); *Nova Express* (1964).

*181*

pears in the chaos, tries to strangle his own voice. But there is something in the work itself which resists and defeats him. He *cannot* destroy the integrity of his work, even though he tries with maniac frenzy. He tries by disguising it as science fiction, as vaudeville, as travelogue; he forces us to wade through endless pages of gibberish where random accumulations of speech blend with dreams and fantasies that have the ring of authentic experience. Constantly, he tries to keep us from learning the truth which he simultaneously *wants* us to know.

Burroughs' claim to originality as a novelist rests on the technique known as the fold in or cut in:

> Pages of text are cut and rearranged to form new combinations of word and image—In writing my last two novels, *Nova Express* and *The Ticket That Exploded*, i have used an extension of the cut up method i call 'the fold in method' —A page of text—my own or some one elses—is folded down the middle and placed on another page—The composite text is then read across half one text and half the other—The fold in method extends to writing the flash back used in films, enabling the writer to move backwards and forwards on his time track—For example i take page one and fold it into page one hundred—I insert the resulting composite as page ten—When the reader reads page ten he is flashing forwards in time to page one hundred and back in time to page one—The deja vu phenomena can so be produced to order—(This method is of course used in music where we are continually moved backwards and forward on the time track by repetition and rearrangements of musical themes—
>
> In using the fold in method i edit delete and rearrange as in any other method of composition—I have frequently had the experience of writing some pages of straight narrative text which were then folded in with other pages and found that the fold ins were clearer and more comprehensible than the original texts—Perfectly clear narrative prose can be produced using the fold in method—Best results are usually obtained by placing pages dealing with similar sub-

jects in juxtaposition—

> *New American Story* (New York:
> Grove Press, 1965), pp. 256-257.

Burroughs never tells us *why* he uses the method, preferring to justify it by pointing out analogies with music and insisting that, after all, it doesn't make the work unintelligible. In this he is correct. Although the fold in method does throw irrelevances into the narrative stream, the fact that they return at regular intervals converts them into a kind of refrain. They become the steady bass chord (like an imbecile voice muttering inanities) that counterpoints the deeper rhythm.

Or rhythms. For there are many rhythms, many voices shouting, screaming, weeping, yearning, cursing, coughing in the junksick industrial dawn through Burroughs' polyphony. The reader listens as best he can, as long as he can bear it. Long enough at least to know that he is Burroughs' *hypocrite lecteur,* his *semblable,* his *frère,* that in this voice the dark side of our nature stands revealed. For Burroughs (who may not be a great social critic or satirist as some make him out to be) reports on the archetypal night of hell. It doesn't matter that this hell sometimes resembles "a kind of mid-western, small town, cracker-barrel, pratfall type of folklore, very much my own background"; [2] it is still the *real* hell, the one Vergil, Dante, and Rimbaud visited.

This is not a personal world of tics or neurotic compulsions, it is more universal than that. Burroughs goes beyond the neurotic and individual to attain the universality of the madman's dream, the prophet's frenzy. There is a deep paradox in this, that in psychosis or delirium—a state in which the individual seems most cut off from others—there is often the expression of profoundly universal dreams, terrors, desires. And so, no matter how strange, Burroughs' voice speaks with a rhythm that we hear as familiar, as somehow *déjà vu.*

The fold in or splice in technique is an effort to destroy form

---

[2] Conrad Knickerbocker, "William Burroughs: An Interview," *The Paris Review,* No. 36, Fall 1965, p. 31.

(and despite the disclaimers it comes close to doing this in the later novels), but even more importantly, it is an effort to *conceal*. Burroughs, who seems to be telling us "everything" is the most secretive of persons. The ambivalence or bipolarity of his work first becomes apparent in the tension between the desire to hide and the desire to reveal. The fold in method hides, under an accompaniment of irrelevances, the dark truths that the other side of Burroughs wants to reveal.

Burroughs, for many years a drug addict, insists on the state of anomie and withdrawal produced by drugs. The addict in terminal state has need of no one and of nothing except junk: "I did absolutely nothing. I could look at the end of my shoe for eight hours ... If a friend came to visit ... I sat there not caring that he had entered my field of vision ... and not caring when he walked out of it." (NL xli) [3]

If the addict withdraws from the external world, it is because he has no need of it, except as supplier of junk. Junk itself gives him everything he needs. Intoxication, according both to Burroughs and psychoanalytic authorities, becomes a sexual aim; the addict attains what Sandór Radó calls "pharmacotoxic orgasm." [4] Distinguished from genital orgasm, this is a state of "euphoria, stupefaction and exhilaration." In this form of "metaeroticism" the need for the genital apparatus disappears. With the genital primacy demolished, the pregenital organizations come to their own. In other words, there is regression to infantile stages of development. The fantasies of violence and perversion which are the substance of Burroughs' novels have the arbitrary power of visions released from the id-world. A purely esthetic account of them would be inadequate; and yet, at the same time, a psychocritique must be severely circumscribed.

First, it must be clear that any judgments I make about the novels will touch Burroughs, the man, only obliquely. The data is not clinical but literary—hence incomplete, deceptive, ar-

---

[3] Titles are abbreviated to initials throughout.

[4] Sandór Radó, "The Psychic Effects of Intoxicants: an attempt to evolve a psychoanalytic theory of morbid cravings," *The International Journal of Psychoanalysis*, Vol. VII, 1926, pp. 396-413.

ranged. We can only guess at the genesis of the strange emotional configurations that repeat themselves from book to book. But we can, through a discussion of repetitive scenes and symbols, show how they connect with each other, setting up a pattern of reciprocal relations, with a specific emotional charge and certain human implications. To attempt more than this would be to minimize the complexity of human personality and to ignore the specificity of the literary work.

*    *    *    *

Burroughs' novels are like a movie screen on which flash repetitive images. These images compose a scene which is deeply sado-masochistic. The scene, characterized by magical role changes, in which now one character, now the other becomes the central figure, usually involves hanging with subsequent orgasm or anal intercourse, or both with variations. A complete re-enactment of the scene can be read beginning on p. 96 of *Naked Lunch.*

The scene begins with "Johnny impaled on Mark's cock." Mark is mocking and cool. Johnny reaches orgasm, here typically associated with vertigo and premonitions of death: "Johnny scream and whimper.... His face disintegrates as if melted from within.... Johnny scream like a mandrake, black out as his sperm spurt, slump against Mark's body an angel on the nod."

The scene then changes to another room, like a gymnasium, in which we are going to witness some sexual acrobatics. "Johnny is led in, hands tied, between Mary and Mark." Johnny sees a gallows which has been set up, and at the sight of it, reaches orgasm again. Now Mary and Mark push Johnny up to the gallows. Mary pulls Johnny off the gallows platform and has intercourse with him while he swings. The hanged boy reaches orgasm, Mark cuts him down, Mary then begins to cannibalize him: "She bites away Johnny's lips and nose and sucks out his eyes with a pop.... She tears off great hunks of cheek.... Now she lunches on his prick...." At this point, Mark kicks her away from the corpse and attacks her. "He leaps on her, fucking her insanely ... they roll from one end of the room to the other, pinwheel end-over-end and leap high in the air like great hooked fish." Now it is Mary's turn to be hanged. While she struggles, Mark pulls her brutally to the gallows, executes her, entering her at the same time. "He sticks his cock up her and waltzes around the platform and off into space swinging in a great arc. . . . 'Wheeeeee!' he screams, turning into Johnny. Her neck snaps. A great fluid wave undulates through her body. Johnny drops to the floor and stands poised and alert like a young animal."

Wilhelm Steckel, the great authority on sado-masochism, tells us that every sadist has a basic scene which is indefinitely repeated in his fantasy life. This scene reproduces, through displaced and disguised images, a period of the child's early existence when he experienced intense jealousy and hate. While some later writers on sado-masochism disagree, Steckel follows Freud in insisting that masochism is the obverse of sadism; that is, hostile feelings, originally directed against a person in the family environment, are introjected and turned back against the self. The basic scene may thus very well have both masochistic and sadistic components—this constant shift between the two neurotic solutions is, for Steckel, the chief source of the bi-polarity typical of the sadist.

In these fantasies the Narrator may identify himself with the active or the passive figure in the fantasy, or with both.

Sadistic behavior originates both in the oral and the anal stages. In the oral stage, it is associated with the appearance of the milk teeth and aggression against the breast. In Burroughs' fiction we find a certain amount of orally-regressed imagery. Willy the Disk has a powerful sucking apparatus:

> If the cops weren't there to restrain him . . . he would suck the juice right out of every junky he ran down. (NL 7)

> The Sailor's face dissolved. His mouth undulated forward on a long tube and sucked in the black fuzz, vibrating in supersonic peristalsis disappeared in a silent, pink explosion. (NL 52)

The alternative to junk is alcohol:
At first I started drinking at five in the afternoon. After

a week, I started drinking at eight in the morning, stayed drunk all day and all night, and woke up drunk the next morning. (J 108)

Radó states that "the psychic manifestations of oral eroticism are always present in a marked form even in those cases of drug-mania in which the drug is not taken by mouth at all. One received the impression that some mysterious bonds exist between the oral zone and intoxication. . . ."
Orality and sucking imply a mother who supplies breast or bottle. For the junkie this is the Connection. The Connection, however, is a mean refusing mother who always makes the baby wait:

> Sometimes you can see maybe fifty ratty-looking junkies squealing sick, running along behind a boy with a harmonica, and there is The Man on a cane seat throwing bread to the swans, a fat queen drag walking his Afghan hound through the East Fifties, an old wino pissing against an El post, a radical Jewish student giving out leaflets in Washington Square, a tree surgeon, an exterminator, an advertising fruit in Nedick's where he calls the counterman by his first name. The world network of junkies, tuned on a cord of rancid jissom, tying up in furnished rooms, shivering in the junk-sick morning. (NL 6)

Since the refusing mother is unconsciously remembered, she can take any form but her own. In the following quote she appears as a man with strongly maternal characteristics:

> So this man walks around in the places where he once exercised his obsolete and unthinkable trade. But he is unperturbed. His eyes are black with an insect's unthinking calm. He looks as if he nourished himself on honey and Levantine syrups that he sucks up through a proboscis. . . . Perhaps he stores something in his body—a substance to prolong life—of which he is periodically milked by his masters. He is as specialized as an insect, for the performing of some inconceivably vile function. (J 100)

Here, in the storing up of a vital substance which the junkie-baby desperately needs, is a transparent identification with the mother. Burroughs may even speak of himself as a baby: "sudden food needs of the kicking addict nursing his baby flesh." (NL 8)

But if the mother does feed her junkie baby, it may be poison. There are many references to junk cut with Saniflush: "Well, I guess one hand didn't know what the other was doing when I give him a jar of Saniflush by error...." (NL 173) Or food may be poisonous or repulsive: "The Clear Camel Piss Soup with boiled Earth Worms/The After-Birth Suprême de Boeuf, cooked in drained crank case oil, etc." (NL 149)

Images of orality are few in number compared with the abundance of images from the anal stage of libido development. It is here that the regression seems to stop and attain a degree of stabilization. Freud associated sadism with anal eroticism and traced it to the child's resentment at being forced to give up the symbolic penis represented by the fecal mass. The delight in excrement and repulsive objects and the celebration of aggressive acts of anal intercourse appear as the emotional core of the novels. The following quotation is a finger exercise in mixing repellent motifs:

> 'Stole an opium suppository out of my grandmother's ass.'/ The hypochondriac lassoes the passer-by and administers a straightjacket and starts talking about his rotting septum: 'An awful purulent discharge is subject to flow out . . . just wait till you see it.'/ .... 'Feel that suppurated swelling in my groin where I got the lymphogranulomas. ... And now I want you to palpate my internal haemorrhoids.' (NL 41)

A variety of causes for the anal fixation may be posited, but since we are not in a therapeutic situation, it is difficult to speak genetically. The child may identify with the mother and wish to be anally penetrated by the father; this is the "negative oedipus" complex. Or he may identify with the pre-oedipal infant who is penetrated by bottle or feces. Or there may be memories of enemas or whippings which are masochistically revived. All we can know here is that we are in the presence of a pronounced anal fixation.

References to anal intercourse are numerous, explicit, pornographic. Various personnae for the Narrator are on the receiving
end—Johnny, Johnny Yen, Bill Lee, etc. Since one participant
is always a boy, the act is heavily laden with narcissism. The
narcissism can be taken as corroboration for the view that this
is a pre-oedipal scene: mother feeding baby. The passive partner
is the baby, the active the mother.

Often these boys are inhuman and reptilian:

> The green boy's penis, which was the same purple color as
> his gills, rose and vibrated into the heavy metal substance
> of the other—The two beings twisted free of human coordi-
> nates rectums merging in a rusty swamp smell—(TTTE 7)

Whenever sexual contact occurs there is the suggestion of something repellent, poisonous, or viscous—so the green boy moves
in swirls of poisonous vapor. The sex act produces images of
messing or smearing:

> Later the boy is sitting in a Waldorf with two colleagues
> dunking pound cake. 'Most distasteful thing I ever stand
> still for,' he says. 'Some way he makes himself all soft like
> a blob of jelly and surround me so nasty. Then he gets
> wet all over like with green slime. So I guess he come to
> some kinda awful climax. . . . I come near wigging with that
> green stuff all over me, and he stink like a old rotten canta-
> loupe. (NL 16)

This fascination with smearing or dirtying is commonly associated with anal-sadistic regression and expresses less the impulse to dirty the object than the autoplastic desire to play
with excrement. There is an undeniable playfulness and enjoyment in the imagining of filthy messes with which Burroughs
entertains us. The psychoanalytic belief that the literary production may be associated with feces, the first "production" of
our chronological lives, seems less absurd when we read Burroughs. It is not only the pleasure with which he revels in

"dirty" subjects, but the very method he has hit upon (of chopping things up and shifting them about) seems to represent an aimless stirring or messing or playing around, delighted in for its own sake. Why indeed resort to a method of production that so threatens coherence both of meaning and emotional effect, if it were not gratifying, more gratifying indeed than the mere writing of a story?

Sometimes the smearing may spread from the anal region to absorb the entire body:

> When I closed my eyes I saw an Oriental face, the lips and nose eaten away by disease. The disease spread, melting the face into an amoeboid mass in which the eyes floated, dull crustacean eyes. Slowly, a new face formed around the eyes. A series of faces, hieroglyphs, distorted and leading to the final place where the human road ends, where the human form can no longer contain the crustacean horror that has grown inside it. (J 112)

Several other elements typical of the anally-regressed individual are apparent. There are traits of what Erich Fromm calls the necrophilious individual who is fascinated with corpses, killing, and death.[5] The scene in which Mary eats Johnny's face is only one of many examples. The necrophile is an anal type—he loves the dead mass of his own excrement which normally becomes repugnant and an object of shame. The necrophiles are cold, distant, remote—as are indeed the characters Burroughs creates. They are "driven by the desire to transform the organic into the inorganic, to approach life mechanically, as if all living persons were things." They are in addition "devotees of law and order." There is, throughout the novels, a constant preoccupation with law and order, especially of an authoritarian kind. Mary McCarthy has stated that Burroughs is a moralist. But the competing authority systems in his novels—the Nova Mobsters, Islam Inc., the Liquefactionist Party, the Factualists, the Divisionists, etc.—

---

[5] Erich Fromm, *The Heart of Man* (New York: Harper & Row, 1964), pp. 40-41.

have no ideological content. They represent the tightening and compressing impulse, typical of the anal-sadistic type; or they may be defenses against guilt feelings; or efforts to control the sado-masochistic drives. Certainly they have nothing to do with any recognizable system of ethics which depends on a stable notion of human nature and behavior. Punishment there is however, enough to revenge all the crimes of the Marquis de Sade.

The anal-sadistic dumbshow occupies center stage in the novels, but for this very reason, were we trying to understand the author of the novels, we would search for deeper, repressed meanings against which the anal-sadistic regression is a defense. But they are not clearly evident, and it would be presumptuous to claim to know what lies *behind* the horrendous scenes we witness. There are, however, a few clues pointing to what lies even deeper than the anal-sadistic regression and, using the viewpoint of Edmund Bergler as an analytic tool, it is possible to speculate on some of these secondary implications.

The explicit role played by women in Burroughs' fantasies is very small, although they often appear in disguise. The Connection is only the first of these disguises. One explicit appearance is of the chopping or castrating woman. There are many references to vaginal teeth or the castrating vaginal grip:

> He was torn in two by a bull dike. Most terrific vaginal grip I ever experienced. She could cave in a lead pipe. It was one of her parlor tricks. (NL 91)

The flippant tone masks a terror that goes back to an infantile misapprehension. "It takes a long time," says Edmund Bergler, "before the young child perceives his mother as good, generous, and loving. Before this impression has been formed, the child builds up a 'septet of baby fears' in which the mother plays the role of a cruel witch. Fantastic as it may seem, the very young child considers himself the innocent victim of a wicked witch who is capable of starving, devouring, poisoning, and choking him, chopping him to pieces, and draining and castrating him."[6]

I think it likely that the giant crabs and centipedes who loom up and attack male victims are images of the enveloping or choking mother. She seems to press upon the infant like "the monster crab with hot claws." (NL 29) There is a whole zoology of such creatures in the novels, who might well be the infantile mother.

The infantile response to the giantess of the nursery is, first, the masochistic take-over of the terrors inflicted by her, so that they seem to stem from the self rather than an outside force. Passive suffering now becomes active suffering, and the child is well on his way to the masochistic use of pain. The writer frees himself from the pre-oedipal mother by becoming his own mother and feeding himself with words. This is illustrated by Burroughs who *invents* images of poison, suffocation, absorption, etc. Maintaining the self-sufficiency of the womb state, and at the same time transmuting passive reception of pain into active enjoyment of it, he feeds himself (and us) with poison words:

> The 'Other Half' is the word. The 'Other Half' is an organism. Word is an organism. The presence of the 'Other Half' a separate organism attached to your nervous system on an air line of words can now be demonstrated experimentally. ... The word may once have been a healthy neural cell. It is now a parasitic organism that invades and damages the central nervous system. (TTTE 49)

If for 'Other Half' we read 'mother' and for 'word' we read milk, then this curiously archaic passage duplicates the pre-oedipal situation described above: the baby is attached to the poisoning mother and blames her for the damage (castration) to his body.

Explicit attacks on women represent a defense against the masochistic desire to submit and be overwhelmed by the infantile mother:

> Mary the Lesbian Governess has slipped to the pub floor on a bloody kotex. ... A three-hundred-pound fag tramples

[6] Edmund Bergler, M.D., *Homosexuality: Disease or Way of Life?* (New York: Collier Books, 1956), p. 36.

her to death with pathetic whinnies. . . ." (NL 127)

Two male homosexuals "know happiness for the first time"
when "Enters the powers of evil. . . ." a wealthy woman.
Brad announces that "Dinner is Lucy Bradshinkel's cunt
saignant cooked in kotex papillon. The boys eat happily
looking into each other's eyes. Blood runs down their
chins." (NL 129-130)

The traumatic discovery of early childhood, so important for
the development of castration terror and the flight from women,
is parodied in fag talk:

'Oh Gertie it's true. It's all true. They've got a horrid gash
instead of a thrilling thing.'/'I can't face it.'/'Enough to turn
a body to stone.' (NL 150)

These episodes mean: I don't really want to be overwhelmed by
mother. Look how much I hate women! But, as in the typical
homosexual pattern, the element of psychic masochism remains
the fundamental psychic fact.

The earliest response to the giantess is aggression in the
form of breast-biting; but there is little breast imagery in Burroughs. All interest in the breast has been transferred to the
male organ (which gives "milk" and can be sucked). This
accounts for the intense aggression directed at the penis:

Every night round about eight-thirty he goes over into
that lot yonder and pulls himself off with steel wool. . . .
(NL 175)

Descent into penis flesh cut off by a group of them. . . . The
boy ejaculates blood over the flower floats. (SM 115)

The penis canal was a jointed iron tube covered by sponge
rubber—Pubic hairs of fine wire crackled with blue sparks
—The dummy cocks rose in magnetic attraction of the wall
symbols. . . . The dummy that was precisely *me* penetrated

> him with a slow magnetic movement—Tingling blue fire
> shot through his genitals transfixed by the magnetic re-
> volving wall symbols—The vibrator switched on as the
> other watched—idiot lust drinking his jissom from screen
> eyes—Sucking cones of color that dissolved his penis in
> orgasms of light—(TTTE 76-77)

The third quote shows the connection between genitality and
machines that appears throughout Burroughs' work. The machine adds an element of impersonal cruelty to the onanistic
act. There are many other examples of cutting, chopping, breaking, or otherwise attacking the penis.

The role of masturbation is, not surprisingly, an important
one. This happy event takes place in the Eden of childhood:

> Wooden cubicles around a hot spring . . . rubble of ruined
> walls in a grove of cottonwoods . . . the benches worn
> smooth as metal by a million masturbating boys. (NL 117)

> . . . his plan called for cinerama film sequences featuring
> the Garden of Delights shows all kinds masturbation and
> self-abuse young boys need it special its all electric and
> very technical you sit down anywhere some sex wheel
> sidles up your ass or clamps onto your spine centers and
> the electronic gallows will just kill you on a conveyor
> belt. . . . (TTTE 3)

Or masturbation may appear in symbolic disguise. Here the hand
is obviously referred to under the circumlocution "Sex Skin":

> . . . I remember this one patrol had been liberating a river
> town and picked up the Sex Skin habit. This Sex Skin
> is a critter found in the rivers here wraps all around you
> like a second skin eats you slow and good. (TTTE 4)

Masturbation, according to Freud, always has an incestuous as
well as a masochistic component. Hence, it is accompanied by
feelings of guilt and desire for punishment. One of the most

unusual punishments devised in Burroughs' chamber of horrors is found in the passage where we see men changed into "penis urns":

> Carl walked a long row of living penis urns made from men whose penis has absorbed the body with vestigial arms and legs breathing through purple fungoid gills and dropping a slow metal excrement like melted solder . . . a vast warehouse of living penis urns slowly transmuting to smooth red terra cotta. (SM 112)

Obviously this is only poetic justice for the abuse of an organ— the organ takes over the functions of the entire body! This same form of punishment occurs in other passages, where it is the mouth that takes over, or even the anus. This seems to be a situation in which instinctual drives, related to one particular organ, emerge victorious from an internal conflict with the ego; this is a classic neurotic solution.

Perhaps now some pattern may be seen to emerge. First, I have insisted on the sado-masochistic flavor to many scenes. Suffering inflicted and received takes many forms, but seems to appear most often in the image of the hanged boy. In the sado-masochistic situation it is the explosion of affect that changes pain into pleasure. Hence, these death scenes are explosively written. The hanged boy's orgasm produces a spurt of pleasure that erases the element of pain. This intoxication of affect is a repetitive element in the novels. It produces a mixed reaction in the reader who reads about disagreeable incidents presented with relish and enjoyment; the same bafflement occurs when we encounter images of smearing and messing. The insistence on slimy, viscous, ectoplasmic contacts is a sign of anal regression dramatized more explicitly in scenes of anal intercourse. Most often enacted between two boys, this scene draws its emotional charge in part from the negative oedipus—the desire to be overwhelmed by the father. Yet since the protagonists are usually boys, it seems to insist on another, deeper component. This is a rehearsal of the nursing scene. The participants are nursing mother and nursed baby, penis being substituted for bottles and anus for mouth.

Finally, some clues suggest a mechanism described as "psychic masochism," different from the sexual masochism that demands acts of physical violence. This complex arises from the infantile misapprehension about the mother who appears as the "giantess of the nursery." Its identification is probably the most speculative or doubtful aspect of this analysis of Burroughs' works.

These various components form a field of emotional forces set up by the books' narrative flow, such as it is. Within this field there is a strong sense of polarization, a pulsing rhythm, a purposeful ambivalence which never relents and comes to be the central fact about Burroughs' novels.

We have already seen ambivalence in the duality of sado-masochism, a duality which resolves in the explosive fusion of affect which accompanies the sado-masochistic scene. Ambivalence also takes other forms in Burroughs' work. Early in *Naked Lunch* we meet a character whose physical shape is unstable or ambivalent:

> The physical changes were slow at first, then jumped forward in black klunks, falling through his slack tissue, washing away the human lines. . . . In his place of total darkness mouth and eyes are one organ that leaps forward to snap with transparent teeth. . . . but no organ is constant as regards either function or position. . . . sex organs sprout anywhere. . . . rectums open, defecate and close. . . . the entire organism changes color and consistency in split-second adjustments. . . (NL 9)

A more purposeful change takes place in the case of the man with the talking anus:

> After a while the ass started talking on its own. . . . Then it developed sort of teeth-like little raspy incurving hooks and started eating. He thought this was cute at first and built an act around it, but the asshole would eat its way through his pants and start talking on the street, shouting out it wanted equal rights. It would get drunk, too, and

have crying jags nobody loved it and it wanted to be
kissed same as any other mouth.... After that he began
waking up in the morning with a transparent jelly like a
tadpole's tail all over his mouth.... So finally his mouth
sealed over, and the whole head would have amputated
spontaneously.... —except for the *eyes* you dig. That's
one thing the asshole *couldn't* do was see. It needed the
eyes. But nerve connections were blocked and infiltrated
and atrophied so the brain couldn't give orders any more.
It was trapped in the skull, sealed off. For a while you could
see the silent, helpless suffering of the brain behind the
eyes, then finally the brain must have died, because the
eyes *went out*, and there was no more feeling in them than
a crab's eyes on the end of a stalk. (NL 132-133)

This brilliant anecdote, which shows Burroughs' tremendous
power of improvisation, actually illustrates the genetic development of the negative oedipus as defense against psychic masochism. There is, first, the struggle between the oral impulse and
the anal impulse. The anal is seen as sadistic and searching for
dominance which it eventually achieves. The face (the seat of
orality) is sealed off by a wall of tissue, and finally "goes out",
i.e., masochistic attachment to the giantess of the nursery becomes completely unconscious. The domination of anal eroticism
then seems complete. However, this domination is only apparent.
The buried oral material retains its power and reappears in the
forms shown.

Another form of ambivalence is the male-female dualism. The
hermaphrodites, the men who become women and vice versa, are
probably representations of the couple as witnessed by the child
in the primal scene:

A penis rose out of the jock and dissolved in pink light back
to a clitoris, balls retract into cunt with a fluid plop. Three
times he did this to wild 'Olés!' from the audience. (SM 73)

The fact that the scene is being witnessed suggests the spying
child of the primal scene. There are many other examples of

characters who change their sex:

> They say his prick didn't synchronize at all so he cut it off and made some kinda awful cunt between the two sides of him. (SM 78)

> The Commandante spread jelly over Carl's naked paralyzed body. The Commandante was molding a woman. Carl could feel his body draining into the woman mold. His genitals dissolving, tits swelling as the Commandante penetrated applying a few touches to face and hair— (SM 109)

Here, the psychic mechanism seems clear: it is submission to the father image (the Commandante) which transforms him into a woman (identification with mother).

The psychological tension is exteriorized—he images a war between the sexes:

> The war between the sexes split the planet into armed camps right down the middle line divides one thing from the other... (SM 157)

But the battle is really inside the divided child, torn between two psychic "strata"—the oral stratum, with its submission to the mother; the anal stratum, with its submission to the father. To this there can be no solution except maturity, a solution Burroughs does not seem to envisage.

All writers are exhibitionists of their fantasy experience, Burroughs more so than most. Even when he puts us on and invents polymorphously perverse scenes out of Kraft-Ebing, he is making complicated demands on us. The demand to reject and revile him, the demand to accept him. Once again we return to the inherent ambivalence of Burroughs' psychic experience; if we can focus our attention on it, it will become clear that this is the source for the pulsing rhythm of his prose and the strange flickering alternation of his vision.

\* \* \* \*

Any appreciation of Burroughs has to answer the question:

does he belong in a major literary tradition? I believe that the preceding analysis aligns Burroughs with novelists, such as Kafka and Beckett, whose major theme is ambivalence and indeterminacy. Like these writers Burroughs has created an esthetic which permits him both to affirm and deny. His characters are simultaneously men and women, simultaneously masochistic and sadistic, simultaneously anal and oral, simultaneously dependent and autarchic, and so on. All psychic phenomena are over-determined, that is, can never be traced to a single cause; and psychic mechanisms have a way of changing into their opposites, due to the censoring activity of the super-ego which forces them to assume disguises. The only kind of equilibrium to be found in the emotional world of such writers as Kafka, Beckett, and Burroughs is an equilibrium of alternation, in which emotional states constantly reform opposing patterns. Here the law of contradiction does not apply—an event may be itself yet not itself at the same time. Nothing can ever be affirmed once and for all; no stable emotion, no stable value can be established. The only law is that of flux, and flux is the essence of Burroughs' novelistic style.

Burroughs' use in his later novels of the fold in method contributes both to the indeterminacy of his work and to its basic two-cycle rhythm. Not only does it create a counterpoint or beat, but it produces junctures and discontinuities which are points at which the two-cycle rhythm can shift. Hence, a theme is always prevented from too lengthy development by a break in continuity which carries the reader off on an opposite current. In this way the powerful ambivalencies of the work are maintained.

Burroughs' novels of ambivalence represent the first truly American contribution to this literature. But this is not all. Far more original than Albee, Burroughs is our only writer of the absurd. Some of his straw-hat routines are as American as apple pie. In his wild meanderings across the world, the ubiquitous tourist stopping at American Express to change his traveler's checks into pounds or pesos or piastres so he can buy junk, Burroughs' picaresque hero is a wanderer more cynical and lost than Bellow's Herzog or Augie March, and he sees deeper into the split psyche that has grown up in this country within sight of the suburban lawns and the progressive schools. Burroughs seems to absorb the environments through which he passes, and like some weird machine of his own invention, his voice modulates with a thousand accents and intonations, producing a style so much no-style that it is entirely his own.

No influence that has affected Burroughs seems to me as important as Rimbaud. Not just the Rimbaud who recounts for us his season in hell. Nor just the Rimbaud of the *Illuminations* whose brilliant discontinuous style Burroughs at his best sometimes attains to. I am thinking rather of the Narrator of "Bateau ivre" who, after his wild, hallucinating journey, suddenly grows tender and yearns for Europe and the contained world of childhood:

> If I desire European waters, it's the puddle
> Black and cold where toward the fragrant evening
> A child crouches full of sadness and sets free
> A paper boat that's frail as a butterfly in May.

There are many moments of such pathos in Burroughs too, moments when he remembers: "that stale summer dawn smell in the garage—vines twisting through steel—bare feet in dog's excrement." (SM 127) Or again: "One morning in April, I woke up a little sick. I lay there looking at shadows on the white plaster ceiling. I remembered a long time ago when I lay in bed beside my mother watching lights from the street move across the ceiling and down the walls. I felt the sharp nostalgia of train whistles, piano music down a city street, burning leaves." (J 107) No more than he has been able to destroy the form of his novels has he been able to destroy that pathos, that tenderness which in an unexpected moment will flash back at us from the page. Instead, just as with Rimbaud, we know that the work grows out of that moment of childish reverie. The work has its genesis there, and even the most violent and aggressive outbursts have something childlike about them.

Like many American writers searching for greatness, Burroughs does not have the stature of Kafka and Beckett, those prototypical writers of the Absurd. There is some intellectual deficiency in his work; and he does not carry as do these two, counterweight to his negating vision, the sense of what the tradition of the West means. There are other crippling limitations. Beckett and Kafka are controlled artists but Burroughs cannot escape—or allow us to escape—from the obsessive monotony of his hallucinations. But a great artist must affirm not only man's bondage but his freedom. Burroughs, returning from the Night with blistered oedipal eyes, crustacean eyes, tender adolescent eyes spewing hate and mistrust, eyes of a sick junkie coughing in the industrial dawn, is unable to free himself from the horror of what he has seen. Conrad's Kurtz died with the words "The horror! The horror!" on his lips; but Conrad threw himself into the hostile element and with his hands and feet kept himself up. Burroughs, carried off on that same tide, turns and shouts over his shoulder the excuse for every unimaginable act ever committed—"Wouldn't *you?*"

**marcus klein**

# John Hawkes'
# Experimental Compositions

*Everything depends, of course, on the
kind of one's sample, and any general
characterization might be sustained. In
the years since the end of World War II
the novel in America has been: nihilistic,
existential, apocalyptic, psychological; it
has asserted the romantic self; it has re-
corded the loss of self; it has explored the
possibilities of social accommodation; it
has withdrawn from social considerations;
it has been radical and conservative. In
form it has been loosely picaresque, it
has returned to its beginning in myth, it
has been contrived with a cunningness of
technique virtually decadent, it has been
purely self-reflexive and respondent to
its own development. And the novel has
died.*

*All of these things and more have been
said credibly. . . . It might be said therefore, given so many contradictory convic-
tions, that as a whole and as a category of
cultural enterprise, the novel in these
years has been essentially aimless and at
best frenetic. No definition is valid when
everything can be maintained.*

MARCUS KLEIN
*THE AMERICAN NOVEL
SINCE WORLD WAR II*

---

All remarks by John Hawkes on his own fiction quoted in this essay
come from the following: "John Hawkes: An Interview," *Wisconsin
Studies in Contemporary Literature*, VI (1965); "Notes on the Wild
Goose Chase," in Marcus Klein (ed.), *The American Novel Since World
War II* (New York, 1969); "Notes on Violence," *Audience*, VII (Spring
1960); "John Hawkes: On His Novels," *Massachusetts Review*, VII
(1966).

"Experiment" in fiction is itself a modern convention, and in the terms of that convention John Hawkes for more than twenty years has been the most unremittingly modern writer in America. That is not to say that he merely recapitulates. Leslie Fiedler is certainly right when he says that Hawkes is "no more an echoer of other men's revolts than he is a subscriber to the recent drift toward neo-middlebrow sentimentality." Nor it is to be said either that Hawkes has been strikingly innovative in composing narrative forms, either by reference to his modern predecessors or in his own progress from book to book. He has not been. It is only with *Second Skin* in 1964, a novel that, paradoxically, moves toward an older conventionality of narrative structure, that he seems to have been engaged in making new rules for himself. But for the rest, his "experimental novel"—a designation which Hawkes himself has used—has been defined by its commitment to such technical aims as opacity of surface, independence of image together with alogical forms of coherence in the work of art, objectivity and detachment on the part of the author, and to such corresponding ideas as the autonomy of art, the purity of the artist's vision and the validity of his nightmares. He has said that he "began to write fiction on the assumption that the true enemies of the novel were plot, character, setting, and theme...." It follows that he began in that position of adversariness to the nineteenth century which was basic to modernism, and which, since Flaubert, has become a tradition. Hawkes is in that sense a traditional writer, and he is also unique because—matters of intelligence and sheer verbal ability aside—none of his contemporaries has seemed to find these limited preceptions so continuously useful.

These modernist attitudes and techniques have from their beginning implied an ambition for, variously, "the 'sculpture' of rhyme," the apples of Cezanne, the dehumanization of art, and, in general, a condition of static, impersonal absoluteness. Art is to become artifact. But this ambition is costly, as a century of avant-gardism in all of the high arts testifies. The greater enemy—beyond such matters as plot and character in fiction— is conceived to be didacticism of any sort, with its implication of the possibility of social and philosophical certainties beyond the work of art. Therefore all ease of communication between personality—that of character, author, *raisonneur*—and a commonly perceived reality, must be eliminated. At worst, the theory of art of this sort descends into a mechanical chatter of inversions—anti-hero, anti-novel, anti-whatever. And when art of this sort is perfectly successful, as of course it never is, it stands free even of the context of its own motivations. It is self-justifying, but also without necessary relationship to anything or anyone else.

So Hawkes, for example, deliberately and habitually writes fiction about places he does not know. He had not been to England when he wrote *The Lime Twig*, which takes place in England. He had not been to that American West which is the setting of *The Beetle Leg*. The "Sasso Fetore" of *The Owl* has some resemblance to a hamlet in Transylvania. Whatever else he may have been doing in those novels, he was not attempting an accurate designation of the sense of those places. Again, the title of his collection of shorter pieces is *Lunar Landscapes*, the phrase apparently taken by Hawkes to be appropriate to the landscapes which in the pieces themselves are named New England, Venice, etc. And although he does not really write plotless novels, the motions of time and sequence in the novels are deliberately baffling. So, in *Charivari* the episode of Henry's escape from his wife is followed without transition by a narrative of events leading to his wedding. In "The Goose on the Grave" (in *Lunar Landscapes*) Brother Bolo is shot on page 242 and reappears without benefit of flashback on page 268, in the same scene that had occurred on page 200. And along with place and time, throughout the fiction all anticipated patterns of distinction and signification and emphasis tend to be distorted. Hawkes has said that the "essential substance" of his writing is in "related or corresponding event, recurring image and recurring action," which would indicate that the essential meaning of the fiction is to be discovered in the patterns of its composition, and emphatically not in any correspondence with outside, actual event. Indeed, in the number of his discursive writings and interviews he repeatedly insists on the idea of the detached singularity of the created work.

On the other hand, Hawkes clearly thinks of himself as a
ruthlessly comic satirist. In his essay "Notes on the Wild Goose
Chase," he says that "the satiric writer, running maliciously
at the head of the mob . . . will serve best the novel's purpose."
His aim, he has said in another place, "has always been . . .
never to let the reader (or myself) off the hook, so to speak,
never to let him think that the picture is any less black than it
is or that there is any easy way out of the nightmare of human
existence." In his brief essay called "Notes on Violence" he
affirms the "attitude that rejects sympathy for the ruined members of our lot, revealing thus the deepest sympathy of all,"
which would argue that the pristine independence of the created
work is not the main thing. The one novelist to whom Hawkes
most frequently refers, for a kind of confirmation, is Nathanael
West, in whom he finds such a sustained vision of the ugliness
of human actuality together with redemptive laughter as presumably he wishes to discover in his own work. And that
discovery is after all available in the work, which despite the
energy and conspicuousness of its commitment in upon itself,
does conscientiously, even obsessively, acknowledge outward
event and historical circumstance.

If Hawkes does not construct landscapes from his own direct
experience, still he writes stories about characters who are
defined culturally. More, there is a repeated tendency in
Hawkes' fiction to discover the exact middle of the projected
culture, by locating its burghers, or its most ordinary citizens.
The action of *The Lime Twig*—in an obvious instance—rests on
the fact that the Bankses are lower middle class Britons with
drab British lower middle class frustrations. The barren, twisted
characters of *The Beetle Leg* are created by the barrenness of
the place in which they exist, with its merely tenuous possibility
of a community. Stella and Zizendorf in *The Cannibal* are seen
as intensified but otherwise normal eventualities of character
in the contemporary history of Germany. Even the protagonists
of the two Italian novellas, the hangman in *The Owl* and the
*ragazzo* in *The Goose on the Grave*, while they are social
extremes, function chiefly as perceivers of the middle part of the
culture in which they are situated. Nor does the realization of

these cultures come about entirely, or even primarily, from the workings of the inner logic of the texts. Hawkes along with everybody else knows a great deal about the actuality of these societies, and he has presented himself with only a limited freedom by refusing to deal in first-hand experience. The cultural conceptions are indeed the less idiosyncratic just because they are a piece of the common knowledge. Still more pertinently, the fiction returns again and again to one moment in real time when public event was particularly undeniable: in five of the seven novels and novellas through *Second Skin*, the year 1945 or thereabouts is taken to create the possibility of the events of the fiction. Hawkes is a post-World War II writer, in the exact sense that the shambles left by the end of the War constitute his familiar terrain.

The engendered vision might be historical or apocalyptic, and in fact it is both. But in a writer so assertively "experimental," it should be surprising that social and historical fact—what we all do really know about the post-war climate of England, Italy, Germany, the United States—has such constant and constricting presence. The paradox has apparently occurred to Hawkes too. Its resolution, he has suggested, lies in that "true purpose of the novel," which is "to assume a significant shape and to objectify the terrifying similarity between the unconscious desires of the solitary man and the disruptive needs of the visible world," wherefore the satirical writer who is running maliciously at the head of the mob will create "the shape of his meaningful psychic paradox as he goes." But obviously this explanation involves some fortuitousness, if not in fact a theory of the Oversoul. It cannot work as a formula: the solitary writer engaged in creating "overheated and demonic images" from his own darkness—as Hawkes has described the matter in another place—might be uninformatively schizophrenic. There is no necessary conjunction between private nightmare and public meaning, except perhaps at the farther reaches of a chicken-and-egg argument. Alternatively, the "terrifying similarity" which is to be objectified proposes essentially a process of illustrations —it has to be assumed that in the first place the similarity already has a kind of objective existence, and what then will remain is exercises in revealing it. And in any event, this formulation suggests a fondling indulgence of ghostly images rising from the foetid unconscious, a posture which Hawkes would deny both in his fiction and explicitly.

The opposing attitudes toward the purpose of fiction remain. Hawkes' object is to write public satires, and to write perfectly self-enclosed, autotelic works of art. Nor is this paradox—this contradiction—resolved in the fiction itself. But it does betray the characteristic motion of Hawkes' stories, and their continuous meaning.

The novels are difficult not because they are unmitigatedly private, nor because they are so formally pristine, but finally because they are neither. In terms of its form, the fiction strives for such integral inner relationships and structure—recurring events and images, and also recurring tonalities in character and in authorial voice—as would make it absolutely static. The materials refuse, however, to be composed so well. They tend to retain their own urgencies and isolations, with the result that form in the fiction becomes a continued struggle against slippage, waywardness, and arbitrariness. For an instance, there is the matter of the quick death of Hencher in *The Lime Twig*. Hencher has seemed to be the protagonist of the novel, but after he is killed, approximately one-third of the way through, he is forgotten until the last brief chapter. The instance is convenient because Hawkes has commented on it in one of his interviews. He says that the quality of Hencher's death was meant to be analogous to all that follows in the novel, and that in fact it seemed to him that "he reappears as Cowles (the murdered fat man) and as the constable." The explanation must be correct because it cannot be just an afterthought, but it is correct only to the point of a suggestiveness. Is Hencher's death analogous to all that follows? It is violent, accidental, and according to fictive convention with its assumption of a purpose in events, it is unexpected. In the novel a number of deaths occur, which are violent, arbitrary if not accidental, and to a lesser degree unexpected. By so much the process of analogies creates its own coherence, its own fictive world dependent on a logic similar to but distinct from the common logic. The other deaths, however, obviously involve other characters in other situations. Hencher is kicked by a horse as he tries to move it out of a van. Cowles—since Hawkes particularly refers to him—is murdered. Only from a special and tenuous perspective are the two adventures analogous. Again, Hencher, Cowles, and the constable are alike in that all three are fat, casually immoral, and perhaps related in the fact that they are ego-less servants of an agent more powerfully malign. To that extent, they do establish a stable pattern of recurrences. But within the text Hawkes also uses these characters to explore quite contrary contingencies. Hencher in one of his aspects is a kind of English *ragazzo*, stunned and orphaned by the war and put on the streets to make his way by guile. Cowles, so briefly as he has a presence in the novel at all, is apparently a case of ruined ambition. We learn in an aside that he had been a student in a college and that he had murdered his proctor. The old village constable perverts usual expectations: he should be the representative of kindly if bumbling authority, and he is impassively brutal.

This is not to say that Hawkes fails to bring these materials together into a desired shape, or that he succeeds, but that the form and tone of the fiction are in the effort. The effort is carried forward by innumerable individual strategies, with the effect of vision grasping at every moment for a tidy comprehension of more fragments and more debris. The novels are organized by a play of major and salient symbols—the prefect's four red-eyed ganders in *The Owl*, for example. (As may be appropriate in a novelist named Hawkes, birds of one sort and another are frequent symbols in the fiction.) Colors—notably red and green—become leit-motifs. More subtly but still more strenuously, the prose itself, in its syntactical and tonal properties, endeavors to bring together disparate characters, images, and events. Within a given novel, all characters tend to talk alike. (This is true even in Hawkes' published plays, where his characters do talk but in the accents of a single soliloquy.) Or— since there is in fact a minimal amount of dialogue in the novels —characters think in nearly identical voices. In the first pages of *The Cannibal*, for instance, the idiot Balamir sits reflecting:

He remembered photographs of the vicious tigers and the days when all men wore spats or silver braid, and from the mountains to the *Brauhaus*, camps and meeting halls sprang up, precision glasses were trained. He thought of a pigtailed donkey and the bones of men ground into food. But now the guardhouse was empty, his father, who had been the Kaiser, was dead, and the nurses had been taken from the institution as corporals.

A few paragraphs later Zizendorf sits reflecting:

Jutta's husband had owned the Paper, but he was lost among thousands in Siberia, and I, Zizendorf, his friend, sat through every hour of the day thinking of the past. I too awaited this hour after midnight when my visitor would come, when I could cease thinking of lines of inverted print, and of the spoils I had found but had never seen again in Paris. I alone was editor, but my fingers were too blunt to punch the keys and I had no paper.

The characters mirror each other in their postures, suspended in a dead moment and counting up memories. Their similarity is confirmed by the periodic and descending rhythms of the prose, cautiously and briefly re-energized near the end by the word "but." Not to press the point too far, the rhythms of these two passages are so modulated as to mitigate against a sense of discreteness in images and ideas, and they thereby confirm and unite these characters at a certain level of awareness—somewhat but not totally numb, emotionally muted, distractible.

The characters are obviously as separable as they are similar, however. Balamir is benign and dreamy. Zizendorf is actively civic-minded. They are obviously invented by way of making the vision of the novel the more extensive. And Hawkes' technical effort then is repeatedly to impose a conjunction upon them and upon all of the other characters and all of the other facts of the novel.

No doubt this effort implies that Hawkes is an "experimental" writer in the sense in which that word is by now traditional. He is doing essentially what French Symbolists did. But the stakes he puts into this effort are quite his own, and the technique of the novels is not their end but is exactly corollary to what the novels have to say. The novels most typically are about communities—wholenesses—which are subject to disruptions. More particularly, they are about communities seen in the attempt to recompose themselves after a devastation which in its turn intensifies the threat of all current intrusions. When they are not, or when the protagonist does not necessarily speak for a community—as in *Second Skin*, for example—then they are about devastated persons put to the same kind of activity, trying to bring past and present terrors into a composed plausibility. The scene of the fiction is one of disarray or of advanced and ineluctable deterioration, come to the point of such severity that everything erratic—any new eventuality of lust or greed or violence or even the birth of a child—is equally unbearable. For that reason there is little variation of pitch in the novels, sentence by sentence. And the same imaginative endeavor which fears disruptive individual assertions, constantly invents them. The fiction must therefore be engaged at each juncture in attempting cohesion, by way of plot, of prosodic strategies, and by way also of a rigorously detached authorial attitude which, as Hawkes has pointed out, has the effect of being comic.

The fictions are not for this reason all alike. Hawkes' various communities do have individual representational realities. They are colloquial in different ways. A German town is not an Italian town, and if Hawkes does not deal in cultural travelogues, still he has allowed his settings to make demands. Moreover, the various communities also present themselves with individual histories of literary usage, which Hawkes tends to acknowledge in parody. His first novella, *Charivari*, plays lightly with the manners of early Aldous Huxley. *The Beetle Leg* is a Western. (A random line from the text reads: "... Luke spread out his neckerchief and said to the Sheriff, 'This here pie's for Maverick. She ain't never seen a wedding.' ") Behind *The Lime Twig*, as Hawkes and others have said, there lies a Graham Greene thriller. The range is remarkable, as is the exuberant fecundity with which Hawkes invents nightmare images.

But the narrative is in all instances created by an endeavor to subdue the anarchy of those images, the endeavor always being contingent upon the next horror. And finally in all instances the stakes are the same. The antagonists are on the one side—the purposive side—an intricately contrived sense of stasis, and on the other side there are irrational marauders. The sense of stasis is a desperate artifice, and it is deathly. It is represented most clearly, perhaps, by Il Gufo, the hangman of *The Owl*. He in turn stands for the ancient traditions of Sasso Fetore, and the peace of the city. The sense of composed stasis is, again, represented by the repaired insane asylum in *The Cannibal*, which signifies the return of normalcy and peace to *Spitzen-on-the-Dein*. The insane inhabitants are once more contained and secure within traditional walls. On the other side, the intolerable marauders are vivid, and instinctual. They are overwhelmingly numerous, and in the amounts of their inherent threatening energies they extend—to take only examples central to the fiction—from the baby in *Charivari* to the great horse in *The Lime Twig*. In *Charivari* the prospective baby threatens the brittle unity of Henry and his wife and their relatives and friends. The banal marriage, dependent for its life on its superficiality, triumphs when the baby is not born. The horse in *The Lime Twig* is the primary token of appetite and adventure for both Hencher and Banks in their dismal cultural confinement, and it kills them. (Hawkes has said that after writing the novel he saw something redemptive in the death of Banks. With arms extended Christ-like, Banks places himself before the rushing beast. But one may question just what it is that is redeemed. By his death Banks stops a crooked horse race, and that is a triumph for sport and morality. The horse is, however, the horse of his dreams, an image of sexual prowess, and money, violence, glamour, and power. He dies in order to frustrate this rich appetancy. And at the same time, because Larry, the head of the gang, has planned to make his fortune and retire in order to pursue a dream of lime trees, Banks' martyrdom is doubly frustrating. That which is redeemed is the landscape of the "Dreary Station" with which the novel begins.)

In the other fictions—again to take only examples which are central—the vital marauders are seen in such figures as, in *The*

*Cannibal,* the dead monkeys in the insane asylum which seem to be alive, and the motorcycles themselves, in fact—which rush into the landscapes of both *The Cannibal* and *The Beetle Leg,* and the hot-rods in *Second Skin,* and in *The Owl* the prisoner who tries to fly away, and in *The Goose on the Grave* for once, the protagonist, Adeppi. At the end Adeppi runs from the city pursued by cries of sacrilege. And in the main part of the narrative of each of these fictions, indeed, with the one exception of *Second Skin,* the violent threat to the stasis of the community is terminated by violence. In *The Owl* the prisoner is hanged, whereupon, at the very end, the covenant drawn between the hangman and the people of Sasso Fetore can be restored. At the end of *The Beetle Leg* the motorcyclists called "Red Devils" are ambushed by the citizenry. This final scene of the narrative is followed by the brief *Envoi* in which Cap Leech refers back to the dominating image of the novel, the corpse buried under the tons of earth of the dam. At the end of *The Cannibal,* the act of cannibalism precedes the reinvestiture of the insane asylum. The act is, as it were, its own terrifying reward, an orgy become a solipsism.

The most recent among these fictions, *Second Skin,* seems by comparison to be written from a perspective of mellowed comic wisdom. Skipper is distinctly both protagonist and narrator. The novel is made by the action of his writing of his memoirs, an action which suggests a humanized composition of disruptive violences. Skipper is, moreover, for once, a poignantly appealing character: a large, shambling, aging man, who has been beyond all reason submitted to the sterile wilfulness of everybody else. He is terribly exposed—witness his bald head. Because he has returned from the War—the major action of this novel takes place once again *circa 1945*—it is implied that he knows much about destruction. He is a good and loving man, who tries to protect everybody from the consequences of their itching for self-destruction, and he suffers ingratitude and violence for his yearning efforts. So he retires, miraculously, to the dusky pastoral of the Wandering Island, and he resolves his suspicions of his own deathliness by becoming perhaps a father and in any event a successful Artificial Inseminator. But even in this novel, the resolution in behalf of love and fruitfulness is ambiguous to the point where it suggests its absolute contradiction. In the last words of the novel Skipper contentedly reports that he has found "The still voice." This voice may be "still voice." This voice may be "still" in two senses—the one sense meaning peace at the center of the whirlwind, the other meaning such a retreat from discrimination of outward event as is akin to suicide. Skipper becomes an *artificial inseminator*, and if this new ability represents an ingenious compromise, still it also confirms the deterioration he has suffered in too many engagements. The Wandering Island itself, obviously, is a fantasy, the more emphatically so because the horrors it contravenes are unrelievedly vulgar. The other, northern island with which it is compared is "rooted fact in the cold and choppy waters of the Altantic." And even so, the Wandering Island with all of its intimations of Atlantis and of Shakespeare's dream of the Bermudas, contains terrifying ironies. One of its features is the infested swamp nearby, where Catalina Kate is forced to submit to the long imperturbable embrace of an iguana. Nearby also is a fisherman's hut in which Kate sometimes sleeps, with fateful inferences of the fisherman's house on the other island, where Skipper's daughter was lured. The final scene of the novel is a fete in behalf of the birth of the baby, but it takes place in the island's cemetery. Kate says that the baby "look like fella in the grave."

The end of the novel contains a vision of death, and in that it is typical of Hawkes' fiction. The logic of Hawkes' plotting of events typically demands such an ending. But more than that, and because plot in the usual sense is not a conspicuous part of the fiction, the ending is intricate with all of the effort of Hawkes' prose. In all of their inner movements all of the fictions strive constantly for a supreme composition, which is deathly. The effort may of course bear any number of thematic implications—moral, political, psychological, religious, and literary. It is in itself none of these, but rather a desperate urgency to impose harmony on the welter of insane human life. Which in itself—add one more irony—is death, and therefore justifies the effort.

# maurice cagnon & stephen smith

# J. M. G. Le Clézio: Fiction's Double Bind

*It has been a long time since I have renounced saying everything I was thinking (I even wonder sometimes if there's such a thing as a thought). I've merely been satisfied to write all that in prose. The poem, the novel, the story are singular antiquities which no longer deceive anyone, or almost. Poems, stories, for what? Writing, that's all that's left, writing, only writing...*

J.M.G. LE CLÉZIO
*FEVER*

In the preface to his first published work, *Le Procès-verbal*, Le Clézio cast his lot squarely with those writers who use fiction to explore its own possibilities, who recognize no valid reality external to that which exists within the individual imagination: "I have paid very little attention to realism (more and more I have the impression that reality does not exist); I would like my story to be taken in the sense of a total fiction, whose only interest would be a certain repercussion (however ephemeral) in the mind of the reader." In the preface to *La Fièvre*, however, after affirming the death of con-

Le Clézio's works discussed here are as follows (English translations available are also indicated): *Le Procès-verbal*, 1963 (*The Interrogation*); *La Fièvre*, 1965 (*Fever*); *Le Déluge*, 1966 (*The Flood*); *L'Extase matérielle*, 1967; *Terra Amata*, 1967; *Le Livre des fuites* (*The Book of Flights*); *La Guerre*, 1970. The original French editions are all published by Gallimard, Paris; English language editions are Atheneum, New York. "Comment j'écris" ("How I write") appeared in *Cahiers du Chemin*, 1 (October, 1967). All quotations from Le Clézio's works have been translated by the authors.

ventional genres, he states that nothing remains but writing, which takes its substance from experience, which seeks out and describes, and which "unsparingly reworks reality."

These apparently contradictory assertions are reconciled in a pasage from *L'Extase matérielle* crucial to the understanding of Le Clézio's esthetics. Recognizing that modern man has not resolved the age-old oppositions between life and thought, between mind and matter, between reality and fiction, he contends that the passage from reality to the imaginary is simply the transhumance from one reality to another. He then concludes: "In fact, there are not two realities. There is only the one which we conceive by means of language. The person who does not submit to this drama, who believes that he can avoid it by creating other connections, by dreaming of a 'total world,' is mistaken. He is lying."

The resolution seems complete. The evidence, nevertheless, suggests that Le Clézio was not persuaded by his own argument. "What can be said," he was to write only two years later, "about the writer who lies by writing that he is lying?" *Le Livre des fuites* patently takes as its subject the effort to pierce the veil which separates man from reality. The barrier is seen to consist largely of those structures and strictures imposed by language, by the necessity to classify and define, by those distinctions which every culture creates in an effort to render the universe intelligible. Le Clézio works from the assumption that these entities exist nowhere but in the mind, that their limits must somehow be exceeded if total reality is to be comprehended. A reexamination of his work reveals that the goal of his art has always been basically transcendental, his theoretical pronouncements to the contrary notwithstanding, but a transcendance to a more basic, rather than to a higher reality.

In an article entitled "Comment j'écris" ("How I Write") Le Clézio stresses that both the source and means of writing are found in the spontaneous recording of stimuli, impressions, and reactions: "There is no room for invention, there is no possibility of truth, nor of untruth. There is only this world, constantly, from one horizon to the other." Le Clézio underscores his view by capitalizing and setting apart typographically the key phrase: "EVERYTHING IS WRITTEN IT SUFFICES TO READ IT." We are to interpret that the entire record of human intelligence is *there* needing only to be understood: signs and symbols written on walls, bits of paper and backs of envelopes, tablecloths and cigarette packs, in telephone directories, newspapers, and books.

The article's opening sentence—"Every time a man wants to write, this is what he must do"—appears almost as programmed instruction in creative writing; the intentional mode (he who *wants* to write) is, however, at some remove from the realm of accomplished fact: the author's acute consciousness of himself as writer, in the throes of an endless creative birth process. Thus the evolution from "You cannot escape from life" to "You cannot escape from life if you know how to write." Le Clézio emphasizes the well-nigh unbridgeable distance from the germinal moment of creativity to the finished artistic construct, between writing as simultaneous transcription and the actual care taken by a skilled craftsman constantly reworking his materials. Positing man as the forever potentially omniscient, omnipresent being, literature as the ultimate possible game, Le Clézio puts forth the underlying notion that one cannot refuse the smallest fraction of the entire spectrum of human complexity: "Accidents, passions, desires, apprehensions, all that is stirring in me. . . . And I, I look on; I create."

By means of an ongoing osmotic process, the writer seeks to become all things. Just as he carries within himself the "eggs of the words which will vanquish," so also does the act of writing itself consist of the search for "the egg, the seed." In Le Clézio's attempt to self-appropriate the cosmos, these then are the interacting forces of the established dialectics: man at once writing and being written: "everywhere . . . I write with my whole body . . . and I am incessantly being written by the world."

The affirmations in "Comment j'écris" become in *Le Livre des fuites* anguished questions. In the first, the act of writing provided the elemental tension of exchange, for words were still modes of possible communication. In the latter there is too often no escape from paralyzing limitations, for words are themselves part of the trap. "How can you escape from language?" Le Clézio asks; "how can you escape, even if only for a single time, even if only from the word KNIFE?" as he seeks to reestablish contact with primal essence by confronting on the most basic level, that of language, the distortions resulting from the necessity to define.

Words are unreliable conveyors of meaning. Identical words and gestures can be called upon to speak "of politics, races, women, cars, discomforts, all at once." Words are incapable of retaining and transmitting a predetermined significance: "Words no longer meant the same thing twice." They can never fully circumscribe intended ideas, and each word might promiscuously embrace all possible meanings, since communication depends entirely on interpretation: "A word once pronounced is another word. I say *woman*, that is *statue*, that is *octopus*, that is *wheel*." If all meanings are possible for any one word, then there is no reason to insist on the *mot juste*; rather, one word can be substituted for another at random: "Here 'table' is written, and there 'mirror,' but it could just as well have been 'cloud' and 'tank truck.' "

The idea that words alone, divorced from context, can have meaning, would seem to lie at the base of many of Le Clézio's extensive enumerative passages: a list of names from the telephone directory, and another of items from a dictionary; a chapter composed solely of insults; eighteen columns of words consisting of 89 nouns and one adverb, followed by 81 terms said to express movements; a lengthy sequence written in "incomprehensible words." Le Clézio, never the dupe of his own imaginings and experiments, struggles in this linguistic bind to seek the appropriate written correlative to intellectual concepts: "it would take words coming from the depths of space at the speed of light . . ., which would crush everything in their path, words like lava flows . . . which would hiss in the air and hollow out huge boiling craters on the earth's surface."

At times the author scornfully disowns norms of language: "dictionaries are horrible, for they are never complete; there is always something which eludes them." While mindful of the inadequacy of words, Le Clézio concedes nevertheless their necessity: "between raw reality and the reconquest of pure reality, there is the entire voyage of the word. But since our knowledge is perfected only by language, we have no choice. We must recapture truth in lies. Our chances of accomplishing this are minimal." Pessimistic though this assessment be, it suggests that truth can somehow be derived from the lie which conceals it, that somewhere within this limitless prison of words lies a secret meaning waiting to be discovered. Le Clézio's entire canon thus far stands as a monument to the sincerity of this belief in the ultimate possibility of elemental knowledge: "What must be guessed is hidden behind words and acts, hidden behind works."

The author's treatment of fictional personages reveals similar reluctance to delimit and abstract, the same attempts to avoid the mutilations and truncations of reality which they entail, yet also the inescapable final return to the individual as the only signifying entity within our culture's mode of expression. The very name of Adam Pollo, the central figure of Le Clézio's first novel, sets the allegorical tone which will dominate in all subsequent characters as well. "Adam," the Hebrew word for "man," reflects an overriding concern for presenting the entire "spectacle of reality," that "permanent exhibition of adventures which tell the little history of the world," and "Pollo," evocative of the Greek word for "many," already hints at an unwillingness to opt for unity at the expense of multiplicity. As though this double epithet were not sufficient in itself to elicit the parabolic reading, Le Clézio stresses the lack of criteria for distinguishing the individual from Everyman. Adam Pollo writes to his mistress Michèle that after having observed her along with every other customer in a bar, acting identically, sharing identical features, he recognized them as "all, all, all alike." He readily admits that he himself is no more differentiable than they: "we are all alike, all brothers . . . , we have the same bodies and the same minds"; his personal ontology corroborates this universal sameness: "there is no difference between sea, tree, and television . . . , TV is ourselves, mankind."

A sporadic fusion appears to characterize Adam's relationship with his surroundings, and, at times, various aspects of the environment one with the other. Often the equivalence can be interpreted as merely metaphorical, a dream, a psychological reference point, or a sexual fantasy. Adam and Michèle make love imagining themselves as spiders or slugs; at a zoo Adam identifies totally with any other species by desiring the female.

Other correspondences, however, offer greater resistance to a figurative analysis. As Adam follows a dog along the beach and through the streets of a city, we are progressively led to believe in the hero's potential metamorphosis. At first he is not a dog, "not yet, perhaps"; he then proceeds to be no longer human, "in any case, never again"; and eventually he too may be able to micturate tranquilly on American cars and No Parking signs, and make love unabashedly in the open.

The rat-killing episode develops the osmotic process significantly. At the outset, Adam noticed that the rat had "a look of kinship with himself"; then, slowly forgetting his own identity, Adam "was transformed into a white rat, but by a bizarre metamorphosis; he still kept his own body." His transmigration of essence is complemented by that of the rat, which, because of its hatred and terror, becomes a man. In other sequences Adam is, variously, a vegetable, moss or lichen, the sea, an oyster.

An episode prefiguring a similar experience in *Le Livre des fuites* shows Adam walking through city streets at night. His self, fragmented and kaleidoscoped, is shared, perhaps, by "four or five thousand adams . . . , wandering around the city. There were some on foot, others on bicycles or in cars . . . a woman-adam . . . other men-adams . . . an old man-adam." The allegorical reading is obligatory here, as it is again at the book's conclusion when the author speaks of "Adam or of some other from among him." Yet in spite of this proliferation of adams, with a small "a," Adam, the individualized incarnation of humanity, remains distinct from the masses, both implicitly in the reader's mind and explicitly by the author's dual typography.

The unremitting motif of transmigration in *Le Procès-verbal* might be rationalized in terms of Adam's insanity, were it not so inextricably involved with Le Clézio's stated desire to create a total fiction. Through Adam he decries that false idea of the universe whereby everything is catalogued, classified, "and by which one can choose as though from a file the appropriate designation for an object." Adam's development, according to the author, is governed by "the double system of multiplication and identification.... Little by little he annihilates himself through self-creation." Le Clézio intended, it would therefore seem, that the reader interpret literally his character's shifts of being. Instead, Adam persists as a rather traditional novelistic person: perhaps necessarily—just as a writer's words cannot but assume some measure of their conventional significance, so must his characters to some extent be seen in interpretable frames of reference. Though Adam strives for an essence perpetually in flux, his author and the reader unhesitatingly agree with his final avowal of the futility of that quest: "Everything is finished. You are yourself and I am myself."

In *Le Déluge* characters continue to attempt flight beyond the normal limits of defined individuality, only to fall back into predictable fictional modes. François Besson becomes alternately a piece of sculptured ebony, the idiot seated opposite him on a bus, the rhythm of the sea and wind, a fly caught by a carnivorous plant, grass, and a "man-motor." Diverse degrees of literalness may be inferred for each of these metamorphoses, but for the character the judgment stands intransigent: "you will not escape from the revelation of your existence.... You are BESSON."

The stories in *La Fièvre* further illustrate the concept of a mutable continuum of being, adumbrating the author's eventual overt linking of the theme with his fascination for thought and its creative powers. Roch Estève, hero of the title story, alone on his bed and sick with fever, "had become that woman," his with Elisabeth. In "Le jour où Beaumont fit connaissance avec sa douleur," the pain from Beaumont's toothache obliterates the contours of his being, at once emptying him of all previously acquired ego ("Your name is Beaumont?" asks the unknown young woman he telephones in terror. "My name was Beaumont, yes") and opening the self to total possibility: "I am everything which takes place on earth, all the horrors and all the pleasures. All that is said and all that is desired ... because I am empty,

empty, empty. And because everything can enter me." Throughout *La Fièvre* fluidity of essence is a usual and natural phenomenon. The author, or some one of his creations, assumes, among numerous additional identities, that of a train, a whirlwind, a multitude of relationships with a box of matches, "a wave, or rather a rhythm," a muted trumpet, or the dry crackle of a fingernail being broken.

A passage deliberately reminiscent of Pascal's projection of the self-image against two infinities, and, perhaps less wittingly so, of Alice's dimensional transmogrifications in Wonderland, centers on the ability to expand into the entire universe, coupled with an equal capacity to contract to that "non-existent point ... which is considered *divine*." Paradoxically, either movement propels one into "the area of total emptiness ... where nothing exists, not even infinity." Total creation leads thus inexorably into absolute negation, and whatever is completely under the control of its creator, be he god or artist, has no existence outside that creator. Only as devisor of that which is exterior to himself can he wreak any veritable effect; yet such effects invariably defy prognosis and control. In the specific case of literature, the writer's finished product is for the reader merely a set of raw materials: "I wrote pins, tobacco, passions, to suffer, nylon, seed. You read zipper, top, beauty, woman, cigarette, cloud." The strongly auto-parodistic story "Martin" in *La Fièvre* underlines "the divine nature of language." Martin-Lucifer, greedy after godhood, manipulates language beyond itself to invent "Elmen ... in which words were twice the same," only to be cast into darkness, symbolized by the loss of his glasses and by night's advancing shadow, and forced to confess: "God, or God! ... I have blasphemed you too much!" The impulse is not, however, diminished by admitting the chimerical nature of its promise, and in all subsequent works Le Clézio explores more deeply the dilemma that creation cannot, but must, transcend its creator.

*Terra Amata*, with renewed emphasis, further expands the theme of multiplicity of selves. Chancelade undergoes an even greater number of metamorphoses than do the characters in any of Le Clézio's preceding works. Near the end of the book the author abruptly dismisses Chancelade completely in order to concentrate on the creative act itself: "But enough has been invented, now. There is no Chancelade, there has never been a Chancelade. There has been only myself, writing these words, knowing that they hide nothing."

*Le Livre des fuites* is on one level a study of the imaginative process, which finds its natural transcription in the metaphor of limitless capacity for change. Here again the character's allegorical name, Jeune Homme Hogan (Young Man Hogan), which cannot but recall Joyce's "Here Comes Everybody," varies as readily as the persona it represents. Multiple modifications of the same name yield at times to completely unrelated cognomina, illustrating in yet another manner the infinitude of possibilities open to any creature of the imagination. Le Clézio calls him Walking Stick, John Traveller, Iskuir, and Daniel Earl Langlois, provides him with other ages and races, other spatial and temporal contexts, and even the other sex.

This character, to a far greater extent than Chancelade, serves as vehicle for inquiries into the very nature of fiction. "Can you imagine that?" introduces not only the work's opening airport sequence but, more essentially, the foremost preoccupation of the entire book. Can one imagine a character whose entelechy itself is merely imagined? If so, then the dilemma of "the one or the many" is resolved, for the character thus is able to encompass anything which can be conceived— that is, he can be "the many" at no loss to unity. A negative response, on the other hand, throws literature as a whole into serious question, along with its purpose and inherent interest, if any.

Le Clézio not unexpectedly admits both answers. He expounds a theory of literature as the direct recording of materials from exterior reality, denying at the same time that such a feat is possible. He denounces his own attempts to imagine: "I wanted to imagine, but that is impossible: one invents nothing," and describes literature as a fruitless effort to communicate when communication must remain an unattainable ideal. Yet he persists in writing and invention, probing and analyzing his motives for doing so, with each successive assertion eliciting its own negation: "Everything which I . . . put on paper . . . is denied at the same time by someone other than myself; a hidden phantom which shakes its head in constant denial."

The multifaceted character is brought into check by Le Clézio, who avows that Hogan is none other than himself: "He is I, only I"; but this oneness is temporary only, and the personage does not cease performing in what would appear to be autonomous fashion. At book's end, his adventures project into the future as he awaits the next bus, and the author chooses to close his "adventure novel" with the words "To be continued."

Bea B., perhaps the only "character" in *La Guerre*, Le Clézio's last work of fiction to date, is as protean and elusive in her repertory of masks as was Hogan. It comes, therefore, as no surprise when we are informed, even before her name is disclosed, that she does not have "a single body and a single soul. She has thousands of them." Like the protagonists of the preceding novels, Bea B. undergoes numerous total transformations of essence, becoming at various moments a mechanical doll, a kind of car, a tower, a manatee, a thought, the sun, or even herself.

Bea B. seeks personal salvation through appropriating endless other beings, disguising herself as "a nurse, a stenographer-typist, a fashion reporter, a movie extra, a nude model for men's magazines, a social worker. She has quantities of names for disappearing." However, in spite of all the diversity which he imagines for her, Le Clézio invests Bea B. with a certain unity of character in the traditional sense, attributing to her a deep-rooted and all-pervasive fear, a rare combination of acuity and naiveté in her life-attitude, an enthusiasm for motorcycles and pornographic magazines. The ultimate source of her unity, as of her diversity, unfolds from an examination of the work's other "character," Monsieur X.

Once again Le Clézio's onomastics are revealing: X, the eternal unknown quantity, a revenant driving "a big BMW 500 cm³ motorcycle," described physically by way of an impressionistic jotting in Bea B.'s diary: "He is ugly, but I find him handsome." We first see the two of them together playing the

favored game of masquerades, their conversation a pastiche
of Ionesco's pastiche of language. Other evocations of this evan-
escent figure occur in Bea B.'s thoughts addressed directly to
him, indirect references to him in her engagement book, and
enigmatic, hallucinatory meetings in which he may or may not
recognize Bea B.—at a dance hall, at an airport, in a sequence
involving a killer-car, where at first the driver "resembled Monsieur X," then suddenly *was* Monsieur X.

He is the one fighter, the eternal war-maker who, incarnated
as a soldier in Vietnam, writes letters to Bea B., the documentary
realism of which is shattered by the author's almost throwaway
closing statement: "That, approximately, is what could have
been written, at that time." When Monsieur X symbolically dies,
Bea B. in her own mind fully assumes his existence. Now trans-
shaped into "Bea X," she serves to heighten an earlier inchoate
awareness of willfully split personality: "Monsieur X is myself.
I didn't know it. I though that Monsieur X was someone else.
I have his hand, it's my own. I have a motorcycle." This central
theme of arbitrarily exchanged identities, of perpetual creation-
negation by "repeated acts of physical and psychical violence,"[1]
at once controls and frees Le Clézio's whole vision of the world.

Bea B. and Monsieur X appear to be indistinguishable—and
indistinguishable from Jeune Homme Hogan or Chancelade or
François Besson or Adam Pollo. The recurrent similarity does
not, however, preclude a manifest progression in Le Clézio's
character portrayal. Up through the point in *Terra Amata* where
he declares that Chancelade never existed, Le Clézio devotes
considerable space in his writing to those details which enable
the reader to "recognize" personages—physical descriptions,
psychological analyses, family backgrounds, and social milieux.
Adam was potentially everybody, but he was essentially Adam.
Hogan, Bea B., and Monsieur X are potentially everybody, but
they are essentially Le Clézio. Less and less does he seek to mask
this self-oriented aspect of his creation. In *Le Livre des fuites* he
shifts from first-person-author to third-person-Hogan: "Enough
of 'I'! It is he, it is myself as a friend, about whom I wish to

---

[1] The expression is taken from Ingmar Bergman's film *The Passion of
Anna* with which striking thematic analogies can be drawn.

speak." Bea B. and Monsieur X can both best be understood as further examples of this same phenomenon. Monsieur X's Malediction, a jeremiad of myriad future calamities, includes, in the typographic form of a cash-register receipt, a parodic outline of the book itself:

| | |
|---|---|
| War | 12 |
| The world is absurd | 06 |
| Everything is beautiful | 10 |
| Monsieur X's Malediction | 04 |
| One day we will be free | 24 |
| Total | 56 |

Monsier X—impossible here to think of him as other than the prolocutor for the author—confesses that perhaps "the war is only in myself," but adds in a crucial aside that "however, even if all that is only in me, it is because it is also in others."

So it is that the paradox may be resolved. As Le Clézio strives with greater success to free his personae from the limits of an imagined reality, they take on more and more the limits of their creator's real imagination. As they lose the peculiarities which allow us to identify them as themselves, they gain those distinctive intellectual traits which enable us to see the author behind the masks. As they become increasingly diverse, we become increasingly aware of their elemental unity, as did Le Clézio himself in *L'Extase matérielle*: "by imagining, I did nothing but endlessly re-create myself."

Though ultimately we must acknowledge that the reality of every fiction lies only in the imagination, we can at the same time perceive the truth of Monsieur X's Jungian assertion that every man's inner universe exists also in the mind of others. Accordingly, this primary reduction of all Le Clézio's characters to their source in the creator's inventive powers does not obviate their multitudinous identities as they, like the words of which they are formed, await coming esthetic reincarnations in writer and reader alike.

# How now?

## jacques ehrmann

# The Death of Literature

*I listen only for the pleasure of repeating.*

**DENIS DIDEROT**

*—Don't you see that Gabriel repeats any old shit without understanding it; he only has to hear it once.*
*—You've gotta hear 'em to repeat 'em, Gabriel snapped back. How the fuck would you go about finding the shit all by yourself?*

**RAYMOND QUENEAU**

## RECIPE

1. Take any scrap of writing. Whichever one comes to hand. A page from a dictionary or a telephone book; a press clipping; an ad; one of Shakespeare's sonnets; a list of books; street names; a Latin sentence.
2. Take another scrap.
3. Etc.
4. Cut up each scrap or recopy it.
5. Choose a title (optional).
6. Arrange each scrap on a clean page.
7. Stop when you've had enough.
8. In this manner you will have made "texts". For instance, like this:

*229*

## A BLANK SPACE

It had ceased to be a blank space of delightful mystery—a white patch for a boy to dream gloriously over. It had become a place of darkness. But there was in it one river especially, a mighty big river that you could see on the map, resembling an immense snake uncoiled, with its head in the sea, its body at rest curving afar over a vast country, and its tail lost in the depths of the land.

## NUMBERS I

0, 1, 2, 3, 4, 5, 6, 7, 8, 9.

## NUMBERS II

zero
one
two
three
four
five
six
seven
eight
nine

## LISTERINE

Antiseptic
Kills germs by Millions on contact
For Bad Breath, Colds and resultant Sore
Throats, Minor Cuts, Scratches, Insect Bites,
Infectious Dandruff.
1 Pint 4 Fluid ounces

## MONOTONICITY

The proof of

$$\int_0^y \varphi_{n+1}\left(\xi \,\Big|\, \frac{n-1}{n}s\right) d\xi > \int_0^y \varphi_n(\xi\,|\,s)\,d\xi, \qquad \text{for } y > 0.$$

is quite simple and again makes use of the monotonicity preserving of densities with a monotone likelihood ratio. Since the characteristic function of the interval $(0, y)$ is a monotone decreasing function of $\xi$, it follows that

$$\int_0^y \varphi_{n+1}\left(\xi \,\Big|\, \frac{n-1}{n}s\right) d\xi = \frac{\displaystyle\int_0^\infty \beta^{n+1} e^{-(n-1)\omega s}\left[\int_0^y e^{-\xi\omega}r(\xi)\,d\xi\right]f(\omega)\,d\omega}{\displaystyle\int_0^\infty \beta^n e^{-(n-1)\omega s}f(\omega)\,d\omega}$$

is a monotone decreasing function of $s$, and therefore

$$\int_0^y \varphi_{n+1}\left(\xi \,\Big|\, \frac{n-1}{n}s\right) d\xi \geqq \int_0^y \varphi_{n+1}\left(\xi \,\Big|\, \frac{n-1}{n}s + \frac{\tau}{n-1}\right) d\xi$$

$$= \frac{\displaystyle\int_0^\infty \beta^{n+1} e^{-(n-1)\omega s}e^{-\tau\omega}\left[\int_0^y e^{-\xi\omega}r(\xi)\,d\xi\right]f(\omega)\,d\omega}{\displaystyle\int_0^\infty \beta^n e^{-(n-1)\omega\tau}e^{-\omega\tau}f(\omega)\,d\omega}$$

or

$$\int_0^y \varphi_{n+1}\left(\xi \,\Big|\, \frac{n-1}{n}s\right) d\xi \cdot \int_0^\infty \beta^n e^{-(n-1)\omega s}e^{-\omega\tau}f(\omega)\,d\omega$$

$$\geqq \int_0^\infty \beta^{n+1} e^{-(n-1)\omega\tau}e^{-\tau\omega}\left[\int_0^y e^{-\xi\omega}r(\xi)\,d\xi\right]f(\omega)\,d\omega,$$

## LIKE

Winston tastes good like a cigarette should.

ETC.

etcetera

Must I clarify? There is no mystery about these "texts." They do not seek to provoke the reader; nor do they require his complicity. They need not be understood; they are what they are. Can as much be said of any other kind of writing?

Irritated by their banality, a typical reader might reject such texts, saying that they are too easily put together—that anyone could do as much. Without realizing it (or rather in complete ignorance) he would thus be expressing both for me and for anyone else the very heart of the matter. What touching simplicity! In so concluding, our reader would not be saying anything personal—nothing that you or I would not say in his place. It is easy to state that everyone is, potentially, capable of putting together similar "texts." We must view this answer not as a solution to a problem but rather as a point of departure for a question which necessarily poses itself: "Who *made* these texts?" We must put to the test the very meaning of this question while attempting at the same time to answer it. In other words: What does it mean to "compose" a text? Who composes a "text"? How is a "text" composed? Or, to formulate the question in yet another manner, "Of what and by whom is a text composed?"

These are just so many questions wherein both "author" and "text" are reciprocally implicated and are functioning both simultaneously and alternatively as subject and object of the question. The "author" and the "text" are thus caught in a movement in which they do not remain distinct (the author and the work; one creator of the other) but rather are transposed and become interchangeable, creating and annulling one another.

Until now, with regard to poetic theory, it has been customary to think in one direction only; going from the author to the work, from the subject who creates to the object created. This (linguistic) object has been recognizable *as a poetic object* to the extent that we have been aware of having to do with a "gratuitous" fabrication of language. It has been doubly differentiated from ordinary language: on the one hand because of the latter's utilitarian character (language as instrument); on the other hand because of the fact that ordinary language is not *produced* (created) by anyone in particular, as opposed to the poetic object (the poem, etymologically, is a preeminently created object) which is fabricated or constructed *by* the one designated as "author."

Underlying this dichotomy which separates ordinary language from poetic language—utilitarian language from gratuitous language—is the theory of intentionality (which, although submitted to indirect criticism has never yet to my knowledge been systematically and radically questioned on that level, to the extent that the relationship between the "author" and the "work" has not been fundamentally rethought). This theory gives an admirable explanation of the operations of a sovereign consciousness situated at the origin of two different *ends*. And so, in order to know if we were dealing with poetry, all we had to do was to go back to the *origin* of the text, that is to say, to the one who had produced it (and to whom the text actually *belonged*) and by deciphering his intention, place this bit of discourse under the category (or heading) of "poetry", if that be the case.

But what if the "author" is no longer to be found at the origin of the "text"? Then to whom does this "text" belong? These are questions to which the theory of intentionality can no longer provide satisfactory answers. Is the problem of the utilization of a text (its purpose) the same as that of its source (or origin)? Both aspects relate to the question of ownership—that is, to the one to whom the text belongs and to the manner in which it is used. This is what we must explain here.

The telephone, the typical means of communication between individuals in our society, will furnish a particularly appropriate example. Who *makes* a telephone book? Who is its author? It is not sufficient to reply that the employees of the telephone company put it together. A telephone book is also made up *of* (and *by*—on reflection there is more to it than a simple play on words) all the subscribers who are listed in it—who have contributed their names to its *making*. To this already impressive (although limited and calculable) list of authors we must add all the possible users (subscribers or not; eventual or actual)—anyone—everyone. In this vast and impersonal network of communications it is the users who *compose*—who are and make—the text;

in other words, who are both its object and subject.

Therefore, if "I" chooses a page of the telephone book *at random*, and if "I" places it alongside other texts chosen according to the same principles, "I" does not emerge from the impersonal, for on the one hand "I" is not at the origin of these texts ("I" did not make them). On the other hand anyone else could have (and would have) done as much in his place. It no longer makes sense to speak of intentionality because the intention is engulfed, drowned in the generality of all the other intentions, either actual or virtual, of the user-fabricators of these pages. One should be able to say that these "texts" are as intact after being extracted from their original context, as they were before.

However . . .

If the pages of a telephone book (or any other text) do not actually belong to me or to anyone else, if, as a result, nothing of my own making enters into this text, any more than it does into the others alongside which it was placed, then the very fact of having isolated them at first, then collected them—of having separated them from their original context in order to reassemble them *in another manner*—presupposes a certain minimum movement, a certain displacement, however slight, comparable to that which attests to the passage of a presence in a room where objects have moved (or better: have been moved) from their usual place.

If, in this respect, it is possible to speak of "poetry", it is in this slight movement of "texts" that we must look for it, discover it, *invent* it. It does not allow itself to be enclosed solely within the stable and conventional forms of poetics inherited from tradition (whose innovations would nevertheless be recognized and recognizable as "poetry" because they have been produced *within* a system that, on the whole, has remained uncontested). One can find it in language in general, because of the simple fact that no language is literal. By this, one must understand not that language sends us to some sort of "elsewhere" beyond language (presupposing a "here"), but that there is built into all communication the distance inherent to its articulation. This distance constitutes the play of language, the possibility of its poetry, that is to say, the irreducible portion of chance, of indeterminateness, of incompleteness, of formlessness which render possible (and ineluctable!) both the dependence of subject and object as a function of their history and structure, and the necessity of their independence.

Therefore, every language awaits its poet—you, I, anyone—who will make poetry surge forth from it. One can no longer say that the poet is at the *origin* of his language, since it is language which creates the poet and not the reverse. Nor can one say henceforth that poetry depends upon the *intention* of the poet on the pretext that he gives the label of "poem" to what he writes and that those who take part in the same history agree to recognize it as such. Poetry (or fiction) is therefore not to be found *within* texts of a given (conventional) type but, virtual and diffuse, within language itself, that is, in the relationship between writer and writing, reading and reader, and, even more generally, in the play of all communication.

Play always implies an alternation of presence and absence (like the two ends of a seesaw which cannot both be simultaneously above or below). I should now like to say a few words on the subject of play.

If we take as a point of departure the one who has gathered the texts, his presence—as we have seen above—is imperceptible, negligible within them; it has now vanished without leaving any trace other than that sliding, glancing touch which alone permits us to divine a passing presence, now *gone* and transformed into absence.

Marks on stone, cuts in wood, wear marks, nicks, scratches, graffiti: these and all other discrete traces of a presence now in ruins. Or, perhaps, blank spaces on the earth now filled with rivers, lakes, and names, like this mighty big river that you could see on the map, resembling an immense snake uncoiled, with its head in the sea, its body at rest curving afar over a vast country, and its tail lost in the depths of the land. Thus the echoes awakened in us by the disturbing remains of a disintegrated past give rise to an emotion as shattering as that which the most accomplished "art" could evoke.

This presence is not there at the center of things, recognizable and sovereign. Its empire has passed. Things have ceased to belong to it. If in any way it does remain at the center of things, it does so in the form of a question—the question of its belonging to the "texts," or of its ownership of them; have things ever belonged to this presence, or has it served simply as a depository, a temporary user, a relay?

"I" is therefore in the "texts," but not as subject at their origin—that is to say, not as their "author—but as their object, the one who must be sought precisely because he is absent from them. Yet it is vain to attempt to discover him for the very reason that he is indeed absent.

If the simple accumulation of "texts" can produce a slight impression which allows us to detect the passing of a presence, the latter is nevertheless reduced to its descriptive minimum. This presence is not, therefore, anonymous; it cannot be so. Inscribed as it is within signs, before pointing to anything else, it points to itself. Thus, by giving the description of a presence, the "texts" indicate the identity of the one who has assembled them, but nothing else. This identity provides no more information than does a passport to a customs officer, an identification card to a police officer, or the entries in a telephone book to the person who consults them. The presence is summed up by this bare minimum of information. There is no emotion involved in this brief summary; neither regret nor pleasure, neither shame nor vanity; there is no effusion or constraint, because "that's the way it is." Every trace hides an absence, which is precisely why it exists as a trace. Instead of trying to go against nature by trying to force the signs to yield a presence which can only remain outside of them, why not opt in favor of the trace by attempting in *so far as possible* to efface all signs of a "presence," knowing all the while that total success is impossible because it is contrary to the very nature of the trace?

One must understand that in such a perspective, where great care has been taken to strip and denude in the most radical fashion, these "texts" cannot appear under the official seal of a signature, because we have just contested the possibility of talking about an "author" in connection with them.

The presence of a reader is no more explicit nor implied than is that of an author. This presence is just as indeterminate because these "texts" are not addressed to any particular public. They are addressed to everyone, to anyone who can make use of something written, to anyone who can read.

Although indefinite, the using public does not remain completely indeterminate; it also manifests itself through slight traces—those to which the coordinates of a history and culture may be reduced. However, the most flexible possible reading is guaranteed, for nothing (or rather the minimum constituted by the text itself) hinders its use or limits its echo. Since the one who has assembled the "texts" has a minimal control over how they are read, everything happens between the lines, in the interval between the words, in the whiteness that separates the "texts," in the semantic space between title and "texts," in a word, in all that, knowingly, has remained silent and that depends upon the user, and will be put into play according to his own system of resonance. In this manner the "text" loses the sacred character which in our culture we have been pleased to confer upon it. Sacred (poetic) language and ordinary language cease to oppose one another like an aristocrat and a plebian. In the same way the opposition ends between the gratuitous and utilitarian aspects of language. Consequently, we no longer confront poetry as though we were standing at the threshold of a church, a place that evokes all that is "sacred" to the profane, that immediately triggers the response: attention, sanctuary!—or its literary equivalent: attention, poetry!— automatically engendering an attitude of constrained respect and stiff decorum in marked contrast to the coarsest profanations and irregularities of everyday life and language. What hypocritical reverence!

From this point of view—if we restrict ourselves to the modern era—Baudelaire must be regarded as one of the principals responsible for this sacralization of poetry. If in one or two generations the characteristics of this sacralization have changed and seem to have lost their sharpness, it is none the less hardy (more so in the language arts than in the plastic arts which have a marked lead on the former).

By incorporating into art elements (objects or fragments of objects either "natural" or "fabricated") that tradition has never previously admitted, the Cubists and the Surrealists have helped to change the frontiers of the artistically sacred. But, although it has been altered and enlarged, the scope of art still remains sacred for them. Like the fairy who transformed a pumpkin into a carriage with a touch of her magic wand, it was enough for the poet or the Surrealist artist to *touch* with his signature the basest of objects (such as Duchamp's "Fountain") to claim to elevate it to the "dignity" of art. Such a procedure, although it serves to demystify in its own way and up to a certain point (as had Hugo's placing a revolutionary bonnet on the dictionary a century earlier), is still situated within a tradition that makes a poet both a magus and a redeemer. The artist continues to be this demiurge whose role consists in saving men from the triteness and baseness of daily life; in *redeeming* them by *offering* them the consolation of a *gratuitous* language; in sacrificing himself in order, as Mallarmé said, "to give a purer meaning to the words of the tribe."

In one form or another it is always the same religion of beauty, this stupid "goddess," mute as a dream in stone; the justification for so much fanaticism and the pretext for so much cowardice. The poet has always offered himself as the high priest of his cult, ready and willing occasionally to become its sacrificial victim, to be its prophet, and sometimes its martyr.

If, in both first and final analysis, these "texts" are not attributable to anyone (neither proceeding from, nor destined for, anyone), their belonging, ownership, or appropriation—and by extension that of any writing at all—no longer conforms to accepted conventions. As a result the criterion of "originality" of artistic production is both modified and contested.[1] To write would be first of all to quote. The "writer" would not be the one who "listens to a voice from within," but rather the one who

[1] Is this such a scandalous claim? This criterion, which we are inclined to believe "essential" to art is, in fact, a recent invention. As we know, up to the French Revolution the property rights of a text (hence, its originality) followed moral and legal conventions very different from our own.

quotes, who puts language in quotes; who both sets it off and calls it to himself, who, in a word, *designates* it as language.

If we stop for a moment to consider the function of quotation marks in discourse, we perceive, in effect, that they serve to isolate a word, an expression, a text by placing it at a distance (is "esthetic distance" anything close?). The "writer" refuses to accept them as they are given to him. This gesture is quite the opposite of an appropriation! However, he also calls them to himself because he incorporates them in his discourse, because he makes of them the subject of his discourse.

The "writer" is therefore neither *inside* nor *outside* his language. He does not pause within it; he merely passes through it. But how can we say it is "his" language since the language he places in quotes is a borrowed one? Far from appropriating language in order to immobilize it, the "writer" suspends language in order to transmit it. By putting it back into circulation, carried along by the quotes, so to speak, he contributes toward making it comprehensible indefinitely. He does this, not through any magical transformation effected with the help of the quotes, but by using the latter to underline the transformable nature of language. Being a "writer" or a "poet" no longer corresponds to any particular identity, but to a particular *situation*, accessible however to everyone.

"Poetic" language is not another language, it is the same language. Or, more precisely, it is language itself whose capacity (and function) to change and expand is suddenly exposed.

But to state (as does one tradition in criticism) that "poetic language" is defined and measured by its degree of variance from "ordinary language" is to claim that all variation of language is poetic and that the absence of variation is necessarily prosaic: this is patently absurd. To maintain that "the poet does not speak like everyone else"—to contrast prose and poetry, natural language and the language of art, the language of science (which is supposed to approach the so-called zero degree of writing) and the language of poets (supposed to vary as far as possible from "zero")—finally, to found the "poeticity" of poetry on a *concensus*, that is, on what the majority (which one?) recognizes as "poetry," only serves to strengthen the prejudices of tradition by dressing it up in a kind of cheap positivism which renders stylistics (these, at any rate!) no more scientific for all that.

If a variance exists—and we are convinced that it does—it is not a variance *in relation to* the norm, but rather a variance *within* the norm. Or, more precisely, the norm (the law of language) is founded on the possibility of variance. This must be understood in two ways:

1) Because the variance is possible, the norm is necessary.

2) Because the variance exists, the norm is possible and is able to exist.

The variance is therefore built into the law. It is its very articulation. The law, as affirmation and articulation of the possibility of variance, contains thereby something unfinished, formless, which eludes it and which is none other than the affirmation and articulation of desire, a desire wherein one must discern the variance (as Lévi-Strauss has shown in the law prohibiting incest), since it both separates and brings together the members of a society.

Thus, anthropology and psychoanalysis meet at this crossroads in order to teach us that language obeys the law of desire and always comes to us from elsewhere (whence its character of echo, of quotation, through which variance manifests itself) and to teach us also that, inversely, desire obeys the law of language. It then becomes evident that to stop at the level of intention in accounting for the poetic is to limit oneself to grasping merely the visible part of the iceberg.

Starting on the one hand with the concepts of desire, of giving and of exchanging as they are proposed by the disciplines we have just examined, and on the other hand with the concept of variance as I have tried to define it from the point of view of the poetics of language, a new field of inquiry opens up to us, intact: that of poetic economy, which I intend merely to label here since it is not a part of my present subject.

Since desire and language are built into one another, they both "speak" *for* and *in place of* each other. This explains their common characteristics of reduplication and reversal and the play inherent in them. This play of language and desire founds language on the poetic. This thesis rejoins that of Jean-Jacques Rousseau who writes in the *Essay on the Origin of Language*: "figurative language was the first to be born"; and "at first people spoke only poetically," which I would be tempted to reformulate in the following manner: language exists because poetry exists, not the reverse.

As echo, the poetic nature of language may be defined by two necessary and sufficient characteristics: displacement and repetition. These are constituent characteristics of all anthropological identity (individual or collective) since, without them, no identification is possible. Repetition and displacement designate both the same and the other within the one. Psychoanalysis, for example, has taught us to formulate this as follows: The son wants to be *the same* as the father, but perceiving himself to be different from him, he experiences himself as *other*. By desiring to repeat the father, that is to put himself in his father's place, he displaces him; and conversely, by displacing him, or setting him aside, he wants to repeat him. But, to account for the identity of a subject, it does not suffice to situate him on a diachronic or historical plane (in his relationship with the father). We must also situate him on a synchronic axis, in the relationship that "each one" has with his "like." According to this second axis, a second form of repetition and displacement manifests itself in the subject: in the *other*, "I" sees the *same* as himself ... and someone else besides him. Without going into greater detail let us simply note that it is possible to superimpose the concepts of time and space upon those of repetition and displacement to account for the variance within the subject, both being doubly inscribed therein.

The same may be said of the echo, a synonym for the variance within language. In fact it is the same spatio-temporal axes which are found in the form of paradigm or syntagm thus giving the echo its dual character of repetition and displacement.

It would be false to think that displacement is situated in relation to the place of origin of a word (or a text), such as a dictionary definition being used as a point of departure for the meaning, from which the word would have deviated for the purpose of "poetic effect." Describing displacement in this fashion would once again permit the supposition that the intention of the interlocutor (poet or reader) accounts for something, that he wanted to give now a "poetic", now a "utilitarian" meaning to the words. If this were the case, all texts labelled "Poetry" would touch us "poetically." This is manifestly not the case. On the contrary, the possibility of displacement is found in the very nature of language, in the fact that language is "semantic," that is, in the vibration or movement that surrounds the words and that no dictionary will ever succeed in "rendering." The possibility of displacement is found in the play of meaning. But, let us not misunderstand what is happening. It is not a question of invoking any so-called mysteries of language and toppling into the aberrations of a mysticism inimical to science. It is solely a question of putting oneself on guard against a reductive rationality which would claim to explain displacement-within-language *by* something else. It is impossible to explain it *by* a history, either individual or collective (two modes of consciousness), precisely because it is intermingled with this history, because it *is* this history, that is to say, all that we can hope to know about it. Since this displacement is time in motion within language, it is no more satisfactory to explain it *by* the structures of metaphor and metonymy—which are obviously the elementary forms of displacement—because it is displacement itself which is at the basis of every structure.

The same is true of repetition; for repetition is a different mode of displacement. It is its musical aspect—its tempo and rhythm—which in traditional prosody takes on the ostensible form of rhyme.

Repetition and displacement are inversions of one another: repetition is a displacement of the *same*, and displacement is repetition of the *other*. But repetition is never exactly the *same*, nor displacement absolutely *other*. This is what makes language what it is: both progression and return of communication—exchange.

A rose is a rose is a rose. . . . An inspired formula which summarizes and illustrates the poeticity of language. At this crossroads of the "simplest" echo—in which paradoxically its dual nature may be discerned—poetry and language re-echo indefinitely.

Contesting an "author's" proprietary rights over his language; breaking down the barriers that separate "literary" from "ordinary" language; upsetting the relationship between language and poetry—such audacities are not without consequences with regard to critical examination of the linguistic material we will have chosen to call "literature." In other words (or in traditional terms—which can only be supported by dint of quotation marks), what will become of "criticism"? How will one situate "critical discourse" in relation to "literary discourse"?[2]

Let us state at the outset that by posing the question in this manner, it becomes a tactical or operational one, the validity of which will have to be contested as the operation progresses, *since,* in *principle,* it is the very validity of the distinction among different types of discourse that is being placed in question here.

In fact, if literary material rightfully extends to all linguistic signs, it is logical to think that every distinction between literary language, ordinary language, and critical language is also rightfully abolished because no inherent difference separates them essentially. The opposition between language and metalanguage would be obliterated thereby from the start. It would yield to a critical unfolding of signs stretching out infinitely and indefinitely, all in the same plane, without any priority being attributed to a particular one because, as we know, there is nothing to prevent any one of these signs from functioning, at any given moment in its career, as a quotation. Because— whatever it may be—it contains the variance which makes it double as an echo. That is its nature. It is useless, therefore, to wish at first to separate the various functions (literary, utilitarian, critical) according to so-called modes of discourse, given and accepted as such before any examination. To pose from the outset the duplex existence of a language and a metalan-

---

[2] Whoever launches into such audacities can scarcely claim exclusive rights to them. Others lead the attack on other fronts, on other levels. And if one had to look for precursors it would be well to direct one's attention toward those who practice the plastic arts.

guage is to indicate the priority and anteriority of the one over
the other, to presuppose the existence of a "first," simple language and a second language which sets itself apart from it.
The validity of the concept of metalanguage is operational
only, for it is evident that at a given moment it becomes necessary to differentiate types of discourse for the purpose of the
epistemological cause—but this "validity" will never be absolute
or permanent. Under these conditions, "literature" has no
rightful existence of its own; consequently, this term only has
meaning in the area (infinitely variable in its delimitation) defined by the conjunction of a particular reading and a particular writing. Critical reading is but an invention and an inventory
of literature. Both become obliterated, however, as soon as they
are constituted: their existence is sustained solely by their conjunction; that is, by the signs they share, put into common use
and in communication, in the course of that very communication.
Nothing else fixes or determines their existence or organization.

  "Literature" then does not distinguish itself from other systems of signs as a privileged mode of discourse, but *is a particular
manner of reading and deciphering signs*. What is literary is
not one text to the exclusion of another, but the texts that the
reader decides to qualify as such.

  If one accepts this thesis, one must of necessity conclude that
a certain conception of "literature"—the one that makes of
certain signs an aristocracy of discourse separated (by what
magical decision?) from the banality and vulgarity of "ordinary
language"—loses all validity, all foundation, on losing its
privileges. This "literature," a dumping ground for fine feelings,
a museum of belles lettres, has had its day. Now, signs, *all
signs*, are open to a new reading—necessarily fragmentary—
but liberated from the shackles of an arbitrary and sterilizing
"taste."

  The cutting or delimitation is effected therefore in an unworn,
unbroken mass, a wave of proliferating signs; a sort of unas-
sembled film which one might designate as the discourse of the
world; an ensemble, heap, accumulation of all the discourses, of
all the signs, of all the traces that no frontier, whether temporal

or spatial, historical or cultural, could hinder by its dotted line. Signs are a mass of all of history's messages, whose uniform and continuous murmuring or stridency would prevent a particular hearing from manifesting itself. In this Babel all meanings are equivalent: non-meaning prior to being cut off (as one speaks of cutting off debate in order to come to a decision); each time meaning is primed, then explodes. It is then that meaning sweeps through the decisive rent. Whether it be delicate or violent, spontaneous or constrained, the incision-decision passes through the global mass of signs, divides them, fragments them, shatters them. From this surgery a meaning bursts forth. This meaning is none other than the very break which opens the sluice gates. A trickle or torrent which does not stop signifying.

In this surge of meaning, everything breaks up at once because everything is disposed of. Everything is disposed of because everything is breaking up.

Meaning is organized within non-meaning; it does not take its place. It neither covers over nor obliterates it. It designates and "presents" it. Therefore, since non-meaning does not efface itself (politely) before meaning, we cannot claim that the latter is ever *established*. Since it cuts, disposes, executes, meaning is never legitimate. That is why it is advisable to denounce it rather than submit to it. But, since that is its inevitable role, we might as well see it played out to the end. Let that tyranny be a terror, that violence a subversion! Then, if meaning *commands* subversion (as one says of a geographical point that it commands a strategic place, that it both forbids and gives access at the same time), if meaning disposes of (and therefore also demands) subversion, then meaning maintains subversion in its revolutionary virulence, its acid intransigence. In this way it takes part in its own subversion. (Such a step alone allows one to avoid relapsing into the quietude of positivism, into the indolence and content of the notion that "everything has been said" —with respect to meaning.)

But one could just as well revise the proposition which has just been advanced and state that subversion *commands* meaning. It is through subversion that meaning can arise. Subversion *calls forth* a meaning, but by drawing the latter to itself, the former contaminates and subverts it. Thus, the meaning is always disappointed. And disappointing. It only manifests itself as loss, as flight: to attempt to arrest it is to allow it to escape; but neither does releasing it allow us to grasp it.

Where and when is meaning? On this side of us in a past of which our memory would be the recapitulation? Beyond, in a future ready to be grasped, in a dawn "to be lived"? Evidently not, for such a past or such a future could only be built upon a fixed, solid present, which is precisely what is lacking. It "is" this lack: the very subversion which undermines presence. Thus in the very process of "presenting" itself, it obliterates itself.

This is a mechanism comparable on all points to the cinematographic process: at what moment in a film is the meaning localized? 1) On the film, before its projection? Its meaning would then be in awaiting the forthcoming projection. 2) On the film after the projection? Its meaning would then be in the recollection of the projection. 3) During the projection? But then, in what sequence, in what image? In choosing one—to fix on it the meaning of the film—we evidently contradict its cinematographic nature by depriving it of its movement. No one of these three hypotheses is satisfactory, since the meaning can never be localized. (It is an error to look for meaning *within* movement itself, for movement is only the condition of its possibility.)

Whether it be past or present, the meaning remains a false meaning; we are setting out on a closed road. We are therefore living in the error (and the wandering) of deciphering signs—their "presence" constituting the very blind spot, the subversive moment par excellence, from which is wrought the subversion, or rather the reversal of the motion of time, whereby "past" and "future" topple over one another. What is there to conclude if not that as a result of these reductions, meaning has lost even its operational value: it is impossible to appeal to it even as the "moment" of subversion. Concurrently and/or in parallel fashion, temporality (which is the other side of the coin, so to speak) also loses all operational value; it is impossible to appeal to it as the "meaning" of subversion.

As for this last term, it is impossible to believe that it is the only one to magically retain a positive value—keystone of the whole edifice. Having played its role (subversion of meaning, subversion of temporality) it no longer supports anything, not even negation. It affects its own obliteration, for want of support by any complement whatever—except, as a last resort, by attributing to itself its own complement: the subversion of subversion.

After this obligatory detour, putting us on guard against the possibility of founding meaning, we should return to the initial question and ask ourselves under what conditions and at what price the reading-writing of signs takes place? Since its only viable status is as subversion, its function can only be a terrorizing one: it consists of setting fire to the powder, of activating the flames—of burning, consuming meaning. By this act, the reading-writing process makes manifest the impossibility of meaning. But let us not go so far as to believe, by trusting in the preceding incendiary metaphors, that our hidden or avowed concern is for purification. On an altogether different level, changing the act but nonetheless allowing it to keep the same role, I could just as well have said that the reading-writing process consists of stirring up shit. It all comes down to the same thing: fire and shit; a childish, childhood game—*but without innocence* as psychoanalysis teaches. It is neither pure nor impure; and yet joyful!

We would be allowing ourselves to be taken in by appearances if we believed that this game is synonymous with irresponsibility. This game is neither completely free nor completely gratuitous, because we are *implicated* in it: we are that very matter and the subjects who stir it up. Our shit is our history—it is, as we say, our business; it is also we who make it. Conversely, our history is our undoing; literally, it decomposes us. Like death. It *is* our death. We are, therefore, the history of our matter at the same time as the matter of our history. We make and unmake ourselves at one and the same time. Without end or beginning. For what is "made" at one end is unmade at the other—just like a loop of film.

Our history is in all its acceptations organic. It digests us and we digest it: it consists in absorbing the signs, which, in turn absorb us; it is the nourishing and fecal matter of the signs that we consume and secrete. That is how the *expenditure* of our energy may be summarized. The chemistry of our history corresponds to the economy of our discourse. A paradoxical circuit through which we both communicate with and escape from ourselves.

But, the consuming process inevitably remains selective, never total. Shit and ashes are matter. Consequently, discourse is reborn from its ashes, fertilized and nourished precisely by this waste of which it is both the product and producer. The *natural* cycle unfolds, by means of which the "leavings" are retrieved as fertilizer, then consumed anew ... but in another form. In the economy of signs, the ruin of discourse remains the condition of its possibility. It is from this failure that the threads of communication are drawn and woven. It is within this break in discourse that history is played out. Or in the break in time that discourse is played out. Historical communication, that is to say discourse in its diachronic aspect, is made up of the entirety of signs produced in a given era. The function of these signs is obviously for the use of the group which produces them. But, if they lose their *meaning* in the process of being used, doubtless this erosion does not affect their *signification* (perhaps, on the contrary, even emphasizing it?) for the "epochs" that follow. Thus history would be manufactured through the exchange of signs, whence its play: The inevitable floating of discourse and its ambiguities, essential dislocation between the echo and the voice, between reading and writing, question and answer—interchangeable but never simultaneously in the same place. This dislocation is a function of the relationship between, on the one hand, the signifying and the signified, on the other, the words and the things which prevail at a given time. Whence the inevitable misunderstandings, the perpetual refocusing, the succession of erasures, amendments, and corrections, of regrets from one age to another.

We cannot therefore make of history an (objective) category of thought, but merely a condition. Like literature, history is constructed: a bottomless text with inexhaustible combinations,[3] of which only a part is utilized, consumed by each "epoch".

In effect that which is consumed—burned, evacuated, sacrificed—is neither arbitrary nor indifferent nor indefinite. Since all these signs could not be consumed at the same time in a given culture and "epoch", we must seek in the process of the selection of signs, in the choice of priorities, in the modes and focal points of the consuming process, the rules of historical play of the "epoch" and culture in question. Their elaboration constitutes the area within which history is invented and determined.

Thus, history and literature have no existence in and of themselves. It is we who constitute them as the object of our understanding. And this object, the fruit of our invention, constitutes us as subjects—being both acting and acted upon, dominating and dominated.

The "meaning of history" (and of literature) is therefore only a myth to which we have clung—perhaps out of our weakness and cowardice or of some visceral desire to believe that life has a foundation that could justify it, out of some obscure need to orient ourselves and thereby attempt to protect ourselves from what our society calls madness.

*Translated from the French*
*by A. James Arnold*

---

[3] Witness the dictionaries, commentaries, translations, biographies, the staging and the questions that science asks itself, all of which require reading and deciphering. which need to be reformulated periodically in order to remain intelligible.

### jonathan culler

# Towards a Theory of Non-Genre Literature

> *There is no question . . . of establishing a theory, a pre-existing mold into which to pour the books of the future. Each novelist, each novel must invent its own form. No recipe can replace this continual reflection.*
>
> ALAIN ROBBE-GRILLET
> *FOR A NEW NOVEL*

If a computer were programmed to print random sequences of English sentences, a study of the texts thus produced would be very instructive. As one asked, repeatedly, "How can I make sense of this text?" one would become aware of the particular appropriateness of this question, for reading under these conditions is a process of making or producing sense by applying to the text a variety of hypotheses, contexts, and codes. Whether or not a text makes sense depends on the possibility of reading it as an instance of one of the types of intelligibility one has learned to look for. "Sense" is not a unitary category: what makes sense as a haiku would not make sense as instructions for a cake-mix. Hence, reading these computer texts would be a process of trial and error, of postulating various functions to see what will suffice.

Some of the most important expectations and requirements for intelligibility are enshrined in the various genres. A genre, one might say, is a set of expectations, a set of instructions about the type of coherence one is to look for and the ways in which sequences are to be read. This definition is quite simply illustrated if one takes a piece of journalistic prose and sets it down on a page as a lyric poem.

Yesterday on Route Seven
A car
Travelling at sixty miles per hour rammed
a sycamore
Its four occupants were
Killed.

The *fait divers* has become exemplary tragedy. "Yesterday" takes on a completely different force. Referring now to the set of possible yesterdays, it suggests a frequent, almost random event. One is likely to give new weight to the wilfulness of "rammed"—the car is the only active, animate force—and to the passivity of "its occupants", defined in relation to their automobile. The lack of detail and explanation connotes a certain absurdity, and the neutral, reportorial style will be read as restraint and resignation. This is clearly different from the way in which one interprets journalistic prose, and these differences can be explained only by reference to a set of expectations with which one approaches lyric poetry: that it is atemporal (hence the new force of "yesterday"), that it should cohere at a symbolic level (hence the re-interpretation of "rammed" and "its occupants"), that it is complete in itself (hence the significance of the absence of explanation), that it expresses an attitude (hence the interest in tone as deliberate posture). Our set of expectations about lyric poetry—our notion of lyric poetry as a genre—leads us to look for these particular types of intelligibility.

There is, of course, an alternative view of genres: that they are simply taxonomic categories in which we place works that share certain features. Since every work has properties, every work, perforce, could be placed in some genre. If a text seems not to fit, this means only that a new category must be postulated. Thus, *non-genre literature* would be an inadmissible concept, or if it were to be admitted, would designate only a residue.

This view of genres seems singularly unhelpful. To treat them as taxonomic classes is to obscure their function as norms in the process of reading. If we begin with the assumption that every work must be accounted for in a literary taxonomy, then our taxonomic classes become artifices of description. But taxonomies must be motivated, and if one literary classification is better than another it is because its genres are, in some sense, natural classes whose reality is grounded in the expectations and procedures of readers. Moreover —and this is particularly crucial for the study of contemporary literature—this approach would make it difficult to account for the importance of those seminal and disquieting works which, falling outside of established genres, would be treated as a residue. As Philippe Sollers, one of the leading theorists and practitioners of this "residual" literature, writes:

> Perhaps the most striking feature of modern literature is the appearance of a new monolithic, comprehensive mode of writing, in which the distinctions among genres, which have been completely abandoned, give way to what are admittedly "books", but books for which, we might say, no method of reading has yet been worked out.

What one requires is a theory which distinguishes between the *readable* and the *unreadable* and assigns an important place to, and explains the significance of, these works which resist our reading: works like Lautréamont's *Les Chants de Maldoror*, Mallarmé's "Un coup de dès", Joyce's *Finnegans Wake*, Raymond Roussel's *Locus Solus* and *Impressions d'Afrique*, Robbe-Grillet's *Instantanées*, Sollers' *Drame* and *Nombres*. This theory, which after Julia Kristeva one might call *théorie du texte*, grows out of what is most radical and interesting in contemporary French literary theory and practice. But I say "grows out of" advisedly, for the members of the *Tel Quel Group*[1] might not care to recognize themselves in the apolitical reflections that follow.

A theory is defined by the questions it asks, and the question

[1] *Tel Quel* is the leading avant-garde review in Paris today. Those who publish in that review are known as the *Tel Quel Group;* their work, both from a theoretical and practical point of view, is extremely disruptive in relation to traditional thought and literature. (Editor's note)

that founds this theory is, "why are our most crucial and tantalizing experiences of literature located at the interstices of genres, in this region of *non-genre literature?* The answer might be found in Wallace Stevens:

> The poem must resist the intelligence
> Almost successfully.

The essence of literature is not representation, not a communicative transparency, but an opacity, a resistance to recuperation which exercises sensibility and intelligence. Just as we would stop playing games if we could master them completely, so our interest in literature depends on what Geoffrey Hartman calls "the differential relation of form to consciousness", the tension between writing and reading. The concept of *text* has been developed to focus attention on literature as a surface. Jacques Derrida has brilliantly exposed what he calls the phonocentrism of Western culture—the assumption that the written word is simply a record of the spoken word and hence represents a communicative intention. But we know, at least since Mallarmé, that this *"métaphysique de la présence"* is ill-suited to literature, which inevitably involves an absence, whether that of emotion recollected in tranquility and evoked by the poem as an absence, or that of *"l'idée même et suave, l'*absente *de tous bouquets."* Spoken language might refer us to a communicative presence, but written language involves an irreducible *différance* (spelled with an "a" to highlight a difference perceptible only within the written language and to emphasize the pun: difference, deferment). The written word is an object in its own right; it is different from meanings which it defers and which cannot be grasped except by other signs that we place in the "empty" space of the *signified.* The text is a region in which characters are placed in relation to one another and inaugurate "a play of meaning". The job of literary theory is to specify the forms of this game: the procedures used to defer meaning, and the procedures of recuperation.

One might say that the attitude which determines contemporary literature is a fascination with the power of words to create thought. When linguists present us with examples of unacceptable sentences, the immediate reaction of the literary sensibility is to imagine contexts in which these could have a meaning. Those who note this astounding recuperative ability of the mind are likely to ask what, if any, are its limits. The writer, thus, hovers on the edge of highly-patterned gibberish, trying to determine exactly where that border lies. Robbe-Grillet has admitted in an interview: "I grant you that *Dans le labyrinthe* can, in fact, be recuperated. If I thought that it could not, I would not continue to write. I would have attained my goal." And of course he is right: although the philosophical acrobatics of recuperation—the *chosistes* versus the subjectivists—are highly amusing, his novels are recuperable.

For more successful examples of resistance one must look elsewhere, for if the essential function of a genre is maintained, radical changes of convention can take place within it without its texts becoming *unreadable*. One has only to think of the varieties of realism that give the novel a history. The novel itself is not called into question by a change from social to psychological realism. As long as one can take the text as about someone and his experience of the world, one can accept the most bizarre alterations of technique. Thus the move from *Portrait of the Artist* to *Ulysses* is easily assimilated, but the shift from *Ulysses* to *Finnegans Wake* takes us outside the genre. *Finnegans Wake* is probably not recuperable—or only for some future audience who might read it as a realism of the process of writing. It cannot be read as a novel but must be read at a metaliterary level: the level at which the acts of reading and writing are posed as problematic.

There are, of course, an increasing number of works which must be read at this level. As Sollers writes, "Today the essential problems are not those of author and work, but those of *writing* and *reading* [*écriture/lecture*]." *Non-genre literature* avoids established relations between *écriture*—production of a surface—and *lecture*—production of sense—and hence, for the reader, is essentially *about* the ways in which he attempts to create order.

*Ecriture* uses a variety of procedures, some of which are mechanical or aleatory. Today we find, writes Julia Kristeva, "literature has reached that maturity in which it can write itself like an automaton and no longer simply 'represent' like a mirror." One might cite the procedures developed by Pataphysicians for altering, rewriting, texts; the mechanical process of description in Claude Ollier's "Panoramic description of a modern neighborhood"; or the procedures that structure Sollers' *Nombres*, altering personal pronouns, ordering words according to a sequence of vowels, fragmenting the discourse—all in ways that suggest an original text and force the reader to grope toward it but finally frustrate his efforts. As Julia Kristeva explains:

> It is because the condensed sequences of *Nombres* do not represent anything to the listener trying to grasp a communicated meaning, because it is impossible to retain the information they proffer, that they awaken the infinite memory of a whole repertory of meaning.

The recourse to mechanical procedures plays two roles: it creates pattern but prevents this pattern from manifesting, directly, a human intentionality. The machine produces a structure but significance is the product of the reader.

Games are another important technique. The writer sets himself the problem of organizing a group of elements selected in some random or irrelevant way. There is, for example, the surrealist game, *l'un dans l'autre*, in which two objects are chosen independently and one must then be described in terms of the other: describe a sewing machine as if it were a sugar cube. This game derives, of course, from the theory that the force and interest of a metaphor is proportional to the distance that separates its two terms. The goal is to investigate whether any materials are so refractory as to resist intelligibility; the result is an explicit exercise of the power of language to create thought.

More interesting and radical are the games developed by Raymond Roussel. Take a sentence, for example, *la peau verdâtre de la prune un peu mûre*, and change one letter to produce *la peau verdâtre de la brune un peu mûre*. Then invent incidents to get you, as if were, from "p" to "b". Or alternatively, take a line of verse, title of a book, etc. and read it as a series of puns: *Napoléon premier est empereur* yields *Nappe olé ombre miettes hampre air heure*, providing elements which must be organized in some way.[2] *Locus Solus*, that enigmatic monument, is really the ultimate game of this sort. It is the story of machines invented to create a world which is itself created by these mechanical linguistic procedures. Thus, the machine that picks up teeth and deposits them in a mosaic is itself produced by punning on *demoiselle à prétendants* to give *demoiselle* (in the sense of "paviour's rammer" or "paving beetle") *à reître en dents*. The work is, of course, really nothing more than a fantastic exercise in the response of imagination to language. As one of Roussel's admirers declares, "Roussel has nothing to say, and he said it badly."[3] We cannot, then, read *Locus Solus* as a novel; it is rather a *text* in a language which sends us nowhere: "a language which says only itself," as Michel Foucault points out in his study of Roussel, and which mocks us in our attempts at recuperation. Only a theory of *non-genre literature* could explain the curious fact that we take such works to be significant.

Another mocking voice is that of Lautréamont. His procedures belong to a slightly different category, although kinship with Roussel becomes apparent at a theoretical level. In Roussel, one might say, language is finally closed, incestuous, self-referential. In Lautréamont the same end is reached but by a different route. By overstating his claims about the way his language impinges upon and affects the world, Lautréamont provokes in the reader a counter-reaction which leads him to emphasize the *clôture* and artificiality of this sequence of marks on the page. The opening line of *Maldoror*, the wish that the reader may become "as ferocious as what he is reading," forces the reader to grapple, whether ferociously or not, with an egregious category mistake, and problems are only compounded when he reads, "I shall establish in a few lines how Maldoror was good during his early years, when he lived happily. There, that's

[2] An attempt to render the first example in English would give: "The wrinkled skin of the old *pear*" and "The wrinkled skin of the old *bear*." (Editor's note. The reader can work out the second example.)

[3] Rayner Heppenstall, *Raymond Roussel* (London, 1966), p. 87.

done." An unaccustomed shock for the reader of novels. In a sense, of course, the narrator is right. By telling us he will establish a particular fact he does establish it. But if we grant him this right, we must agree to read his verbs as performatives, accomplishing textual actions rather than reporting others, and we must abandon all hope of distinguishing between the "I" and "he". In short, we must read the book as an act of what Roland Barthes calls "the consciousness of the unreality of language" and violate the implicit contract between author and reader that forms the basis of the novel as a genre.

Of course we do continue to read Lautréamont, despite these problems. And that is perhaps what is most fascinating: the astonishing human capacity to recuperate the deviant, to invent new conventions and functions so as to overcome that which resists our efforts. These texts which fall at the interstices of genres enable us to read ourselves in the limits of our understanding. "We are nothing more than this movement, nocturnal and diurnal, of the readable and the unreadable, in us, outside of us," says Philippe Sollers. Our most profound experiences may be those of frustration. That is why it would be interesting to study the random texts produced by a computer and why *non-genre literature* is not just a residue but central to the contemporary experience of literature.

Many of the most interesting French writers, including those who, like Butor and Robbe-Grillet, previously wrote "novels", seem recently to have joined Sollers and the *Tel Quel Group* in the production of texts destined to bear out Maurice Blanchot's predictions about *Le Livre à Venir* and to show the justice of his observation that "when one encounters a novel written according to all the rules of the past historic tense and third person narration, one has not, of course, encountered 'literature'."[4]

---

[4] Maurice Blanchot, *Le Livre à Venir* (Paris, 1959), p. 254.

the scriptive imagination. It is this intense, obsessive multiplication that Sollers specifically underlines:

> *But if he tried to write.... And if he tried to read, even*
> *the simplest passages would soon stand out, open out, as*
> *if possessed of some extra-ordinary power: "The sky is*
> *blue", for example, would be metamorphosed into images,*
> *memories, journeys or sensations of multiplied transversal*
> *presences; everything began to move, to merge into every-*
> *thing else, to follow everything else in rapid succession,*
> it made him feel dizzy, submerging him, as if the flattest
> form was at the same time the deepest, where he could get
> lost, *but also see, watch the functioning of his own organism.*

Lastly, each one of the obsessive features, image-promoters,
will be written anew (establishing an analogical alignment of
images) every time one of the images it has elicited becomes the
reason for an additional paragraph. Its initial potential is thereby
multiplied. In order to keep the exposition within reasonable
compass, we shall leave aside the developments themselves, and
concentrate instead, for purposes of schematization, on the
starting point of one of the innumerable strings of associations:

> Or rather they suggest, perhaps, scenes half sketched, and
> immediately interrupted, places just indicated by a *colored*
> *detail, but by that very color related to each other*, places
> *connected by an invisible thread.*

II.  GAUGING THE LINES
> What should I take as a *gauge?* the feel of the linen, the
> placing of the lights, the smell of the different pillows, the
> colors of the wallpaper.

Here the color red is a privileged thread. It appears four times
in the opening lines (quoted earlier) of the text. We find it
again on page 10:

> Mine is the only room with a light on—the *red* lamp

but also page 13:

> The light *reddened* by the lampshade

page 16:

> *red* Bangal flares

a little farther on, page 19:

> the sky *reddened* by the lights of the town

and quite regularly throughout the rest of the book.

One problem remains to be solved, however. If the designation of a written detail (here, red) immediately starts a prodigious series of images with red objects as their common denominator, how is one particular image, rather than another, actuallly selected? Limiting our examination to the first four paragraphs of the book, we find that the phenomena of selection may be reduced to three types:

a) Highlighted by the description, the factor red goes right to work. With the brief evocation of the woman left for the time being in suspense, it is the *female body* (the face) that selects from the series of possibilities of red. The lips thus chosen attain written status in the same evocatory movement. Their origin is so obvious that the qualification red is left out, which would here have resulted in a manner of pleonasm. The "exorbitant" power of the color red is thus reinforced, and starts another, more intense series, from which the diamond shape and the red traffic light are soon extracted according to more complex but nonetheless distinct criteria.

b) The idea that red is the common denominator of the images it promotes may be formulated as follows: *images line up around it*. The red light at the intersection is therefore selected not only by the street evoked by the descriptive trajectory (that is the previous phenomenon), but by analogy with the serial phenomenon itself. The cars, *like the images*, "regroup in three *lanes* at the red light." Phonetically a relative of *line*, the word *lane*

underscores this deliberately [in the French: *filière* and *fil*—
Trans. note]. It is a case of the fiction providing an *allegory* of
the function that is producing it.

c) By orienting the only physical detail specified here, the
lips, the red of the woman's dress fashions her face and becomes,
as it were, her *sign*. The woman is specifically introduced as "the
woman in red". The spatial (the conversation) and emotional
("by smiling") union that takes place between the man and
the woman entails a uniting of their *signs*. (It is therefore not
a matter of indifference whether the word is pronounced.) It is
for its quality as a masculine emblem that the diamond shape
[the red sign that hangs outside all tobacco stores in France—
Trans. note] is chosen from the series of red objects. That
selection again reinforces the initial choice made by the description of the street [the tobacco sign hangs from the store-
front, i.e. in the street—Trans. note]. And the appropriateness
of that sign is such that it elicits the following image (the appearance, as if by *magic*, of the cigarette) which strengthens
and reconfirms it:

> He makes a gesture with his left hand, in which he is
> holding a cigarette.

That confirmation of the uniting of their signs, and consequently of the partners themselves, engenders a growing *intimacy*. The smile, a simple mark of politeness, perhaps, turns
into inextinguishable laughter:

> the woman throws her head back .... bursting with laughter,
> bends suddenly forward.

III. GENERAL REGULATORY MECHANISMS

The selection of the scriptive material is consequently the
result of two complementary mechanisms. While the richness of
the analogical material never ceases to increase, specific local
requirements relentlessly select the image with the strongest
analogical determination.

What happens then is that, as the text progresses, both the

image proposals and the specific determinants increase in such proportions that the composition would soon be swamped by the ensuing disorder if it were not subjected to certain general regulatory mechanisms established at the level of the text as a whole. Here are two examples:

*La Peau de chagrin:* "I chose a notebook; I divided it into two parts." This strictly material measure metes out the physical space allotted the writing for its development, and regulates the writing itself. Each written sentence builds its unity word by word, controls its respiration by an intuition of its prescribed length, is inscribed inside a hollow sentence-frame, complies with the requirements of its own rhythm. This apprehension of its length (and of its own self as it were prior to itself) regularly excludes from the sentence, whatever its length and complexity, a whole series of incidents. And the prior choice of a volume engenders a similar phenomenon, but scaled to the size of the book. Just as each group of words is located in relation to the capital at the beginning and the period at the end, so each page, here, and each paragraph, has its place determined with reference to the first page and the last, yet to come, but already assigned by the thickness of the notebook. A multitude of incidents (all the continuously proliferating crossroads) are consequently eliminated. And, limited, the paper's surface becomes a precious space with an economy of its own. There is an immediate play between two inversely proportional dimensions, the analogical material endlessly accumulating, and the blank page, *"peau de chagrin"*, inexorably shrinking to an end. The ceaseless increase of the selective power accruing to the paper counterbalances the ever-expanding proliferation of analogical material. Note, for instance, at the end of the first part, page 51:

(I am near the end of the page, I must finish soon with a *short*, obvious *sentence*).

*One night, one day:* "I chose a notebook; I divided it into two parts." This essential division of the book has another motive. An assertion of the rights of writing, obviously, and a concrete regulation, but also a general regulation by reason of

the stringent "temporal" organization it institutes. The first
part of the book corresponds to the Night; it begins:

> The sky above the long, gleaming avenues is *dark blue*.
> Later on, I shall go out. I shall walk in the direction of
> the sun until it finally disappears

and ends, page 51, with the words:

> It is five o'clock in the morning.

The second part marks the Day, from the first line page 52:

> Open, then shut, they should have seen the close whiteness
> of the pillows that my cheek rubs against *as I wake*

to the last, page 96:

> Yet, in the evening of this day, when the air is still warm . . .

Nevertheless, the point here is certainly not to offer an ordinary
succession of events occurring during the course of an astro-
nomical day. A more attentive reading in fact reveals that *Night
and Day do not follow each other immediately*. Page 7 indicates
that it is an *Autumn* Night:

> But look again at the street and its *yellowing* trees,

and page 53 clearly implies that it is a *Spring* (or Summer) Day:

> the foliage of the plane-trees which form a kind of long,
> *dark green* tunnel.

The Night selects all the images evoked in the first part, the
Day in the second, as overtones of each of their hours (e.g. the
dinner hour) according to very strict regulations:

> It would be forty days and forty nights (a single day, a

single night).

The laws of the universe thus obtained are rather more complex. There, everything is in a state of continuous relationship; everything is implicated in a fabric of analogies. Insofar as it is based on the idea of an essential autonomy, i.e. an independence with regard to the continuity of the analogical fabric, the classic notion of the fictional character no longer applies. Everything that might imply it (first and last names: otherwise they would be subject to strange metamorphoses) is missing. There are nothing but generic evocations (man, woman, child), and personal pronouns (he, she, it).

If we insist on having characters, then, we shall have to call them pronominal. This displacement is by no means inconsequential. The general term "woman", for instance, is soon revealed to be the common denominator of a certain number of women, so that here and there a brief description is required to choose from the various possible feminine evocations. The pronoun *she* accentuates the phenomenon by becoming, through its frequent indetermination, a focus of multiple evocations, a locus of exchange allowing the writer to begin talking about one woman and end up with another, a *grammatical creation* of this analogical continuity. Take for instance the following paragraph:

> ... since there are no more air battles ( ... ) or air-raids
> ... : since the sirens are now silent (he sees again the
> *woman* sitting on the grass, wrapped in a *red eiderdown*).
> A miracle, that's what it was, a great comfortable catastrophe ... the last carefully selected species, the survivors,
> among whom, of course, he counts himself ... reading on,
> as the room grows gradually darker; and he gets up to
> *switch on the crystal chandelier*. It has stopped raining,
> *the sun is shining.* She puts on her mac and her boots ...
> (I can see her profile, her unruly brown hair, her *red
> jacket* ...).

The transition from one paragraph to the other is effected by analogy. The chandelier pierces shadows as the sun does clouds. The pronoun *she* is indeterminate. Since no other woman has appeared during the several preceding pages, grammatically *she* can only be referring to that victim of an air raid, several years prior to the last scene, several years after the scene of the boy reading. That is naturally impossible: it must therefore be another woman, but one who has inherited, from that grammatical relation, the *red* jacket. The groups *man-he-him* and *child-he-him* are the object of analogous associations that play, for instance, on the various periods of childhood.

But what about *I*? Itself annexed by the scriptive world, it could not possibly refer to some "antecedent" from the everyday world, notably the author. Confronted with the pronominal characters—*objects*, it represents a sort of pronominal character —*subject*. It is the law of writing incarnate. As such, it is in essential contact with the other pronouns and objects. The book successively proposes several allegories of that communication. On page 34, "I" 's face becomes "hers" through, appropriately enough, a resemblance between their eyes. On page 35:

> But the inaccessible spectator, who witnessed the drama for a few moments, could, if not intervene, *experience the thoughts and feelings of the victim.*

On page 35 as well, this paragraph with a Borgesian cast:

> Similarly, in the cinema, I find myself at once among the characters before me on the screen ... I became that wall. A crack in that wall. I was that leaf-strewn path; that stretch of stagnant water by which an invading army passed. I was the queen's comb; the ship's flag.

Or again, page 42:

> listening to a night that became the only night, to a bedroom that opened on to all bedrooms, to a body, mine, that became every body. Eyes closed in the dark, there is, at the other side of the room, that body, also dressed, and im-

agined far from here, moving through the town, standing against yet another landscape seen again ...

## IV. THE INTERSTITIAL SPACE
As if he wished to persist in the *space between*, beyond the permitted limits.

But the scriptive process by which an analogical universe is engendered, is not limited to being embodied by the pronoun "I". It also secretes *its own ideology* which is intuitively revealed whenever some privileged circumstance appears.

This scriptive universe naturally eludes the rather summary laws of the Euclidian one. Its continuity, for instance, provides for instantaneous displacements in time and space, which notions are thereby simultaneously recognized and abolished. Any one thing is always, in some way, already another thing, a multitude of other things. A sort of permanent ubiquity characterizes each of the elements of this universe. Analogy blurs essences. A chandelier, in our everyday world, is in no wise the sun; but, in the scriptive world, after a fashion, it is.

A score of images, where what we should have to call an almost successful ubiquity exercises its sway, signal that equation. For instance, the sheet of paper observed in transparency (the back is *seen* from the front), the mirror, the eye being observed, and that ideal arrangement of the material space where writing is at work:

> From this balcony, opening the two doors of the French windows out towards me, I can also see into my room through the net curtains. Better still, by going out through another room in the flat, which, on the fifth floor, is rounded at the corner and thus provides a view of both the avenue and the little dark street, I could circle the building on the outside and return to my starting-point.

Thus here not only is it possible, and with a minimum of movement, to contemplate the *outside* (the avenue *and* the dark, narrow street), but also the *inside*, the room. *Better still* (this value judgment should not be ignored), it is likewise *almost possible*—for this, I think, is the meaning of the circular movement—to come face to face with oneself, as if on either side of a mirror. Here is effect we might recall A. Lichnerowicz's statement, quoted by Sollers in *L'Intermédiaire:*

> One of the questions we may ask concerning the universe, in topological terms, is precisely whether or not it may be oriented. In practice, that means that, in the case of a negative answer, by making a circular trip in the universe, and going all the way round, you would return to your point of departure, not identical to yourself, but *symmetrical* to what you were at the start.

These privileged images bring us nearer to the critical juncture of Sollers' novel—

> the central image( . . . ), commanding, unseen, everything else: a proximity, an unexampled freedom, the narration . . .

They converge toward the mystics' supreme point, where contraries cease to be perceived contradictorily, the pivotal point where opposites cancel out:

> Outside and inside, night and day; or rather, at the *pivotal point*, outside and night, inside and day: neither one nor the other; both at once.

[p. 85, where we have corrected Mr. Smith's mistaken translation of *charnière*: hinge, pivot, by "ossuary": *charnier*—Trans. note.]

Here, then, is the ultimate reason for *The Park*'s being constructed according to the two sides of Day and Night. Whenever one side is "enclosed" within the other, we shall have come closest to the essential. For instance the cinema—Day in Night —which generates the mystical paragraph just quoted. For instance the opening of the closet—Night in Day—which induces the unforgettable experience:

I shut the green velvet curtains. I open the closet; and *it* happens. At the bottom of the darkness and the clothes a cyclic perspective *at last* unfolds. Gravitating in the void which has just opened on the absolute other-side: what happened—the confused, century-old mass; a mass murmuring louder and louder.

Let's return, then, one last time, since we're not too far from the center of the book, to the statement: "I chose a notebook; I divided it into two parts." The division it underlines exactly determines the ideal place where the transmutation occurs that transcends, at their point of junction, both Night and Day. It is page 51, at the end of the first period of the book:

(I am near the end of the page, I must finish soon with a short, *obvious* sentence); the explosion comes at last, tearing at one side, at one arm; the breath stops in an inaudible cry (*nobody will have realized it;* there are two seconds left) and, closing his eyes,

a large blank, here, detaching from the first part:

It is five o'clock in the morning.

So it is at the precise instant when *Night* and *Day* most intimately merge—where the *World* (Autumn's *nocturnal* hour) and *Writing* (night's *morning* formula) unite, at this ideal center of the book enclosed on either side, but their forces joined, by the *World*:

The sky above the long, gleaming avenues is *dark blue* (first sentence)

and *Writing*:

The exercise-book with the orange cover, patiently filled, weighed down with regular handwriting and leading to this page, this sentence, this full stop, by the old pen frequently and mechanically dipped into the *blue-black* ink (last sentence)

(the sky borrowing its color from the ink)—that, between obverse and reverse, there occurs that supreme interstice around which the entire book *revolves*, without its ever being named: the exact instant of death.

*Translated from the French by Erica Freiberg*

*TRANSLATOR'S NOTE:* For the quotations from *The Park,* I have used A.M. Sheridan Smith's translation (Calder & Boyar, London, 1968), which, however, in order to retain the sense of Jean Ricardou's analysis and to respect the original French, I have had to modify slightly (for instance, Smith's translation of *"assister à son propre fonctionnement"* by: "aided by *(assisté par)* the functioning of his own organism", which should read: "watch the functioning...", etc.). In order not to distract the reader's attention, I have done so without comment except in one crucial instance ("ossuary" instead of "pivotal point" for *charnière*), where I felt it necessary to point out to the eventual reader of the English version of the novel that Ricardou has not taken any liberties with the original text in his quotations.

Incidentally, it is interesting to note the subliminal pun that appears in the translation: death, the occurrence suggested by the crucial, pivotal point, is implied but never explicitly mentioned by Sollers—except insofar as *"charnière"* (pivot) contains *"charnier"* (ossuary). So, actually, the mistranslation is only relative, as Smith thereby inadvertently makes the pun apparent, while making the main meaning disappear.

## jochen gerz
# Towards a Language
# of Doing

**1.**

Our language is closely tied to the evolution of western thought
and philosophy since Aristotle. It corresponds to this tradition
insofar as it is a means of introverting the contradictions of the
external world or, in other words, insofar as it represents the
demands of the external world on the individual.

Moreover it also corresponds to that tradition in making of
the external world a reflection of itself. That is to say that the
external world is such as it is "said" to be. In replacing it with
its own interpretation and in forwarding the interests of its own
interpretation with the individual, our language mechanically
assures the domination of representation over life.

**2.**

Our language assures this domination by division. It divides
life into "reality" and "idea". In creating a division between
the two, it sets itself up as an indispensable and unique medium,
and as it takes over the gap created between the individual and
external world by this division, little by little, it replaces almost
totally all direct and primary communication by the "representative" information of the medium, by its monologue. Insofar as the medium comes to represent the external world to the
point of replacing it, the individual becomes dependent on it
and is forced to abandon his rights to the world.

As long as "what is happening" only corresponds to "what
has always happened," and the increasingly autonomous representation weighs down on the present moment, our language
manages the incompatibility (in order to hide it) of the individual's wish to communicate with the external world and
of its own representative character which imposes what "should
be" the wish of the individual: to put up with the world.

Since humanist ideology, of which Aristotle was the true prophet, has taken the stage, our language, as far as the individual is concerned, has proved itself a vehicle of this ideology of dispossession and alienation.

### 3.

All searching for a new language which is viewed exclusively in terms of a search for a new poetical code can only be considered as a development of traditional thought and cannot escape being reproached for having deepened and enlarged the range of possibilities of the domination of life by representation. The visual poetry movement—which has never, properly speaking, been just a literary movement in the sense that it pursued or announced aims which could be related to academic or anti-academic positions of its time—has, for the first time perhaps, set itself up in opposition to more than a poetical code by putting into us auto-informative elements. It has tackled the whole "balance of power" as it is maintained and recreated in the language of our thought and consequently, in our society.

To the extent which the language feeds the individual's incomprehension of the external world of which he is part, (and yet to which he becomes a stranger), the visual poets claim to make the world live—not through something from "on high", or by representation (the abuse of the world becoming an object of interpolation), but by its own determination to understand and to decipher itself. Visual poetry, and fiction—the term is used in accordance with the "definition" given by Emmet Williams of concrete poetry ("concrete poetry is what concrete poets do")—conveys the evidence which is encompassed by the external world, and it does so to the extent that the individual and the external world form part of the same vision of life.

### 4.

The practice of a writing constantly publishing itself, a writing which at the same time has become its only content, led quite naturally to the discovery of innumerable elements of information outside the signal material of the alphabet—the photographic image, gestures far away from paper, every situation of lived life. On the condition that everything existing "speaks" through its own material existence, communication arises. For "visual writing" this signifies that it has a necessity outside of itself and "a real reflection in the external world" (Dick Higgins).

5.

In representing the demands of the external world, as it is and as it has always been, on the individual (and not vice versa), our language incorporates it into its interpretation of the external world. The individual becomes, instead of a holder of language, as we stated, language's object and as such a speechless part of the contradictory order established by it. Thus it cannot be a question of replacing this language by another "representative" code, which on its part would only intensify the transformation of life into speechlessness: each instant of time, everything without exception must be saved from its anonymity, from its wariness, by its own language, by its own will to be.

*Translated from the French*
*by Deliah Davin*

# richard kostelanetz

# Twenty-Five
# Fictional Hypotheses

*The key question to be asked now is how can intelligent writing (and the serious writer) survive an incipiently terminal situation? The hard truth is that we need not only to write literature that will be read again and again but to create conditions that will insure that such works be available and remembered.*

RICHARD KOSTELANETZ
"What Is To Be Done?"
*CHICAGO REVIEW* (1971)

I.) *Fiction* n. 1. a making up of imaginary happenings; feigning. 2. anything made up or imagined, as a statement, story, etc. 3. a) any literary work portraying imaginary characters and events. b) such works collectively; esp. novels and stories.—*Webster's New World Dictionary* (1966).

II.) *Fiction* 1. The action or product of fashioning or imitating —1784. 2. Feigning; deceit, dissimulation, pretence—1609. 3. a) The action of feigning or inventing imaginary existences, events, states of things, etc.—1605. b) that which is feigned or invented; invention as opposed to fact. c) A statement proceeding from mere invention; such statements collectively—1611. 4. Fictitious composition. Now usually prose novels and stories collectively, or the composition of such works—1599. *Oxford English Dictionary* (1933).

III.) There are no definite limits upon the extrinsic materials available to the teller of stories; the practical limits upon fictional possibility are intrinsic in the creative imagination and one's chosen medium.

IV.) As the stuff of fiction is invention, so fiction comes from the invention of stuff—this observation suggesting that writers so far have scarcely sampled all the possible ways of stuffing "fiction."

V.) Words need not be the building blocks of fiction, or sentences the glue, or paragraphs the frames, or human beings the "characters"; for realized fiction, no matter how unusual, cannot but create its own subject, its own style, its own "events," its own life.

VI.) The primary subject of the best printed literature has always been capabilities indigenous to the medium—effects that come from special language and/or the turning of pages; but just as neither pages nor prose are absolutely essential to fiction, so this mediumistic emphasis does not deny the possibility, or value, of extrinsic references.

VII.) Even the most innovative fictions embody at least *one* element of the classic literary art, whether that be heightened language, the semblance of narrative, credible detail, or developed characterizations; but it is highly unlikely, though not impossible, that a story containing all these elements will be unquestionably new.

VIII.) Perhaps the line will supercede the word, the page the sentence, the chapter the paragraph, and the binding the chapter, as the basic fictional units—or vice versa, the word the line, the sentence the page, etc.; but these changes in scale notwithstanding, the telling result of new fiction will be a synthetic and yet self-consistent world.

IX.) Fiction created for sequential printed pages is likely to emulate in form the dominant communications vehicles of the age—in our time, newspapers, film, television; yet the best literary art necessarily eschews contents already familiar to these new media.

X.) Fictions alone cannot change the world, though they are forever infiltrating, if not liberating, the imaginations of those who do and might; and though artists are clearly indebted to popular art, in the end the mass media (and much else) remain far more influenced by great art.

XI.) The consequential fictions have always touched upon

essential themes—history, nature, growth and decay, communication and relationship, reality and illusion, imagination, fate, etc.; but unfamiliar artifice often puts a surmountable block between such meanings and superficial or oblivious readers.

XII.) A passion for the medium itself and visions of its possible uses are by now the primary reasons for creating fictions; everything else, such as narrative, for instance, is inevitably secondary.

XIII.) The use of imposed constraints, as in traditional poetic forms, forces the creative imagination to resist the easy way, if not cliches as well, and encourages problem-solving and other processes of playfulness, in addition to challenging the reader to discern sense and significance in what at first seems inscrutable.

XIV.) Certain new works are so original that at first they scarcely resemble any "fiction" we know; but since only a philistine would dare dismiss an unfamiliar creation as "not-fiction," art once again forces us to review our standards of literary convention and esthetic appropriateness.

XV.) Formal advances in a particular art often come from adapting the ideas and procedures developed in another field; and sometimes out of this process of cross-fertilization blossoms not just a new step in the art but a true hybrid, in this case between literature and something else.

XVI.) Can it be that presenting a painter's work in chronological succession tells the story of his creative life—the fictions he wrought—so definitively that nothing more need be written; in that case, doesn't everyone carry his "autobiography" snugly in his head?

XVII.) Specificity signals the end of art and the beginning of journalism, history, sociology, or some other form of non-fiction; fiction at its best is neither factual nor familiar but feigned.

XVIII.) Literary fiction could be characterized as the residue of the confrontation between a fictionalizing intelligence and the printed page; but the rectangular paper frame is so plainly the most indomitable constraint upon those imaginations that seem eager to burst through the page.

XIX.) There can be no end to fiction before the demise of imagination, which is to say that as long as man survives there will be new forms of fictionalizing—though that historical form called "the novel" may be judged "dead," fiction isn't.

XX.) A measure of artistry in fiction is personal touch, even though nothing about the author himself need be revealed; the crucial question is this: Could—even would—any other name sign this work?

XXI.) The canon of modernist fiction—Stein, Lissitzky, Faulkner, Joyce, Beckett, Borges—established a tradition of the new that must in turn be artistically surpassed in the present.

XXII.) The new fiction of today need be no more different from the old than, say, 1970 differs from 1960, whose automobiles, clothes, hair styles, advertisements, machines, etc., clearly belong, we know, in junk shops or museums.

XXIII.) The only evidence of true madness in creative art is a breakthrough, because much that pretends to originality is merely capricious eccentricity or exploitative faddishness; insanity itself, however, is generally counter-productive.

XXIV.) Modern art at its best deals not in the manipulation of conventions but in their conspicuous neglect, because familiar forms are the most common counters of commerce; one test of genuine innovation in art, even today, is its resistance to an immediate sale.

XXV.) New fiction bears little superficial resemblance to old fiction, while the experience of "reading" radical work is also profoundly different; so too must radically change the standards and perhaps the language of fiction's criticism.

# jean-françois bory

# Notes

*The fact that the book, as we know it today, has rendered the greatest services to the mind for centuries, does not imply that it is indispensable or irreplacable.*

MICHEL BUTOR
*REPERTORY II*

PRELIMINARY NOTE

Most of my texts are concerned with the assimilation or rejection of one information-medium by another. This approach takes advantage of the dual aspect which characterizes all information or communication-sign or signal; and this duality is particularly stressed in my texts-in-progress. In other words, the text, in its progression from page to page, goes through two kinds of change, one of which is comprehensible to the sensibility and emotional experience; the other kind is understood primarily by the intellect. These two fundamental aspects of the text necessarily polarize and attract one another. However, it is not essential, in my opinion, to explicate these texts in order to understand them (or, better yet, to experience them), since they allow themselves to develop their own potential for a future world, which is already visible beyond the confines of knowledge.

POSTLIMINARY NOTE NUMBER ONE

The impact of Kleist, Novalis, and Mallarmé has given us the idea of grasping total reality, the totality of experience, through the act of literature. Since then, everything leads us to believe that with the end of writing there would be no more reason to write. Caught up in this furious attempt to recapture total reality, writers no longer regard sentences, or even words, as essential. What should be most important is the whole, and the whole is the book—the book inasmuch as the sentence, inasmuch as writing is a temporal development, the book insofar as modulation is concerned.

The book of the past analyzed a situation; the new book translates a state of being. Moreover, at the present, the aim of the author is to achieve this state of being. To write is to want to say everything, and to want to say everything is to want, in the final analysis, to speak no more. Thus, the end purpose of the book is an end to books.

It is a matter no longer of understanding or expressing, but of being caught up in the very text and texture of the everyday world. Each visual book is a key book, a method, somewhat like the first page of an inventory. Therefore, with new books, the reader will begin to read his own text, his environmental text around him, into which he is permanently plunged. And so the endless reading begins.

Today, the spirit balks at reading a traditional linear text; for it is, from now onwards, a matter of reading the world-text. Soon, even the understanding of this book, simply by reading of its text, will become impossible.

POSTLIMINARY NOTE NUMBER TWO

It is likely that countless numbers of books will eddy and swirl in the void of libraries. Such books will be unlike ours; their pages and words will be fundamentally different. They might have, for example, characters or signs that are not apparently linked, that are never repeated but are nevertheless language; writing that is perpetually evolving, not over a period of centuries, like our language, but in minutes, changing from page to page. There will be books in which the signs of language will consist of the spaces between the words; books without pages, or even books without end; books with thousands and thousands of pages that never stop at a cover; books through which the light will move as slowly as words are pronounced; books where the text begins to form from the blank page; books in which the page will form, will grow from signs; books without breaks to separate the letters one from the other and books in which words will know more separation than in ours; books in which words will be read and where each page will be a God; fluid books that will branch out in time—one part of the book readable now, another in five centuries . . .; books of jungles or of vines or of roads; books that are different according to every fundamental law.

For beyond one finds the book!

# Contributors

JOHN BARTH, a member of the Department of English at Johns Hopkins University, is the author of *The End of the Road*, *The Floating Opera*, *The Sot-Weed Factor*, *Giles Goat-Boy*, *Lost in the Funhouse*, and more recently *Chimera*. In 1972, he was co-recipient of the National Book Award for fiction.

JEAN-FRANÇOIS BORY, one of the leading figures in the concrete poetry movement in France, lives in Paris where he edits *Approaches*. His own books include *Saga, Heights, Texts & Zone*, and *Bientôt*. He also compiled the anthology *Once Again* for New Directions.

MAURICE CAGNON received his Ph.D. from the University of Pennsylvania, and is Associate Professor of French at Montclair State College, New Jersey. He has published widely in the field of French literature. Under a grant from the National Endowment for the Humanities he is currently writing a book on recent directions in French fiction.

ITALO CALVINO, one of the leading Italian writers of his generation, is an essayist, journalist, and the author of many stories, who has had six books published in English: *The Path to the Nest of Spiders, Adam One Afternoon and Other Stories, The Baron in the Tress, The Nonexistent Knight & The Cloven Viscount, Cosmicomics*, and *t zero*. His new work of fiction is entitled *War*.

JONATHAN CULLER is a Fellow and Director of Studies in Modern Languages at Selwyn College, Cambridge, and author of a forthcoming book on Structuralism.

JACQUES EHRMANN was a member of the French Department at Yale University. He died, at the age of 41, early in May 1972, after a long illness. Author of many fine, provocative essays

on contemporary thought and literature, he also published
three books: *Un Paradis désespéré, La France contemporaine*
(with Michael Beaujour), and in 1971 *La Mort de la littérature*. The three issues of the *Yale French Studies*, which he
edited to introduce Structuralism in America, "Structuralism", "Literature and Revolution", "Game, Play, Literature",
have been reprinted in book form. He will be deeply missed by
all those who knew him and respected his work.

RAYMOND FEDERMAN, Professor of English and Comparative Literature at SUNY, Buffalo, is the author of *Journey to Chaos:
Samuel Beckett's Early Fiction; Samuel Beckett: His Works
and His Critics* (with John Fletcher); and an anthology of
contemporary French stories, *Cinq Nouvelles Nouvelles*. A bi-
lingual volume of his poems appeared in Paris under the title
*Among the Beasts*. His first novel, *Double or Nothing*, was
published by Swallow Press in November 1971. His second
novel (in French), *Amer Eldorado*, appeared in Paris in May
1974. He is now completing another novel entitled *Take It or
Leave It*.

JOCHEN GERZ, born in Berlin in 1940, currently lives in Paris,
where he is co-editor of the Agentzia series of publications.
His work has been published (and exhibited) around the
world. A proponent of visual literature, his *Theory of Mobile
Texts* was originally produced in a limited edition by John
Furnival at Openings Press.

MARCUS KLEIN is Professor of English at the State University of
New York at Buffalo. He has contributed to *The New York
Times Book Review, The Nation, The Reporter, Hudson Re-
view, Kenyon Review*, and many other periodicals. He is well
known for his *After Alienation: American Novels in Mid-
Century*. He also edited several anthologies of stories, and
essays on fiction, among these, *The American Novel Since
World War II*. He is currently at work on a study of twentieth
century literature tentatively entitled *The Contemporary
Traditions*.

JEROME KLINKOWITZ has written on novelists from Hawthorne's day to the present for *American Transcendental Quarterly, Critique, Studies in the Novel, Chicago Review, Modern Fiction Studies*, and other journals. His books include *Innovative Fiction, The Vonnegut Statement*, a Vonnegut bibliography, and an edition of uncollected stories, essays, and drama by Kurt Vonnegut, Jr. He teaches at Northern Iowa University.

RICHARD KOSTELANETZ, poet, critic, cultural historian, is the author of two novellas, *In the Beginning* and *Accounting*, and word-image poetry collected as *Visual Language*. He has also edited numerous anthologies of modern writing such as *Imaged Words & Worded Images, Future's Fictions*, and more recently *Breakthrough Fictioneers*. His own fiction has appeared in *Panache, Assembling, Approaches, Abyss*, as well as the anthologies *Experimental Prose, Once Again*, and *This Book Is a Movie*.

NEAL OXENHANDLER, Professor of French at Dartmouth College, has published many essays on various aspects of contemporary literature. His books include a study of Jean Cocteau, *Scandal and Parade*, and a novel entitled *A Change of God*. He is currently at work on another novel.

RICHARD PEARCE, Professor of English at Wheaton College in Massachusetts, is the author of *Stages of the Clown: Perspectives on Modern Fiction from Dostoyevsky to Beckett, William Styron*, and a contributor to *Partisan Review, Massachusetts Review, Modern Fiction Studies, Tri-Quarterly*, and other journals.

ROBERT PYNSENT is a member of the English Seminars at Cologne University. He is thoroughly familiar with all aspects of experimental writing not only in Germany, but also in most Eastern European countries.

JEAN RICARDOU has published several works of fiction: *Les Lieux-*

dits, *Petit Guide d'un voyage dans le livre; L'Observatoire de Cannes; La Prise de Constantinople; Révolutions minuscules;* but it is as a controversial, leading theoretician of the new fiction that he has established his reputation in such volumes of essays as *Problèmes du nouveau roman* and *Pour une théorie du nouveau roman.*

STEPHEN SMITH received his Ph.D. from the University of Pennsylvania, and is Associate Professor of French and Chairman of the Modern Language Department at Central Connecticut State College. He divides his interest between Medieval and Contemporary French literature, and will publish shortly his critical edition of *La Mule sanz frain.*

PHILIPPE SOLLERS, the leading figure in the avant-garde literary *Tel Quel Group* in Paris, has published several novels: *Une Curieuse Solitude, Le Parc, L'Intermédiaire, Drame, Nombres, Lois,* and most recently the much-discussed *H.* Among his many volumes of essays, *Logiques* is the most controversial.

RONALD SUKENICK has taught creative writing at the University of California at Irvine. *Wallace Stevens: Musing the Obscure* (1967) was his first book. Since then he has published *UP,* his first full-length fictional work; *The Death of the Novel and Other Stories;* and *OUT,* published in 1973 by Swallow Press. He has just completed another noval entitled *98.6.*

# jean ricardou

# Writing Between the Lines

*Knowledge consists in composing collections of evocative singularities. The king's garden or preserve should include all the animal and plant curiosities contained in the universe. Those which no prospector is able to find should nevertheless be represented: sculptured or drawn. The collections aim at being complete, especially in monstrosities, since their purpose is less to serve knowledge than power, and the most effective collections consist not of real things but of emblems. He who possesses the emblem can influence reality. The symbol takes the place of the real. Accordingly, there is a concern for reality and facts, not in order to observe sequences and quantitative variations, but rather to possess and have available emblematic categories and tables of recurrences established solely on the basis of symbolic interdependencies.*

MARCEL GRANET
*CHINESE CIVILIZATION*

When questioned about their works, innumerable authors today seem somewhat unduly concerned to hide, in the first place, that their novel is a book. If they are so eager to lavish comment on characters, passions, events, it seems to be with the sole purpose of making us forget that all these are *written.*

Philippe Sollers, on the contrary, stresses the scriptive activity by calling our attention to its creative powers instead of con-

cealing them, by declaring to a reporter: "I chose a notebook;
I divided it into two parts", by insisting several times in *The
Park* on the material act of writing:

> Here, on the paper of the exercise-book I have chosen
> because of its color, the sentences slowly follow each
> other, written in blue-black ink with an old pen, in small
> fine handwriting that slopes to the right and which takes
> up only three-quarters of the page; slowly, patiently, with
> frequent crossings-out ... and, sometimes, long passages
> without any corrections, which no doubt denote an unex-
> pected speed, and in which the letters are badly formed,
> lose their individual shape, run together and soon become
> indecipherable.

and on learning to write:

> The hand shakes, as does the shadow of the pen on the
> white surface divided into squares by fine blue lines,
> crossed on the left-hand side by a vertical red line,

The present essay will not attempt to describe any more than
very simple, fragmentary phenomena, facsimiles of the integral
*modus operandi* of this kind of creative writing. Here are the
opening lines of *The Park* (italics mine):

> The sky above the long, gleaming avenues is dark blue.
> Later on, I shall go out. I shall walk in the direction of the
> sun until it finally disappears from view. The city is
> suddenly alive, moving, full of noise and night. I shall go
> now. But look again at the street and its yellowing trees
> and at the building opposite with its colonnades, its semi-
> circular balconies, its fresh zinc roofing, its distant, brightly-
> lit rooms where women are laying the tables for dinner. A
> sitting-room, a dining-room, a kitchen, another kitchen,
> another sitting-room. . . .

> In a leather arm-chair, to the right of the fireplace and

the standard lamp, a man is sitting in profile, glass in hand. In front of him is a woman. I can see her *red dress* through the net curtains, her animated gestures, the movement of her *lips* when she speaks, his slight inclination of the head as he listens to her, and I think I can hear him as he says, in his usual preoccupied way, "Of course". No, nothing will escape my attention if I sit in the small arm-chair on the narrow balcony, where, stretching my legs sideways, I can put my feet up on the wrought-iron balustrade, with its foliage transfixed along rounded, blackened stems that move symmetrically now one way, now another. Above, thin trails of dark smoke can still be seen rising from the chimneys placed in disorderly rows along the roofs. . . . Below, the noise of cars and buses . . . ; the brightly lit shop-windows (only the base of the buildings is continuously visible); the neon signs (*red, diamond-shaped sign* of the tobacconist); and *immediately opposite*, the man and woman who are talking and smiling in the large, bright flat. He makes a gesture with his left hand, in which he is holding *a cigarette*, probably in order to emphasize what he is saying, and the woman *throws her head back*, lifts her arms, then, *bursting with laughter*, bends suddenly forward.

The man stands up and puts his glass on the low table. The woman also gets up, makes a slight movement of the head, and they walk together to the end of the room, where they disappear through a door. . . . Another woman comes on to the scene . . . comes out to the stone balcony, where she leans over watching the cars that flash their headlamps as they cross the junction in the road, then *regroup in three lanes at the red light*.

## I. ASPECTS OF SCRIPTIVE CREATION

Imagining, and *imagining pen in hand* are two entirely distinct activities. Some of their differences should be underlined.

Ordinary imagination elicits evolving images according to a flow whose evolution is based on a continual evanescence. The spontaneous or partially preconcerted themes, the phantasms that may be proposed as vectors of organization, gradually lose their directive power. They themselves evolve, collide, and are finally lost in patterns so complex, so rapidly overlapping, that the mind is soon no longer able to follow them. The metamorphosis entails this prompt obliteration. The imaginative flow eludes any protracted control. Exercising the imagination while at the same time apprehending its movement—such is the privilege that writing seems to enjoy. The written fragment is not flight, mobility, disappearance, but rather inscription, a stable reference. With it, imagination changes status.

Whatever their differences, visual and mental images may both be defined as an immediate synthesis in which each detail loses its autonomy. Description, on the other hand, is a construction elaborated on the basis of analytic elements, a synthesis deferred. The details which emerged in the image, in a description are intensified, particularized, highlighted. The passage:

> In front of him is a woman. I can see her *red dress* through the net curtains, her animated gestures, the movement of her lips when she speaks

brings into prominence, for example, the elements "*red* dress" and "lips" (red), to the exact extent that the image is composed from them by stages.

The analogical elements which constitute the links of the mental image's associative chain consequently differ radically from those which direct the activity of the scriptive imagination. The former exploit the unity which, by definition, characterizes the synthetic image, provoking consecutive images which eclipse one another. The latter go to work instead on each individual detail of the descriptive image, tending to populate the imagination with as many series of analogical images as there are details —and this as many times as the mind refers back, at will, to the original fragment.

Present in each of the images of the mental series it provoked, each of the written attributes (red, for instance) has the importance already granted it by the fact of its being written down, multiplied to the point of obsession by the exercise of